dBASE IV Programming Language Syntax Symbols

Italics

Italicized items indicate that you must fill in specific information. Examples used in many commands follow:

alias Specifies a database that is currently open in some work area other than the current one. *alias* can be the work area name (A through J for the first 10 work areas), the work area number (1 through 40), the alias name specified in the USE...ALIAS command, the actual database name, or a memory variable containing the alias name.

condition An expression indicating database records to be included in an operation (for example, **LastName = "Smith"**).

file name A valid dBASE file name is required.

list Multiple items, separated by commas, may be included.

scope Scope options are **ALL** for all records; **REST** for all records starting from the current record to the end of a file; **RECORD** *n* for a specific record; and **NEXT** *n* for a group of records starting at the current record, where *n* must be a number or expression that results in a number.

skeleton Supports wildcard names, where ? stands for any single character, and * stands for any group of characters (as in DOS commands).

( ) Square brackets indicate that the item is an optional part of the command, which may be used or omitted. Do not type brackets as part of the command (except when using the DECLARE and PUBLIC ARRAY commands).

/ A slash separates mutually exclusive options, only one of which may be used in a single command. Do not type the slash into the command.

dBASE IV 2.0 Programmer's Reference

dBASE IV® 2.0 Programmer's Reference

Virginia Andersen

toExcel
New York San Jose Lincoln Shanghai

SYBEX®
San Francisco • Paris • Düsseldorf • Soest

DBASE IV 2.0 Programmer's Reference

This edition published by toExcel Press,
an imprint of iUniverse.com, Inc.

For information address:
iUniverse.com, Inc.
620 North 48th Street
Suite 201
Lincoln, NE 68504-3467
www.iuniverse.com

ISBN: 1-58348-396-9

LCCN: 99-65500

Acknowledgments

To produce a book that is useful, readable, and technically accurate takes a team with many talents. I had such a team in the preparation of this book and my thanks go to them all:

Special thanks to my friend and colleague Alan Simpson for the use of material from the *dBASE IV 1.1 Programmer's Instant Reference.*

Thanks also to everyone who moved the book from an idea to rough manuscript to finished product:David Peal, developmental editor; Michelle Nance, editor; Kurt Hampe, technical editor; Kristin Amlie, proofreader/production assistant; Lisa Jaffe, typesetter; Suzanne Albertson, production artist; and Cuong Le, screen graphics.

Thanks to the knowledgeable technical support at Borland who helped me through the Beta and Gamma testing of dBASE IV 2.0.

At Waterside Productions, my literary agency, I would like to thank Bill Gladstone and Matt Wagner.

Finally, but certainly not an afterthought, I thank my husband Jack, who patiently kept all the computers running.

Table of Contents

Appendix A

Installing and Configuring dBASE IV

467

Appendix B

dBASE IV File Name Extensions

483

Appendix C

dBASE IV Specifications

487

Appendix D

Using the dBASE Compiler

493

Index

507

Introduction

The dBASE IV programming language consists of over 375 commands and functions, as well as several dozen system memory variables and Config.DB commands. Few of us, including the real power users, can remember the details of every command and function. Similarly, few of us want to lug the whole set of dBASE IV manuals from one place to another. For these reasons, this "pocket reference" was created.

This book is a concise discussion of only the dBASE IV Version 2.0 programming language. It assumes that you are already familiar with writing dBASE IV programs. Features not directly related to programming, such as the Control Center, the design screens, the Applications Generator, SQL, and the Template Language, are not covered in this book. (If they were, it would be several pounds heavier!)

HOW TO USE THIS BOOK

The major commands in this book are grouped by topic. Use Part 1 of the book to quickly find all commands, such as those for printing reports or creating custom screens, that relate to a particular task. Part 1 also contains alphabetized lists of dBASE functions grouped by usage.

The programming commands, the SET commands, and the dBASE functions are listed alphabetically for easy reference in Parts 2, 3, and 4, respectively.

Appendices provide instructions for installing and configuring dBASE IV (Appendix A) and using Borland's new dBASE Compiler (Appendix D). You'll also find a convenient list of file name extensions (Appendix B) and dBASE specifications (Appendix C).

The index includes all the commands and functions, as well as additional relevant topics for individual features. This makes it easier to locate information, even when you don't know which command or function you want to use.

FORMAT OF THE COMMAND ENTRIES

Each command entry includes most or all of the following items:

COMMAND NAME

The Entry's Main Heading

• SYNTAX

A representation of the command's required syntax, in the form

COMMAND *parameter* (/?) (*optional element*</>)

where **boldface** type indicates characters (including any punctuation) to be literally typed in as part of the command; *italics* indicate placeholders for variable text such as file names or field lists to be typed in; and square brackets ([ ]) mark items that are optional in the command syntax, whether literals or (as above) placeholders. The slash (/) gives an "either/or" choice. The question mark (?) can be substituted for an unknown file name and will generate a pick list.

• USAGE This section describes how to use the command, suggests possible applications, and provides details on the command's options.

• EXAMPLE This section uses either a practical routine or one or more sample commands to demonstrate how to use the command at the dot prompt, in a command file, or both.

See Also This section provides a list of related entries.

AN IMPORTANT NOTE ON COMMAND LENGTH

Although your computer screen is 80 columns wide, the size of this page cannot accommodate lines of that length. In sample command lines that would extend beyond the margins in this book, lines are broken using the dBASE semicolon continuation symbol. For example, a command that ends with

```
report? " GET ToPrint PICTURE "L"
```

might be shown as

```
@ 1,5 SAY "Print report? ";
GET ToPrint PICTURE "L"
```

When entering long lines like this one into a program, you can use the exact format shown, breaking the long line into two lines with the semicolon (;). However, when entering long commands such as this at the dot prompt, you cannot use the semicolon to split the lines. Type commands in as one long line, including only a blank space where you see the semicolon.

Part 1

Using dBASE IV Commands and Functions

The dBASE IV 2.0 programming language contains hundreds of commands and functions for a variety of applications. To make it easier for you to find the right command or function for your purpose, they are grouped in Part 1 by usage. Parts 2 through 4 contain alphabetized lists of the program commands, the SET commands, and the functions, respectively.

dBASE PROGRAM COMMANDS

The dBASE IV 2.0 program commands include commands for creating and manipulating database files, locating stored data, building custom screens, printing reports, adding windows and menus to your application, and numerous other program uses. The following pages list these commands by application.

USER-ASSISTANCE COMMANDS

dBASE IV offers two kinds of user assistance. The first, the Control Center, provides an easy user interface based on pull-down menus rather than commands. The Control Center is primarily for non-programmers and is therefore not covered extensively in this book. The second user-assistance feature is the built-in help system, which provides quick reminders of the syntax and options of all commands and functions.

Commands:

ASSIST   HELP

CREATING, USING, AND MANAGING FILES

CREATE and USE, the commands for creating and using database files, will be old hat to most experienced dBASE users. However, they do provide some advanced options, such as the use of ALIAS with USE, and of FROM with CREATE, that may be news to even experienced users.

There are also general-purpose commands for managing database files, text files, and keystroke macro files stored on disk, as well as commands such as CLEAR and CLOSE for managing objects in memory.

Commands:

CLEAR	CREATE/MODIFY STRUCTURE	LIST
CLOSE	DELETE FILE	PLAY MACRO
COPY	DEXPORT	RENAME
COPY FILE	DIRECTORY	RESTORE MACROS
COPY MEMO	DISPLAY	SAVE MACROS
COPY STRUCTURE	ERASE	SELECT
COPY STRUCTURE EXTENDED	EXPORT	SKIP
CREATE	GO/GOTO	TYPE
CREATE FROM	IMPORT	USE

ADDING, EDITING, AND DELETING DATA

There are two techniques for adding data to a dBASE database: typing in new data and copying data from existing files. In the first, you type new information, record by record, onto the screen. Add new data in this way with the APPEND and INSERT commands. Both APPEND and INSERT automatically present simple screens for entering data.

For more sophisticated applications, such simplified screens are rarely sufficient. Instead, you'll want to create forms that are visually appealing, easy to use, accurate, and efficient for entering and editing data. The @...SAY command has over a dozen options for creating custom screens for user communication and data entry. These custom forms usually include prompts that are more descriptive than the field names alone. They may also employ a variety of enhancements, including color, boxes, data checking, and validation.

In the second technique, you add new data to a database by copying data from one file to another with the APPEND FROM and IMPORT commands. Use APPEND FROM to append data from one dBASE database to another, or to import data from spreadsheets and ASCII files into dBASE databases. IMPORT creates a new database structure and imports data into it.

Data in databases must be maintained over time—addresses must be changed in mailing lists, inactive customer files must be deleted, and prices in inventory files must be updated. dBASE offers many techniques for tasks involving *editing* (changing) and deleting data. You can specify certain restrictions on editing data with the EDIT command. In addition, you can easily pinpoint the exact record (or records) to change or delete using *scope* options and the FOR and WHILE query options.

Commands:

@...SAY	APPEND MEMO	INSERT
@...CLEAR	BEGIN/END TRANSACTION	PACK
@...FILL	BLANK	READ
@...SCROLL	BROWSE	RECALL
@...TO	CHANGE	REPLACE
ACCEPT	COPY MEMO	RESET
APPEND	CREATE/MODIFY SCREEN	ROLLBACK
APPEND BLANK	DELETE	WAIT
APPEND FROM	EDIT	ZAP
APPEND FROM ARRAY	INPUT	

SORTING AND INDEXING

In database management, the term *sorting* means to put the records in a database into some meaningful order, such as alphabetical order by name, chronological order by date, or numerical order by amount.

dBASE offers two techniques for displaying database records in sorted order. The faster of the two methods, *indexing*, creates a sorted list of values in a field (or fields), with a pointer to the appropriate record in the database file. This is similar to the index at the back of a book, which lists each topic in alphabetical order and includes a page number that "points to" the location of that topic in the book.

When an index is *active*, it is stored in memory, and dBASE automatically uses the index to display records as though they were in sorted order. Even though you can use only one index at a time to control the sort order, you can create several indexes for a database file. These can be stored together in a multiple index file, which has the file name extension .MDX, or as separate files, each with the file name extension .NDX.

dBASE automatically updates all active indexes during an edit session, which takes time. If you have an index that is rarely used, save time by storing it as a separate file (.NDX) and updating it as needed.

As an alternative to indexing, you can use sorting, the second technique, to rearrange records in a database file. The sorting method produces a copy of the database with records arranged in the sorted order. This takes longer and requires more disk space than indexing because it makes a complete copy of the database file. In addition, a sorted file must be resorted each time the database file is changed, in order to be current. Finally, finding an entry in an index is easier than finding a record in a whole file. Indexing is a more efficient method of ordering records in a database file, but there are some applications in which a separate, sorted file is required.

If you're making the transition from dBASE III PLUS to dBASE IV, you should also be aware of some differences in the way the new version manages index files. dBASE III PLUS stored all indexes in separate database files and made the user responsible for keeping them current. dBASE IV stores all indexes in a single production index file with the same name as the database file, but with the extension .MDX (unless you specify a separate .NDX file). As soon as you open a database file, the production index file is automatically opened and all indexes are adjusted to changes in the database as they happen.

The COPY INDEXES command lets you convert existing dBASE III PLUS .NDX index files to tag in a dBASE IV multiple index with an .MDX extension.

dBASE IV also supports both ascending and descending index sort orders.

Commands:

COPY INDEXES	INDEX	SORT
COPY TAG	REINDEX	USE...ORDER
DELETE TAG		

LOCATING AND QUERYING DATA

dBASE offers many techniques for finding data (*querying* a database), including those listed below. In addition, commands such as REPORT FORM, LABEL FORM, LIST, DISPLAY, DELETE, RECALL, REPLACE, and EDIT support the FOR, WHILE, and scope options so that the commands apply only to specified data.

The commands below are used for locating a particular record or a group of records that match search criteria. To find a particular record, use the LOCATE and CONTINUE commands if the field being searched is not indexed, or the FIND and SEEK commands if the field is indexed. To hide records that do not meet search criteria, use a FOR or WHILE option, or the CREATE/MODIFY QUERY command.

Commands:

CONTINUE	GO/GOTO	SEEK
CREATE/MODIFY QUERY/VIEW	LOCATE	SKIP
FIND		

PRINTING REPORTS

The commands that you use to display dBASE reports allow you to create report and label form designs so you can print formatted reports and mailing labels without programming. In addition, dBASE gives you control over the printed output with the PRINTJOB...ENDPRINTJOB and related programming commands.

Commands:

?, ??, and ???	EJECT	PRINTJOB... ENDPRINTJOB
CREATE/MODIFY LABEL	LABEL FORM	REPORT FORM
CREATE/MODIFY REPORT	ON PAGE	TEXT and ENDTEXT
DEFINE BOX		

PERFORMING CALCULATIONS

There are several commands that perform statistical and financial calculations on database data, including a CALCULATE command. With CALCULATE, you can perform a variety of operations including sum, average, count, highest value, lowest value, standard deviation, variance, and net present value, in a single pass through the database file. To provide compatibility with dBASE III PLUS, dBASE IV also includes the SUM, AVERAGE, and COUNT commands; however, you can perform the calculations that these commands provide with the CALCULATE command.

Commands:

AVERAGE	COUNT	TOTAL
CALCULATE	SUM	

MANAGING MULTIPLE FILES

dBASE provides commands to help you manage multiple related database files. Related database files must each have at least one field that has the same name, data type, width, and decimal. The common field needs to be indexed in at least one of the databases, but it's best to index it in both databases.

Commands:

CREATE VIEW FROM ENVIRONMENT	SELECT	UPDATE
JOIN		

PROGRAM CONTROL COMMANDS

Program control commands are used to control the flow of processing in command files. The MODIFY COMMAND, DO, DEBUG, COMPILE, and other programming commands help you to create, debug, and run command files.

Within command files, commands such as ACCEPT, INPUT, and WAIT enable you to present prompts to the user and store the user's response. Commands such as DO WHILE...ENDDO, IF...ELSE...ENDIF and DO CASE...ENDCASE, let you control the logical flow of a program.

You can also incorporate event processing and error trapping into your dBASE command files. *Event processing* allows a command file to respond to a keystroke or mouse operation, regardless of the task the program is performing at the time. *Error trapping* allows a command file to respond to an error condition without returning to the dot prompt.

Many related commands such as ON PAD and ON SELECTION are used strictly with menus. The ON PAGE command is used only during printing.

Commands:

*, &&, and NOTE	EXIT	ON MOUSE
ACCEPT	IF...ELSE... ENDIF	ON READERROR

BEGIN/END TRANSACTION	INPUT	RESET
CANCEL	KEYBOARD	RESUME
COMPILE	LOOP	RETURN
DEBUG	MODIFY COMAND/ FILE	ROLLBACK
DISPLAY/LIST HISTORY	ON ERROR	SCAN...ENDSCAN
DO	ON ESCAPE	SUSPEND
DO CASE...ENDCASE	ON KEY	WAIT
DO WHILE...ENDDO		

CREATING WINDOWS AND MENUS

A window can add a professional touch to your applications. You can use windows to temporarily display error messages, prompts, and Yes/No option messages such as *"Print now?"* The window disappears when the user responds.

Horizontal, pop-up, and pull-down menus can be used to give the user choices in processing and using data. dBASE provides powerful tools to create and customize windows and menus, and to define the options they contain.

Commands:

ACTIVATE MENU	DEFINE WINDOW	ON SELECTION PAD
ACTIVATE POPUP	MOVE WINDOW	ON SELECTION POPUP
ACTIVATE SCREEN	ON BAR	RELEASE MENUS

ACTIVATE WINDOW	ON EXIT BAR	RELEASE POPUPS
CREATE/ MODIFY APPLICATION	ON EXIT MENU	RELEASE SCREENS
DEACTIVATE MENU	ON EXIT PAD	RELEASE WINDOWS
DEACTIVATE POPUP	ON EXIT POPUP	RESTORE SCREEN
DEACTIVATE WINDOW	ON MENU	RESTORE WINDOW
DEFINE BAR	ON PAD	SAVE SCREEN
DEFINE MENU	ON POPUP	SAVE WINDOWS
DEFINE PAD	ON SELECTION BAR	SHOW MENU
DEFINE POPUP	ON SELECTION MENU	SHOW POPUP

USING PROCEDURES AND USER-DEFINED FUNCTIONS

Procedures and user-defined functions (UDFs) provide many advantages to the programmer. For one, they allow you to better modularize your code into small, specific tasks that are easy to access, test, and debug. Also, you can use the PARAMETERS command to create procedures and user-defined functions that can operate on any data. In a sense, a procedure is like a custom command, and a user-defined function is a dBASE IV function that you've added to the dBASE IV programming language.

You can store procedures and user-defined functions within either a command file or a *procedure file*. Once you open a procedure file, you can access its contents at any time—from the dot prompt or any command file. User-defined functions that you store in an open procedure file are just as accessible as the built-in dBASE IV functions. You can even use them in the design screens. Procedures and UDFs stored in command files are less globally available.

Commands:

DO...WITH	FUNCTION	PARAMETERS
CLOSE PROCEDURE	PROCEDURE	RETURN

MEMORY VARIABLE AND ARRAY COMMANDS

Information stored in a database file is stored on disk. With dBASE IV, you can also temporarily store information in the computer's main memory, or *RAM*. Data is stored in RAM as *memory variables* (memvars). Unlike database data, data items stored in memory variables are temporary and usually are erased as soon as you exit dBASE.

An *array* is a group of memory variables, each with the same name but a different subscript (or subscripts). The DECLARE and PUBLIC ARRAY commands allow you to define an array. Once the array is defined, you can treat elements in the array just as you would treat any other memory variable.

Commands:

APPEND FROM ARRAY	DISPLAY MEMORY	REPLACE FROM ARRAY
CLEAR MEMORY	PRIVATE	RESTORE
COPY TO ARRAY	PUBLIC	SAVE
DECLARE	RELEASE	STORE

RUNNING EXTERNAL PROGRAMS

dBASE IV offers commands that provide direct access to DOS and any program that you can execute from the DOS prompt. This allows you to change DOS settings, such as the system date and time, and to perform DOS operations, such as formatting a disk, without leaving dBASE. You can also access a word processor or spreadsheet program without leaving dBASE IV, provided that your computer has sufficient memory.

In addition, your dBASE command files can use external subroutines written in assembly language. This is useful if you want your program to do something that the dBASE language doesn't provide for, or to perform some task at a much faster speed than dBASE can achieve on its own. Some examples of applications for assembly language subroutines include music or sound effects, data logging from special-purpose hardware, specialized mathematical calculations, animated color graphics, high-speed data communication, and control of laboratory experiments.

Commands:

CALL	LOAD	RUN and !

NETWORKING COMMANDS

dBASE provides commands that are used primarily in multiuser network applications. Note that dBASE also includes several functions and SET commands specifically designed for networks, as listed in the See Also sections following the description of each command in Part 2.

Commands:

CONVERT	LOGOUT	RETRY
DISPLAY/LIST STATUS	PROTECT	UNLOCK
DISPLAY/LIST USERS		

SET COMMANDS

The SET commands allow you to define general parameters that affect your current dBASE IV session. When you issue a SET command, it stays in effect until you either quit dBASE or change the status of the parameter with another SET command. Many of the SET commands have the TO option as well as the ON/OFF option. See Part 3 for a complete description of the SET commands with practical examples.

You can also predefine most SET parameters so they are automatically activated when you first run dBASE. To do so, you need to modify the Config.DB file, as covered in Appendix A.

SET Commands:

SET	SET ENCRYPTION	SET NEAR
SET ALTERNATE	SET ESCAPE	SET ODOMETER
SET AUTOSAVE	SET EXACT	SET ORDER
SET BELL	SET EXCLUSIVE	SET PATH
SET BLOCKSIZE	SET FIELDS	SET PAUSE
SET BORDER	SET FILTER	SET POINT
SET CARRY	SET FIXED	SET PRECISION
SET CATALOG	SET FORMAT	SET PROCEDURE
SET CENTURY	SET FULLPATH	SET REFRESH
SET CLOCK	SET FUNCTION	SET RELATION
SET COLOR	SET HEADINGS	SET REPROCESS
SET CONFIRM	SET HELP	SET SAFETY
SET CONSOLE	SET HISTORY	SET SCOREBOARD
SET CURRENCY	SET HOURS	SET SEPARATOR
SET CURSOR	SET IBLOCK	SET SKIP

SET DATE	SET INDEX	SET SPACE
SET DBTRAP	SET INSTRUCT	SET SQL
SET DEBUG	SET INTENSITY	SET STATUS
SET DECIMALS	SET KEY	SET STEP
SET DEFAULT	SET LDCHECK	SET TALK
SET DELETED	SET LIBRARY	SET TITLE
SET DELIMITERS	SET LOCK	SET TRAP
SET DESIGN	SET MARGIN	SET TYPEAHEAD
SET DEVELOP-MENT	SET MARK	SET UNIQUE
SET DEVICE	SET MBLOCK	SET VIEW
SET DIRECTORY	SET MEMOWIDTH	SET WINDOW OF MEMO
SET DISPLAY	SET MENU	
SET DOHISTORY	SET MESSAGE	
SET ECHO	SET MOUSE	

dBASE FUNCTIONS

Use the dBASE functions in conjunction with dBASE commands to perform operations on individual data items, known as *arguments,* which are always placed within parentheses. Functions that do not accept arguments still require parentheses. If there is not a built-in function to perform a particular job, you can create your own user-defined functions with the FUNCTION command.

All functions return some value. The data type of the value returned depends on the individual function.

As with the program commands, the dBASE functions are grouped by usage and listed below. See Part 4 for complete descriptions and practical examples of the dBASE functions.

DATE FUNCTIONS

The date functions listed below operate on fields of the Date data type, and return numeric, date, or character results, dependent upon the function.

Functions:

CDOW()	DMY()	MONTH()
CMONTH()	DOW()	TIME()
DATE()	DTOS()	YEAR()
DAY()	MDY()	

STRING FUNCTIONS

The string functions let you manipulate character data called strings. Many functions manipulate substrings embedded in larger strings. You can determine the length of a string, excerpt characters from the right, left, or center of a string, search for specific characters within text, and perform many more operations with these functions.

Functions:

&	LOWER()	STUFF()
$	LTRIM()	SUBSTR()
ASC()	RAT()	TAG()
AT()	REPLICATE()	TRANSFORM()
CHR()	RIGHT()	TRIM()
DIFFERENCE()	RTRIM()	UPPER()
LEFT()	SOUNDEX()	
LEN()	SPACE()	

MEMO FIELD FUNCTIONS

Memo field functions return information about the size and text of the menu field.

Functions:

MEMLINES() MLINE()

MATHEMATICAL AND FINANCIAL FUNCTIONS

Mathematical functions include numeric and trigonometric functions that return the results of calculations on the Numeric or Float data types. The trigonometric functions assume the angles are expressed in radians. dBASE provides the DTOR() function to convert degrees to radians and the RTOD() function to convert them back again. The financial functions perform common financial calculations such as net present value and payment amounts.

Functions:

ABS()	FV()	PV()
ACOS()	INT()	RAND()
ASIN()	LOG()	ROUND()
ATAN()	LOG10()	RTOD()
ATN2()	MAX()	SIGN()
CEILING()	MIN()	SIN()
COS()	MOD()	SQRT()
DTOR()	NPV()	TAN()
EXP()	PAYMENT()	
FLOOR()	PI()	

DATA TYPE CONVERSION FUNCTIONS

The data type conversion functions change field values from one data type to another.

Functions:

CTOD()	FIXED()	VAL()
DTOC()	FLOAT()	
DTOS()	STR()	

KEYPRESS FUNCTIONS

The keypress functions return information about the most recent keypress.

Functions:

INKEY()	LASTKEY()	READKEY()

MENU FUNCTIONS

Menu functions return information about any of the horizontal bar, pop-up, and pull-down menus used in your application.

Functions:

BAR()	MENU()	POPUP()
BARCOUNT()	PAD()	PROMPT()
BARPROMPT()	PADPROMPT()	

IDENTIFICATION AND TESTING FUNCTIONS

The identification and testing functions return information about the current processing environment.

Functions:

ALIAS()	FOUND()	ORDER()
BOF()	GETENV()	OS()
CATALOG()	HOME()	PCOL()
CERROR()	IF()	PCOUNT()

COL()
COMPLETED()
DBF()
DELETED()
DESCENDING()
DISKSPACE()
EOF()
ERROR()
FDATE()
FTIME()
FSIZE()
FIELD()
FILE()
FKLABEL()
FKMAX()
FLDCOUNT()
FLDLIST()
FOR()
ISALPHA()
ISBLANK()
ISCOLOR()
ISLOWER()
ISMARKED()
ISMOUSE()
ISUPPER()
KEY()
KEYMATCH()
LIKE()
LINO()
LUPDATE()
MDX()
MCOL()
MEMORY()
MESSAGE()
MROW()
NDX()
PRINTSTATUS()
PROGRAM()
PROW()
RECCOUNT()
RECNO()
RECSIZE()
ROLLBACK()
ROW()
SELECT()
SET()
TAGCOUNT()
TAGNO()
TYPE()
UNIQUE()
VARREAD()
VERSION()
WINDOW()

FUNCTIONS THAT MIMIC COMMANDS

These functions operate much like their namesake commands.

Functions:

CALL() SEEK() RUN()
LOOKUP()

NETWORK FUNCTIONS

The network functions can be used in a multiuser environment for applications that run on a network. They provide information such as which users are currently logged on or which files are locked.

Functions:

ACCESS()	ID()	NETWORK()
CHANGE()	LKSYS()	RLOCK()
FLOCK()	LOCK()	USER()

LOW-LEVEL FILE INPUT/OUTPUT FUNCTIONS

The new low-level file input and output functions allow you full access to sequential file operations, including creating and opening a file, reading from and writing to a file, and moving the record pointer within a file.

Functions:

FCLOSE()	FFLUSH()	FREAD()
FCREATE()	FGETS()	FSEEK()
FEOF()	FOPEN()	FWRITE()
FERROR()	FPUTS()	

The dBASE IV commands and functions have been grouped in this part so you can easily see which ones apply to your application. Part 2 contains a complete description of each command with correct syntax and examples, arranged in alphabetical order. Part 3 provides the same information for the SET commands, and Part 4 covers dBASE functions.

Part 2

dBASE IV Program Commands

The dBASE programming language includes nearly 200 commands for data storage, management, and retrieval; file maintenance, exporting, and importing; report generation and custom form design; custom user interfacing, including multiuser networks; and mathematical and financial computations.

All of the dBASE IV 2.0 commands are described in this part, except for the special-purpose SET commands which are described in Part 3. The commands are arranged in alphabetical order and each description includes the correct syntax, options, an explanation of the purpose of the command, and a practical example of its usage. In addition, there are references to related commands and functions.

?, ??, AND ???

Displaying Fields, Variables, and Results

• SYNTAX

?/?? *(expression 1* **(PICTURE** *template)* **(FUNCTION** function list) **(AT** *column)* **(STYLE** *style code and/or font number)) (, expression 2...) (,)*

or

??? *code*

• USAGE A single ? command always prints its data at the start of a new line. The ? command alone (with no expression) prints a blank line.

The ?? command prints its data at the current cursor position (or print-head position of the printer). If SET PRINT is on, output from ? and ?? is channeled to the printer. If SET ALTERNATE is on, output is channeled to the file named in the SET ALTERNATE TO command.

The ??? command sends printer control codes to the printer without moving the print head.

The PICTURE and FUNCTION options operate as they do with the @ command. The following functions work uniquely with the ? and ?? commands:

H	Horizontally stretches or shrinks field width to accommodate data
V*n*	Vertically stretches and word wraps long fields (where *n* is a number representing the width of the printed column)
B	Left aligns data in template
I	Centers data in template

J Right aligns data in template

T Trims leading and trailing blanks

The AT option specifies the column location on the current line to which to print.

The STYLE option determines the type style of printed output and of the display on some monitors. Type style options are

B Boldface

I Italic

U Underlined

R Raised (superscript)

L Lowered (subscript)

You can also use the numbers 1 through 5 with the STYLE option to specify a printing font. The numbers must correspond to fonts that you have previously defined via the DBSETUP program (or in the Config.DB file).

If you end a ? command with a comma, the first line of any vertically stretched field is displayed. However, additional lines are maintained in memory until you execute either a RETURN, ENDPRINTJOB, or ?/?? command not ending with a comma.

The ??? command lets you send printer codes directly to the printer without moving the print head or printing text. These codes allow you to use special printer features (as defined in your printer's user's manual). You can use either ASCII number codes, key names enclosed in curly braces, or a combination of the two, as listed in Table 2.1.

- **EXAMPLE** The commands

```
? "The cube root of 127 is " ?? 127^(1/3);
   PICTURE "9.999999999999"
```

produce the screen output:

```
The cube root of 127 is 5.026525695313
```

Table 2.1: ASCII Codes and Key Names Used with ???

ASCII Code	Key Name
0	{NULL} or {CTRL-@}
1 through 6	{CTRL-A} through {CTRL-F}
7	{BELL} or {CTRL-G}
8	{BACKSPACE} or {CTRL-H}
9	{TAB} or {CTRL-I}
10	{LINEFEED} or {CTRL-J}
11	{HOME} or {CTRL-K}
12	{CTRL-L}
13	{RETURN} or {CTRL-M}
14 through 26	{CTRL-N} through {CTRL-Z}
27	{ESC} or {ESCAPE} or {CTRL-[}
28	{CTRL-\}
29	{CTRL-]}
30	{CTRL-^}
31	{CTRL-_}
127	{DEL} or {DELETE}

The following commands:

```
SET TALK OFF ShortText = "Hello     "
LongText = "This is a long character string."
Amount = 1234.56
SET PRINTER ON

? ShortText AT 5, ;
  LongText FUNCTION "V15" ;
  STYLE "I" AT 15, ;
  Amount FUNCTION "$" ;
  PICTURE "99,999.99" AT 32

SET PRINTER OFF
```

produce the output:

Hello *This is a long* $1,234.56
character
string.

The next command makes a Hewlett-Packard LaserJet printer switch to compressed landscape mode (Esc E Esc &l1O Esc &k2S):

```
??? "{Esc}E{Esc}&l1O{Esc}&k2S"
```

See Also @...SAY, PRINTJOB...ENDPRINTJOB, SET CURRENCY, SET PRINTER, TEXT...ENDTEXT

*, &&, and NOTE

Adding Programmer Comments

- **SYNTAX**

NOTE *any text*
* *any text*

&& *any text*

- **USAGE** These commands mark text in command files as programmer comments, to be ignored by the compiler. You must use NOTE and * as the first characters in a programmer comment. You can use && to the right of a command line.

- **EXAMPLE** In the following example, only the command

```
ExtPrice = Qty * UnitPrice
```

is compiled:

```
NOTE -- ExtPrice is the extended price of the transaction.

*-- Qty is the Quantity, UnitPrice is unit price.

ExtPrice = Qty * UnitPrice  && Calculate extended price.
```

See Also MODIFY COMMAND/FILE, PROCEDURE

@...SAY...GET

Displaying and Entering Data

• SYNTAX

```
@ row,col (SAY message
   (PICTURE template)
   (FUNCTION function list))
(GET field/variable name
   ((OPEN) WINDOW window name)
   (PICTURE template)
   (FUNCTION function list)
   (RANGE (REQUIRED) (low),(high]]
   (VALID (REQUIRED) condition (ERROR) message))
   (WHEN condition)
   (DEFAULT value)
   (MESSAGE message))
(COLOR (standard)(,enhanced))
```

• USAGE Each component of the @ command is discussed separately in the following sections.

@ ROW,COL

The first component of the @ command positions the cursor (or printer head) at the row and column position specified by *row* and *col*. The *row* and *col* parameters can be numbers, variables, fields, expressions, or functions that evaluate to numbers.

The upper-left corner on the computer screen is row 0, column 0. On a standard 24-line screen, the lower-right corner is row 23, column 79. If a window is active, row 0, column 0 is the upper-left corner of the window, and the lower-right corner is determined according to the size of the window. For example, in an active window defined by the command

```
DEFINE WINDOW Window1 FROM 10,20 TO 20,60
```

the upper-left corner is row 0, column 0, and the lower-right corner is row 8, column 38, because the area within the window border consists of nine rows, numbered 0 through 8, and 39 columns, numbered 0 through 38.

If you attempt to position the cursor outside of the active window, dBASE displays the error message *Position out of window*.

The ROW() function returns the current row position of the cursor and the COL() function returns the current column position of the cursor. You can use these functions in the @ command for relative addressing. For example, the command

```
@ ROW(),COL()+ 5 SAY "Hello"
```

displays the word "Hello" at the current row, five columns to the right of the current cursor position.

When you issue the command

```
SET DEVICE TO PRINT
```

the output from @...SAY commands is routed to the printer (the GET portion of the command is never displayed). When you send text to the printer, the maximum row and column coordinates are each 255.

The PROW() and PCOL() functions are the printer equivalents of the screen's ROW() and COL() functions. You can use them in the same manner for calculating relative rows and addresses. Note, however, that if you attempt to print data above the current line, the printer ejects to the next page before printing the new line.

SAY

The optional SAY portion of the @ command displays any text or the contents of any database field or memory variable (but not memo fields). Use the PICTURE template with the SAY command to format the displayed text. Literal text must be enclosed in quotes, as follows:

```
@ 2,40 SAY "This is printed literally"
```

SAY can display information from the currently open database, as well as from related databases.

Only the plus sign (+) concatenator is allowed in SAY commands to join literals and variables. For example, the *Up* memory variable in the following example contains the character string for displaying an up arrow (↑). The @ command below it displays the up arrow in mid-sentence.

```
Up = CHR(24)
@ 20,1 SAY "Press"+Up+" to make corrections."
```

If the data to be concatenated is not character data, you must convert it to character data.

GET

The optional GET component of the @ command displays the contents of an existing field or memory variable in a template that matches the size and data type of the field or variable. When you issue a READ, APPEND, EDIT, INSERT, or CHANGE command, the user can change the contents of the field or variable displayed in the GET command.

Unlike the SAY command, you can use the GET command to read data into a memo field. However, data can be read into a memo field only when the GET command appears in a format file that you open with the SET FORMAT command.

Unlike the STORE command (and assignment operator), GET cannot create a new variable from scratch. If the field or variable that GET is attempting to display does not exist in memory or in the currently selected database, the error message *Variable not found*

Table 2.2: Picture Function Characters Used with the PICTURE Clause

Symbol	Data Types	Effect in Say	Effect in Get
(	N,F	Displays negative number in parentheses	None
^	N,F	Displays number in scientific format	Displays number in scientific format
!	C	Displays all letters in uppercase	Converts all letters to uppercase
$	N,F	Displays data in currency format	Displays data in currency format
A	C	None	Permits only alphabetic characters to be entered
B	N,F	Left-justifies a number in display	Left-justifies a number in display
C	N,F	Displays CR (credit) after positive number	None
D	D	Displays date in U.S. MM/DD/YY format	Displays date in U.S. MM/DD/YY format, though date is stored in SET DATE format

Table 2.2: Picture Function Characters Used with the PICTURE Clause (Continued)

Symbol	Data Types	Effect in Say	Effect in Get
E	D	Displays date in European DD/MM/YY format	Displays date in European DD/MM/YY format, though date is stored in SET DATE format
I	C	Centers text in allotted field width	None
J	C	Right-aligns text in allotted field width	None
L	N,F	Displays leading zeros	Displays leading zeros
M	C,N	None	Allows user to select from predefined options
R	C	Inserts template characters into displayed data	Displays template characters in highlight, but does not store them in file

appears on the screen. If you use GET to read in a variable, you must predefine the variable.

Table 2.2: Picture Function Characters Used with the PICTURE Clause (Continued)

Symbol	Data Types	Effect in Say	Effect in Get
S*n*	C	Displays the left *n* characters of the data	Creates a highlight that is *n* spaces wide; if data are longer than *n* spaces wide, user can scroll with arrow keys
T	C	Trims leading and trailing blanks from field	Trims leading and trailing blanks from field
X	N,F	Displays DB (debit) after negative number	None
Z	N,F	Displays a zero as a blank space	Displays a zero as a blank space

Unlike data you enter into a memory variable in an ACCEPT command, any data you enter into a memory variable through GET retains its original size. For example, if in response to the commands

```
AnyName = SPACE(15)
ACCEPT "Enter name " TO AnyName
```

you enter **Albert**, the AnyName variable simply contains Albert. However, if in response to the commands

```
AnyName = SPACE(15)
@ 2,2 SAY "Enter name " GET AnyName
READ
```

you enter **Albert**, the variable AnyName actually contains Albert plus nine spaces, because GET retains the original length of 15 characters. This subtle difference can cause confusion in application programs, particularly in memory variables used with the SEEK command. To remove the trailing blanks from the memory variable when you use SEEK, use the TRIM() function, as follows:

```
@AnyName = SPACE(15)
@ 2,2 SAY "Enter name " GET AnyName
READ
SEEK TRIM(AnyName)
```

FUNCTION

The FUNCTION option specifies a general format for the display. Table 2.2 displays the function symbols, the data types they are used for, and the effects they have on displayed data.

The function symbol must be enclosed in quotes and placed to the right of the FUNCTION statement in the command. You can combine functions within a single FUNCTION statement. For example, the command

```
@ 2,1 SAY Amount FUNCTION "CX"
```

displays the contents of the Amount field or variable with the letters DB to the right of negative numbers, and CR to the right of positive numbers.

The $ function displays a currency sign with a numeric field. By default, the $ symbol is placed before the number. You can change the currency sign and its position by using the SET CURRENCY command. The M function specifies a multiple-choice field, with each field separated by a comma. For example, the command

```
@ 5,20 GET State FUNCTION "M AK,CA,NE,WA"
```

displays the contents of the State field and allows the user to select an option by pressing the spacebar or by typing the first letter of the desired state. To include a blank as an option, place two commas next to each other in the options list.

PICTURE

The PICTURE option lets you design a template for the data being displayed or edited. Unlike FUNCTION, a PICTURE template affects individual characters within the data. For example, the command

```
@ 2,5 GET PartCode  PICTURE "A-999"
```

accepts only part codes that begin with a letter, followed by a hyphen, and a three-digit number (the hyphen is inserted automatically).

Table 2.3 lists the available template characters. Literal characters (those not listed as template characters) are inserted into the field automatically. For example, the command

```
@ 5,5 GET Phone PICTURE "(999)999-9999"
```

accepts data into a field or variable named Phone. If the user types **8185550143**, the template automatically converts the entry to (818)555-0143.

You can combine picture templates and functions in the PICTURE command if you precede the function symbol with an @ character and follow it with a blank space. For example, the command

```
@ 5,1 GET PartCode FUNCTION "!" PICTURE; "A-999"
```

can be abbreviated as

```
@ 5,1 GET PartCode PICTURE "@! A-999"
```

RANGE (REQUIRED)

The optional RANGE component of the @ command specifies an acceptable range of numbers or dates for an entry. The lowest acceptable value is listed first, followed by a comma and the highest acceptable value. If you include only a single number as the specified range, that value becomes the lowest acceptable value and there is assumed to be no upper limit. If you include a comma

Table 2.3: Picture Template Characters Used with the PICTURE Clause

Character	Data Types	Effect in Say	Effect in Get
!	C	Displays the letter in uppercase	Converts the letter to uppercase
#	C,N,F	None	Accepts only a number, space, decimal point, plus sign, or minus sign
$	N,F	Displays leading $ in front of number if space permits	Fills highlight with leading dollar signs
*	N,F	Displays asterisks in place of leading zeros	Displays asterisks in place of leading zeros
,	N,F	Displays comma if digits are present on both sides	Diplays comma if digits are present on both sides
9	C,N	None	Accepts only a number
A	C	None	Accepts only an alphabetic character

Table 2.3: Picture Template Characters Used with the PICTURE Clause (Continued)

Character	Data Types	Effect in Say	Effect in Get
L	C,L	None	Accepts only uppercase or lowercase T, F, Y, or N
N	C	None	Allows letters (A-Z) and digits (0-9) only
X	C	None	Accepts any character
Y	C,L	Converts .T. to Y and .F. to N	Accepts only Y or N, and converts lowercase to uppercase
Other	C	Any other characters are added as template characters	Any other characters are added as template characters
Other	N,F	Inserts symbol in data	Displays symbol, but does not store it

followed by a number, the number is assumed to be the upper limit, with no lower limit assumed.

The REQUIRED option automatically checks for the allowable range parameters when the cursor moves into the GET field whether you change it or not. It indicates that the RANGE criteria must be met.

When you actually execute the @...GET...RANGE command and enter a value that falls outside of the acceptable range, dBASE beeps and displays an error message, along with the lowest and highest acceptable values, near the bottom of the screen. To try again, press the spacebar.

OPEN WINDOW

The WINDOW option lets you use a predefined window for editing data in memo fields. If OPEN is included with the WINDOW option, the contents of the memo field are displayed in the opened window. If OPEN is not included, only the *memo* marker is displayed, and the user must press **Ctrl-Home** to open the window (and **Ctrl-End** to close it).

For example, if the database currently open contains a memo field named Abstract, you can use the DEFINE WINDOW command to create a window for editing the memo field.

```
DEFINE WINDOW MemWindo FROM 5,5 TO 15,60
```

Later in the command file (or in a separate format file), you can include a command such as:

```
@ 5,5 GET Abstract OPEN WINDOW MemWindo
```

DEFAULT

The DEFAULT option defines a default value for a variable or field, which is displayed automatically when new data is being entered into a field. The default value can be literal data, an expression, or a dBASE function. Accept the default value by leaving it unchanged on the screen, or type in a new value.

The following command example allows the user to enter new data into a date field named StartDate and presents the current date as the default date:

```
@ 10,5 GET StartDate DEFAULT DATE()
```

The default value is displayed only while you append new records. If SET CARRY is on, the value carried forward from the previous record overrides the DEFAULT value.

MESSAGE

The MESSAGE option defines a message that is displayed at the bottom of the screen whenever a particular field is being edited. The message can be up to 79 characters and must be enclosed in quotes, as in the command

```
@ 10,5 GET StartDate DEFAULT DATE() MESSAGE;
   "Press Enter to accept suggested date;
   or type in a new date"
```

WHEN

The WHEN option lets you define an expression that determines when a field can and cannot be edited. If the expressions results in .T. (true), you can move the cursor into the field and edit its contents. If the expression evaluates to .F. (false), the cursor skips the field.

In the next example, you can edit the Amount field only when the Posted field contains .F.

```
@ 5,4 GET Amount WHEN .NOT. Posted
```

In the next example, you can edit the Tax field only if the field named TaxRate contains a number greater than 0.

```
@ 2,20 GET Tax WHEN TaxRate > 0
```

VALID (REQUIRED) (ERROR)

The VALID option lets you define an expression to validate data entered into a field or memory variable. If the expression yields .T., the value is accepted and the cursor moves to the next field. If the expression yields .F., the entry is rejected, an error message is displayed, and the cursor does not move to the next field. The error message is either the default message, *Editing condition not satisfied (press SPACE)*, or an error message that you specify with the ERROR option.

If you use the REQUIRED option, dBASE checks for the VALID condition when the cursor moves into the GET field whether you change it or not. It indicates that the VALID condition must always be met.

Note that you can specify a user-defined function as the VALID expression for greater control over validating data. You can also include @...SAY commands in the user-defined function to display on-screen calculations as data is entered and edited.

In the following routine, the user is entering data into a database named Orders. When the user enters a part code, the VALID option searches the PartList database for the entered part code. If none is found, the entry is rejected and the error message *No such part code* is displayed at the bottom of the screen:

```
USE Orders IN 1
USE PartList ORDER PartNo IN 2

SELECT 1

@ 5,1 GET PartNo PICTURE "!-999" ;
  VALID SEEK(PartNo,"PartList") ;
  ERROR "No such part code!"

READ
```

COLOR

You can individually color the text and/or highlight in an @...SAY...GET command by using the COLOR option. The first color combination affects the SAY portion of the command and the second color combination affects the GET portion. You must specify valid color codes, as described in **SET COLOR**.

The following command examples show the SAY portion with red letters on a white background and the GET portion with bright white letters on a red background:

```
X=0
@ 5,1 SAY "Enter a number " GET X ;
  COLOR R/W,W+/R
READ
```

If you omit one color combination, the current screen colors are used. For example, the command

@ 20,40 SAY "Total due " GET Amount COLOR ,RB/G

displays *Total due* in the current screen color, and the Amount field highlighted as magenta letters on a green background.

Tip: You can use user-defined functions to develop data-entry screens with features such as help windows, on-screen calculations, and multifile lookup and validation.

• EXAMPLE The DemoGet.PRG command file shown in Figure 2.1 demonstrates several @...SAY...GET commands. For a demonstration of the various @...SAY...GET commands and options, key the program in exactly as shown in the figure, then run it.

See Also @...CLEAR, @...TO, APPEND, CLEAR, CREATE/MODIFY SCREEN, EDIT, FUNCTION, INSERT, READ, SET COLOR, SET DATE, SET DELIMITERS, SET DEVICE, SET FORMAT, SET INTENSITY

THE @...CLEAR COMMAND

Clearing a Portion of the Screen

• SYNTAX

@ *row1,col1* (**CLEAR** (**TO** *row2,col2*))

• USAGE The @...CLEAR command clears text from a portion of the screen or currently active window. If you omit the CLEAR TO and second screen coordinates from the command, dBASE clears the screen from the specified row and column position to the end of the line. If you omit the TO and second screen coordinates, dBASE

```
Page #     1

****************************  DemoGet.PRG
*----- Demonstrate @..SAY..GET commands.
CLEAR
SET TALK OFF
SET STATUS OFF
SET CONFIRM ON
*- Initialize memory variables.
SSN = 123456789
PosNumb = 12345.67
NegNumb = -8765.432
Logical = .T.
Today = DATE()
Right = CHR(26)
Left = CHR(27)
Text1 = "Press "+Right+" to scroll this line."

*- Demonstrate scrolling field.
@ 1,1 TO 3,79 DOUBLE
@ 2,5 SAY "Sample screen with @..SAY..GET commands"
@ 5,5 GET Text1 FUNCTION "S17"
@ 19,1 TO 23,79 DOUBLE
@ 20,5 SAY "Test the "+Right+" and "+Left+" arrow keys."
@ 21,5 SAY "Then press "+CHR(17)+CHR(196)+CHR(217)
READ

*- Demonstrate Multiple-Choice field.
@ 20,2 CLEAR TO 21,78
DayOfWeek = SPACE(10)
@ 20,5 SAY "You can press the space bar to scroll through"
@ 21,5 SAY "options, or press the first letter of a day."
@ 22,5 SAY "Then press "+CHR(17)+CHR(196)+CHR(217)
@ 7,5 SAY "Select a weekday ";
    GET DayOfWeek FUNCTION "M Sunday,Monday,Tuesday,;
    Wednesday,Thursday,Friday,Saturday" COLOR ,W+/N
READ

*- Demonstrate miscellaneous templates and functions.
@ 9,5 GET SSN PICTURE "999-99-9999"
@ 11,5 GET PosNumb PICTURE "$99,999.99"
@ 13,5 SAY NegNumb FUNCTION "X" PICTURE "99,999.99"
@ 15,5 SAY "Today's date, European-style, is "
@ 15,39 GET Today FUNCTION "E"
CLEAR GETS

@ 20,2 CLEAR TO 22,70
@ 20,2 FILL TO 22,78 COLOR R/BG
@ 21,2 SAY "Press any key to view window...";
    COLOR R+/BG
WAIT " "

DEFINE WINDOW Wind1 FROM 10,20 TO 15,60 ;
    COLOR W+/R,R/W,N/G
ACTIVATE WINDOW WIND1
@ 0,0 SAY "This sentence starts at row 0, column 0"
@ 2,5
WAIT "Press any key to remove window..."
RELEASE WINDOW Wind1
```

Figure 2.1: The DemoGet.PRG Command File

clears the screen from the specified coordinates to the bottom of the screen.

- **EXAMPLE** The command

@ 10,5 CLEAR TO 15,50

clears the portion of the screen from row 10, column 5, to row 15, column 50.

See Also CLEAR, @...FILL

THE @...FILL COMMAND

Coloring a Portion of the Screen

• SYNTAX

@ *row1, col1* **FILL TO** *row2,col2* (**COLOR** *codes*)

• USAGE The @...FILL command changes the text and background color of any rectangular portion of the screen or active window. The command affects only existing text, not text displayed by subsequent commands.

The color codes available for this command are the same as those used by the SET COLOR TO command. If no color is specified, @...FILL behaves exactly like @...CLEAR.

If you try to color an area that is larger than the screen or the currently active window, dBASE displays the error message *Coordinates are off the screen.*

• EXAMPLE If you have a color monitor, enter the following commands at the dot prompt for a demonstration of the @...FILL command:

```
SET COLOR TO GR+/B
LIST MEMORY
@ 3,5 FILL TO 16,40 COLOR R+/W
@ 10,10 SAY "Back to yellow on blue"
```

See Also @...SAY, @...CLEAR, SET COLOR

@...SCROLL

Scrolling Contents of a Window

• SYNTAX

@ *row1,col1* **TO** *row2,col2* **SCROLL**
*(***UP/DOWN/LEFT/RIGHT***)* *(***BY** *number)* *(***WRAP***)*

• USAGE @...SCROLL shifts the contents of a portion of the screen or active window so that you can view more information than the space allows. You can shift up, down, left, or right by a specified number of rows or columns. The row and column numbers refer to a rectangular area of the screen. If you are using a window, the row and column numbers are relative to the window boundaries. You can also use negative numbers to reverse the direction of the shift.

The WRAP option rewrites the scrolled characters on the opposite side of the space rather than inserting blanks.

• EXAMPLE The commands

```
@ 1,1 SAY "1234567890"
@ 2,1 SAY "0987654321"
@ 1,1 TO 4,10 SCROLL DOWN BY 3
```

shifts lines one and two down three rows. The area defined by the @...SCROLL command is only four rows deep, therefore the string "0987654321" disappears from the screen, and "1234567890" is displayed in row four. However, using the WRAP option in the command

```
@ 1,1 TO 4,10 SCROLL DOWN BY 3 WRAP
```

rewrites "0987654321" at the top of the area in row one.

See Also @...CLEAR, SET COLOR

THE @...TO COMMAND

Drawing Lines and Boxes

• SYNTAX

@ row1, col1 **TO** *row2,col2 (***DOUBLE/PANEL/***ASCII codes)*
*(***COLOR** *codes)*

• USAGE Use @...TO to draw lines and boxes on the screen. By default, both are drawn with single-line characters unless you have changed the default setting with the SET BORDER command. If you specify the DOUBLE option, the border is drawn with double lines. If you specify the PANEL option, the border is displayed in reverse video.

You can use other characters for box borders by specifying a list of characters enclosed in quotes or ASCII numbers to represent parts of the box. They must be given in the following order: top of the box, bottom, left, right, top left corner, top right corner, bottom left corner, bottom right corner. The ASCII numbers must be in the range of 0 to 255, must be separated with commas, and should not be enclosed in quotes. If you specify only the first character (top of the box in the preceding list), that character is used for the entire box.

The COLOR option defines the foreground and background color for the box or line border. Use the same codes that you use with the SET COLOR command to define the colors.

Tip: To view a list of ASCII characters and the numbers assigned to them, you can enter the forms design screen (using the MODIFY SCREEN command), select **Box** from the Layout pull-down menu, and **Using Specified Character** from the submenu. The number in the leftmost column of the display is the one you use with the @...TO command.

• EXAMPLE This command displays a box with a doubleline border:

@ 2,1 TO 4,78 DOUBLE

The next command draws a box that uses arrows for the top, bottom, left, and right edges, and slashes and backslashes for the corners. The border is displayed as bright blinking red on a black background.

@ 5,10 TO 15,50 26,27,24,25,47,92,92,47 COLOR R+*/W

The command

@ 10,10 TO 20,75 , , , ,63,63,63,63

draws a box with single lines at the sides and questions marks at the four corners.

The following command draws a single horizontal bar using a solid panel:

@ 18,10 TO 18,60 PANEL

See Also @...CLEAR, @...FILL, DEFINE BOX, SET BORDER, SET COLOR

ACCEPT

Asking the User a Question

• SYNTAX

ACCEPT *(prompt)* **TO** *memory variable*

• USAGE ACCEPT presents a prompt to the user and waits for a response followed by a press on the ↵ key. The user's response is stored in a memory variable of the character data type. The data stored in the memory variable can be from 1 to 254 characters long.

The optional prompt can be a character string surrounded by quotation marks, apostrophes, or square brackets. To embed an apostrophe or other character within the prompt, just use a different character for the outside delimiters. The prompt can also be stored in a character memory variable.

If the user presses ↵ in response to the ACCEPT command without first typing any text, the length of the memory variable will be 0. No delimiters are required for the response.

• **EXAMPLE** The following commands present the prompt *What's your name* to the user, wait for a response, and store the response in a variable called Name:

ACCEPT "What's your name " TO Name

See Also @...READ, INKEY(), INPUT, SET ESCAPE, WAIT

ACTIVATE MENU

Using a Horizontal Bar Menu

• **SYNTAX**

ACTIVATE MENU *menu name* **(PAD** *pad name)*

• **USAGE** ACTIVATE MENU displays a horizontal bar menu you've defined. You should issue the command only after using the DEFINE MENU, DEFINE PAD, and ON SELECTION commands to fully define the menu.

Unless you use the PAD option, the first option of the menu is highlighted when the menu is displayed. Otherwise, the specified pad is highlighted on the menu.

When the menu is active on the screen, the user can move the highlight from one option to the next with the ← and → keys, and press ↵ to select an option. The name of the selected option is stored in the PAD() function and the text is stored in the PROMPT() function.

A horizontal bar remains active on the screen until a DEACTIVATE MENU command is executed, another menu is activated, or the user presses **Esc**.

• EXAMPLE Assuming that a menu named MainMnu has already been fully defined, the next command activates the menu, with the highlight on Option2:

```
ACTIVATE MENU MainMnu PAD Option2
```

See Also BAR(), BARCOUNT(), BARPROMPT(), DEACTIVATE MENU, DEFINE MENU, MENU(), ON EXIT MENU/PAD, ON PAD, ON SELECTION PAD, PAD(), PADPROMPT(), PROMPT(), SHOW MENU

ACTIVATE POPUP

Using a Pop-Up Menu

• SYNTAX

ACTIVATE POPUP *popup name*

• USAGE ACTIVATE POPUP displays and activates a previously defined pop-up menu, (including pull-down menus and pick lists). After the user selects an option from a pop-up menu, the PROMPT() function contains the text of the menu option and the BAR() function contains the row number of the selected option.

The pop-up menu is active on-screen until a DEACTIVATE POPUP command is executed or the user presses **Esc**. Only one pop-up menu may be active at a time.

• EXAMPLE The following command activates a previously defined pop-up menu named GetJob:

```
ACTIVATE POPUP GetJob
```

See Also BAR(), BARCOUNT(), DEACTIVATE POPUP, DEFINE POPUP, ON BAR, ON EXIT BAR/POPUP, ON SELECTION POPUP, PADPROMPT(), POPUP(), PROMPT(), SHOW POPUP

ACTIVATE SCREEN

Using the Whole Screen

• SYNTAX

ACTIVATE SCREEN

• USAGE The ACTIVATE SCREEN command deactivates all pop-up menus and windows without erasing their contents from the screen. The full screen becomes accessible for displaying text. @...SAY...GET positioning refers to the full screen (rows 0 through 24, columns 0 through 79) rather than to any windows displayed on the screen.

• EXAMPLE Assuming that the window named Help1 has already been defined and the file HelpMsg.TXT contains text, the following commands display the help message in a window and immediately return control to the full screen:

```
ACTIVATE WINDOW Help1
TYPE HelpMsg.TXT
ACTIVATE SCREEN
```

See Also ACTIVATE WINDOW, DEACTIVATE WINDOW, DEFINE WINDOW

ACTIVATE WINDOW

Using a Window

• SYNTAX

ACTIVATE WINDOW *window name list*/**ALL**

• USAGE ACTIVATE WINDOW displays and activates a previously defined window. When the window is active, displayed text is wrapped to fit inside the window, and @...SAY...GET coordinates refer to the screen area within the window (with @ 0,0 referring to the upper-left corner of the window). All subsequent screen output appears in the active window.

If the window name list contains several window names, all of the windows in the list are displayed, but only the window listed last is activated. If you use the ALL option, all currently defined windows are displayed, and the window defined last becomes the active window.

Activating a window that is covered by other windows brings that window to the forefront.

• EXAMPLE The following command activates three previously defined windows named Help1, Help2, and Help3:

ACTIVATE WINDOW Help1,Help2,Help3

See Also ACTIVATE SCREEN, CLEAR, DEACTIVATE WINDOW, DEFINE WINDOW, MOVE WINDOW, RESTORE WINDOW, SAVE WINDOW, SET BORDER, SET WINDOW OF MEMO

APPEND

Adding New Records to a Database

• SYNTAX

APPEND *[***BLANK***]/[***NOORGANIZE***]*

• USAGE The APPEND command initiates full-screen data entry mode for adding new records to the currently selected database. If no database is opened, dBASE prompts you for one. Use the command keys shown in Table 2.4 to control the screen and cursor. These work both for the simple screen that APPEND shows automatically and for custom screens that you design yourself with the MODIFY SCREEN command.

With APPEND, you can add data only to a single database file. If several database files are open and related, APPEND adds data only to the currently selected file.

Indexes in the production index file are automatically updated. Any inactive index files are not updated and will need to be rebuilt with the INDEX ON or REINDEX command.

The master index, if any, controls the order in which PgUp and PgDn scroll through records. If there is no active index file, scrolling takes place in sequential record number order.

Some newly added records are stored in a buffer before being written to disk. A CLOSE DATABASES, CLOSE ALL, USE, or QUIT command transfers all new records from the buffer to the database file.

If the SET CARRY option is on, data entered into a record is automatically carried over to the next newly added record.

The BLANK option adds a single blank record to the current database file, without displaying a data entry screen. You can use the REPLACE or APPEND FROM ARRAY command to copy data from memory variables into the new blank record.

Table 2.4: Command Keys Used with the APPEND Command

Key	Alternate	Effect
Return		Finishes data entry in one field and moves cursor to next field
Num Lock		Toggles number/arrow keys on numeric keypad
→	Ctrl-D	Moves cursor right one character
←	Ctrl-S	Moves cursor left one character
Home	Ctrl-Z	Moves cursor to start of field
Ctrl-←	Ctrl-A	Moves cursor to previous word, previous field, or beginning of previous record, depending on cursor position
End	Ctrl-B	Moves cursor to end of field
Ctrl-→	Ctrl-F	Moves cursor to next word or start of next field, depending on cursor position
PgUp	Ctrl-R	Scrolls to previous page or record, if any
PgDn	Ctrl-C	Scrolls to next page or record, if any
↑ or Shift-Tab	Ctrl-E	Moves cursor to previous field or beginning of previous record, depending on cursor position
↓ or Tab	Ctrl-X	Moves cursor to next field
Ins	Ctrl-V	Toggles insert mode on/off
Del	Ctrl-G	Deletes character at cursor
Backspace		Moves cursor to left, erasing existing character
Ctrl-T		Deletes word to right
Ctrl-Y		Deletes all characters to right
Ctrl-U		Toggles record deletion marker

Table 2.4: Command Keys Used with the APPEND Command (Continued)

Key	Alternate	Effect
Esc	Ctrl-Q	Aborts last entry and exits Edit mode
Ctrl-End	Ctrl-W	Saves entry and exits Edit mode
Ctrl-PgDn		Moves to last record in file
Ctrl-PgUp		Moves to first record in file

The NOORGANIZE option prevents the user from reindexing or sorting the data during an application by disabling the Organize menu option. NOORGANIZE cannot be used with the BLANK option.

• **EXAMPLE** The following commands open the Mail database and MailScr format file and allow you to add new, but not to rearrange, records using the screen defined in the format file. The CLOSE FORMAT command returns the screen to its default state.

```
USE Mail
SET FORMAT TO MailScr
APPEND NOORGANIZE
CLOSE FORMAT
```

See Also APPEND BLANK, APPEND FROM, BROWSE, CLOSE, EDIT, INSERT, READ, SET AUTOSAVE, SET FORMAT, SET WINDOW

APPEND FROM

Adding Records from Another Database

• SYNTAX

APPEND FROM *file name(***(TYPE)***file type)* **(REINDEX)** **(FOR** *condition)*

• USAGE When you append data from one dBASE database to another, only data with identical field names in both databases is appended to the currently active database. If the width of a field in the active database is less than the width of the database being read, character data will be truncated to fit the new width. Large numbers that do not fit into the currently active database are replaced with asterisks.

The current disk drive and directory are assumed, unless you specify otherwise in the *file name* parameter. The .DBF extension is assumed in the file name being read, unless otherwise specified in *file name.* If the database from which you are reading does not have a file name extension, place a period at the end of the file name in the APPEND FROM command.

If SET DELETED is off, records marked for deletion are read into the current database but are *not* marked for deletion in the current database. If SET DELETED is on, records marked for deletion are not read into the active database file.

The FOR expression works only with fields that exist in both database files.

The REINDEX option delays updating all active noncontrolling indexes until all the records have been added to the active database file.

The TYPE expression defines the structure of a non-dBASE data file and allows you to import data from foreign software systems into an existing dBASE database. Table 2.5 lists options used with TYPE, and the types of files imported.

Table 2.5: Keys Used at the Control Center

Option	Type of File
DBASEII	dBASE II (must have .DB2 file name extension)
DELIMITED	ASCII text file with individual fields separated by commas, and records separated by carriage return/line feed (CRLF)
DELIMITED WITH *character*	ASCII text file with individual fields separated by the specified *character*, and records separated by a CRLF
DELIMITED WITH BLANK	ASCII text file with individual fields separated by a blank space, and records separated by CRLF
DIF	Visicalc Data Interchange Format files with .DIF extension
FW2	Framework II (.FW2) files
RPD	RapidFile data (.RPD) file
SYLK	Multiplan files with .SLK extension
Text Fixed Length Fields	ASCII text file with fixed field length, no delimiters between fields, and records separated by a CRLF with file extension .TXT (called SDF format in earlier versions of dBASE)
WKS	Lotus 1-2-3, version 1A spreadsheet files with .WKS extension

When you import spreadsheet files, dBASE expects the data to be in columns and rows that can be converted into fields and records. If you attempt to import a spreadsheet file whose data is not stored in even columns and rows, the format of the imported data will be unpredictable.

Tip: You can store newly entered records in a temporary database file and then use APPEND FROM to read these records into the actual database. This method is often preferred in networking environments or when data needs to be verified before being processed in the final database.

• **EXAMPLE** The following commands append records from the OrdTemp.DBF database into the currently open Orders.DBF database. However, records marked for deletion in OrdTemp and records that have no entry in the PartNo field are *not* appended (both Orders and OrdTemp have a character field named PartNo). After all the records have been appended, the noncontrolling Orders indexes are updated. Then all records are removed from the OrdTemp database with the ZAP command, so a future APPEND FROM command does not read these records again.

```
Use Orders
SET DELETED ON
*------ Append records from OrdTemp.dbf
APPEND FROM OrdTemp REINDEX FOR PartNo # " "
*------ Empty the OrdTemp database
USE OrdTemp
SET SAFETY OFF
ZAP
```

The following commands open a database file named Master.DBF and read in records from an ASCII text file named Master.TXT. In this example, the file to be imported is stored in Framework II format. When all the records have been added, the active, noncontrolling indexes are updated.

```
USE Master
APPEND FROM Master.txt TYPE FW2 REINDEX
```

See Also APPEND, APPEND FROM ARRAY, BLANK, COPY, DELETED(), IMPORT, SET DELETED

APPEND FROM ARRAY

Copying Array Data to a Database

• SYNTAX

APPEND FROM ARRAY *array name (***REINDEX***) (***FOR** *condition)*

• USAGE The APPEND FROM ARRAY command adds each row from an array to the bottom of the current database file. The first column in the array becomes the first field in each new record, the second array column becomes the second field, and so forth. If there are more array columns than database fields, the extra columns are ignored. If there are more database fields than array columns, the extra fields are left blank.

The array columns being added to the database file must have the same data types as the fields in the database.

The REINDEX option delays updating all active noncontrolling indexes until after all the records have been added.

The FOR option limits the appending to specific records, and must refer to a field in the database file, not to the values in the array.

Tip: Remember that the DECLARE and PUBLIC ARRAY commands automatically create array elements that contain .F. (the logical data type). You cannot append one of these values into a database field that is not of the logical data type.

• EXAMPLE Figure 2.2 shows a sample routine that creates an array of memory variables, displays them on the screen for editing,

```
Page #     1

****************************** ArrayMan.PRG
*-- Program to manipulate arrays

SET TALK OFF
DECLARE OrdArray[10,5]

CLEAR
@ 4,1 SAY "Invoice  Customer   Part        Qty      Paid"

*-- Display fields on screen
Counter = 1
DO WHILE Counter<=10
        STORE 0 TO OrdArray[Counter,1],OrdArray[Counter,2],;
                  OrdArray[Counter,4]
        OrdArray[Counter,3] = SPACE(6)
        @ Counter+5,1 GET OrdArray[Counter,1] PICTURE "999999"
        @ ROW(),10 GET OrdArray[Counter,2] PICTURE "9999"
        @ ROW(),20 GET OrdArray[Counter,3] PICTURE "!!!!!!"
        @ ROW(),30 GET OrdArray[Counter,4] PICTURE "999"
        @ ROW(),40 GET OrdArray[Counter,5] PICTURE "Y"
        Counter = Counter+1
ENDDO
RELEASE Counter
READ

*-- Append array elements to end of the database file
USE NewOrder
APPEND FROM ARRAY OrdArray FOR Invoice > 0
```

Figure 2.2: Sample routine using the APPEND FROM ARRAY command

and then adds records from the array to the bottom of the NewOrder.DBF database. Note that NewOrder has the database structure shown below.

Field	Field Name	Type	Width	Dec	Index
1	INVOICE	Numeric	6		Y
2	CUSTNO	Numeric	4		N
3	PARTNO	Character	6		Y
4	QTYORDERED	Numeric	3		N
5	PAID	Logical	1		N

The DECLARE command defines the array, and the DO WHILE loop displays all of the array elements on the screen. Note that all array elements are initialized to match the data types of the database fields, and that the PICTURE options in the @...GET commands format the display to resemble the field widths of the database fields.

See Also APPEND, COPY TO ARRAY, DECLARE, PUBLIC, STORE

APPEND MEMO

Copying Memo Field Data

• SYNTAX

APPEND MEMO *memo field name* **FROM** *file name* *(***OVERWRITE***)*

• USAGE The APPEND MEMO command reads the contents of an external text file into the memo field of the current database record. By default, the contents of the external file are appended to any text that is already in the memo field. If you use the OVERWRITE option, however, the text currently in the memo field is erased before the incoming text is appended.

If you do not include an extension with the file name, the .TXT extension is assumed.

• EXAMPLE The following commands open a database file named Employee.DBF, position the record pointer to record number 10, and read the contents of a file named Smith.TXT into the memo field named Resume:

```
USE Employee
GOTO 10
APPEND MEMO Resume FROM Smith.txt
```

See Also COPY MEMO, MODIFY COMMAND/FILE

ASSIST

Accessing the Control Center

• SYNTAX

```
ASSIST
```

• USAGE The ASSIST command takes you from the dot prompt to the dBASE IV Control Center, which provides a pull-down menu interface for interacting with dBASE IV. The Control Center displays the names of files in the current catalog in *panels* in the workspace. These panels are labeled Data, Queries, Forms, Reports, Labels, and Applications. The <create> option at the top of each panel lets you create a new file of the given type and places it into the current catalog.

To select an option from the Control Center, position the highlight with the →, ←, ↑, and ↓ keys, and press ↵. Other special keys that you can use at the Control Center are listed in the navigation line at the bottom of your screen, and in Table 2.6

To leave the Control Center and return to the dot prompt, select **Exit to Dot Prompt** from the Exit pull-down menu, or press **Esc** and select **Yes**.

• EXAMPLE To leave the dot prompt and access the Control Center, press the **F2** key, or type the command

```
ASSIST
```

and press ↵.

See Also HELP, CREATE, MODIFY

Table 2.6: Keys Used at the Control Center

Key	Purpose
F1	Help
↑ ↓ → ←	Move highlight
↵	Select
F2	View data
Shift-F2	View/modify design
Shift-F9	Print Quick Report
F10	Access pull-down menus

AVERAGE

Calculating the Average

• SYNTAX

AVERAGE *(field names/expressions) (scope)* (**WHILE** *condition)*(**FOR** *condition)* (**TO** *memory variables/* **TO ARRAY** *array name)*

• USAGE The AVERAGE command calculates the average of a numeric field or fields. You can include up to five field names or expressions, separated by commas. If you specify no field names or expressions, all numeric fields are averaged. All records are included unless you have specified a scope, WHILE, or FOR condition.

Results of the calculation are displayed only if SET TALK is on. You can optionally store calculation results in memory variables by using the TO option, or in an array by using the TO ARRAY option.

Records hidden by a SET FILTER, MODIFY QUERY, or SET DELETED ON command are excluded from the calculation.

• EXAMPLE The command

AVERAGE ExtPrice, Qty TO AvgPrice, AvgQty

calculates the average of the numeric fields ExtPrice and Qty and stores the results in numeric memory variables named AvgPrice and AvgQty.

See Also CALCULATE

BEGIN/END TRANSACTION

Recording Changes to a Database File

• SYNTAX

BEGIN TRANSACTION *(transaction file path name)*
transaction commands
END TRANSACTION

• USAGE You can use BEGIN TRANSACTION and END TRANSACTION at the dot prompt or in a command file to record changes made to a database file. If, for some reason, an error occurs during the changes but before the END TRANSACTION command is executed, you can use the ROLLBACK command to restore database records to the state they were in before the BEGIN TRANSACTION command was executed.

Changes made to the database are recorded in a file named Transact.LOG on single-user computers, and *work station name*.LOG on a network (where *work station name* is the name of the computer that began the transaction). If you do not specify a path name in the BEGIN TRANSACTION command, the transaction file is stored on the current directory.

The END TRANSACTION command commits all changes made since the BEGIN TRANSACTION command was executed and terminates the transaction. To be effective, the ROLLBACK command must be issued after BEGIN TRANSACTION but before END TRANSACTION.

Commands that update the transaction file include APPEND, BROWSE, CHANGE, DELETE, EDIT, RECALL, REPLACE, and UPDATE. dBASE IV commands that close open files (including CREATE [FROM], IMPORT, INDEX ON, SET CATALOG TO, SET INDEX TO, SORT, and USE) are allowed during a transaction only if you make sure that they will not close a file that was open before the transaction process began.

Commands that are never allowed during a transaction are CLEAR ALL, CLOSE ALL, CLOSE DATABASES, CLOSE INDEX, CONVERT, CREATE, VIEW, DELETE FILE, ERASE, INSERT, MODIFY STRUCTURE, PACK, RENAME, and ZAP. On a network, the UNLOCK command will not produce an error, but it will not have any effect while the transaction is in progress.

Only one transaction at a time can be active. Once you issue a BEGIN TRANSACTION command, you must close the transaction by issuing an END TRANSACTION command before entering another BEGIN TRANSACTION command.

You should make a copy of the database before executing the BEGIN TRANSACTION command. This way, if an error prevents the ROLLBACK command from being successful, you can still copy the backup database to the original file name to restore the changes.

During transaction processing on a network, you cannot have two users logged-in with the same name.

• **EXAMPLE** The following routine increases the UnitPrice field by 10 percent for part number A-111, displays all records with that part number, and asks the user if the changes are OK. If the answer is **Yes**, the new data is saved. If the answer is **No**, the ROLLBACK command restores the data to its original state:

```
BEGIN TRANSACTION
  USE Orders

  REPLACE ALL UnitPrice WITH 1.10*UnitPrice ;
```

```
        FOR PartNo = "A-111"
      CLEAR
      LIST PartNo,UnitPrice FOR PartNo = "A-111"

      SET TALK OFF
      Ok = .F.
      @ 21,10 SAY "Ok to commit? (Y/N) " ;
        GET Ok PICTURE "Y"
      READ

      *--- If changes unsatisfactory, undo them.
      IF .NOT. Ok
        ROLLBACK
      ENDIF

    END TRANSACTION
    CLEAR

    ? "Final status..."
    ?
    LIST PartNo, UnitPrice FOR PartNo = "A-111"
```

See Also CHANGE(), COMPLETED(), ISMARKED(), RESET, ROLLBACK, ROLLBACK()

BLANK

Filling Fields and Record with Blanks

• SYNTAX

BLANK (**FIELDS** *field list*/**LIKE**/**EXCEPT** *skeleton*) (**REINDEX**) *(scope)* (**FOR** *condition*) (**WHILE** *condition*)

• USAGE BLANK is used to insert blanks into selected fields or into whole records in the active database file. No records are deleted, they are just filled with blanks. The blank value is dependent upon the data type of the field. With a LIST or DISPLAY command, blank fields are displayed as shown below:

Data Type	**Blank Value**
Character	All spaces
Date	{ / / }
Float or Numeric	No data entered
Logical	.F.
Memo	No data entered

In BROWSE or EDIT, blank logical fields are displayed as blank. If you evaluate a numeric field, it will appear as 0 rather than blank.

The FIELDS option specifies which fields in the database to fill with blanks. Whole records will be blanked if FIELDS is not used.

The REINDEX option delays the updating of all noncontrolling indexes until all records and fields have been filled with blanks.

• EXAMPLE The commands below open the CustList database file and insert blanks into the field AmtDue in every record that has .T. in the field named Paid.

```
USE CustList
BLANK FIELDS AmtDue FOR Paid=".T."
```

See Also ISBLANK()

BROWSE

Displaying and Editing Records

• SYNTAX

BROWSE (**NOINIT**) (**NOFOLLOW**) (**NOAPPEND**) (**NOMENU**) (**NOORGANIZE**) (**NOEDIT**) (**NODELETE**) (**NOCLEAR**) (**COMPRESS**) (**FORMAT**) (**LOCK** *number of columns*) (**WIDTH** *maximum column width*) (**FREEZE** *field name*) (**WINDOW** *window name*) ((**FIELDS** *field name 1* (/**R**) (/column width) /calculated field name 1 = expression 1)...)*

• USAGE BROWSE provides a full-screen, spreadsheet-like interface for editing data. The keys for editing and scrolling are virtually identical to those you use with the EDIT command. You can scroll the highlight past the last record displayed to add new records.

Table 2.7 lists options for the BROWSE command. Many of these options are available on pull-down menus while the browse table is on the screen.

To see the entire contents of a record on the screen, move the highlight to that record and press **F2** (Data). F2 is actually a toggle with which you can switch back and forth between the Browse and Edit screens.

Table 2.8 shows the cursor control keys used in the BROWSE and EDIT screens.

• EXAMPLE In the following commands, the Orders.DBF database contains a record for each order placed by customers. The Master.DBF database contains information about parts in the inventory.

The OrdForm.FMT format file was created using the Orders database and the forms design screen, and includes features such as field templates, picture functions, and edit options (such as VALID, RANGE, and DEFAULT). When you execute the BROWSE

Table 2.7: Browse Command Options

Option	Effect
NOINIT	Tells dBASE to use command line options from the previous BROWSE command, rather than reinitializing all those options.
NOFOLLOW	Prevents the cursor from following a record to its new sort position when you are editing a key field in the controlling index.
NOAPPEND	Prevents addition of new records at the Browse screen.
NOMENU	Prevents access to the menu bar by disabling the F10 key.
NOORGANIZE	Prevents the user from changing the index or sorting the database file by disabling the Organize menu.
NOEDIT	Allows records to be added or deleted, but prevents changes to existing data.
NODELETE	Prevents you from marking records for deletion in the Browse screen.
NOCLEAR	Leaves the browse table on the screen after exiting.
COMPRESS	Slightly reduces border spacing to allow 19, rather than 17, records to be displayed.
FORMAT	Instructs BROWSE to use picture templates, functions, default values, VALID definitions, and other features of a format file.
LOCK	Specifies the number of adjacent fields on the left of the Browse screen that are not scrolled off the screen as the user pans to the right.

Table 2.7: Browse Command Options (Continued)

Option	Effect
WIDTH	Specifies the largest width for any field other than memo and logical fields.
FREEZE	Specifies a field name in which to lock the cursor. You can view other fields, but can edit only the frozen field.
WINDOW	Activates a previously defined window, displaying the browse table within that window.
FIELDS	Lists names of fields to include in the Browse screen. The /R option makes the field read-only. The /*column width* option specifies the width of the field from 4 to 100 (both [/R] and [/*column width*] require the slash mark). You can include a *calculated field*, using a unique field name followed by an equal sign and an expression.

command, it uses the custom features of the form, but not the row and column coordinates.

Rather than using the entire screen, the browse table is displayed within the coordinates defined for the window named Details. Any text or @...SAY...GETS that are on screen remain while the browse table is displayed, though any that are displayed within the coordinates of the Details window are overwritten.

Note also that two calculated fields are displayed by the Browse screen. PName displays the appropriate part name from the Master database. TotSale is the result of multiplying the Qty field by the UnitPrice field.

```
USE Orders IN 1
USE Master ORDER PartNo IN 2

SELECT 1
```

```
SET RELATION TO PartNo INTO Master

DEFINE WINDOW Details FROM 7,5 TO 20,75

SET FORMAT TO OrdForm

BROWSE NOMENU NODELETE FORMAT WINDOW Details ;
    FIELDS CustNo, PartNo, ;
    Part=Master->PartName /10, Qty ;
    UnitPrice, TotSale = Qty*UnitPrice
```

See Also EDIT, SET MEMOWIDTH, SET REFRESH, SET WINDOW

Table 2.8: Editing Keys for the BROWSE and EDIT Commands

Key	Action
Esc	Abandon changes and exit
F10	Access pull-down menus
Shift-F8	Copy data from previous record (Ditto)
Del or Delete	Delete a character
Ctrl-Y	Delete to end of field
Ctrl-T	Delete word to right
Ctrl-Home or F9	Edit memo field
F1	Help
Ctrl-U	Mark/unmark for deletion
→, ←	Move cursor one character right or left
↑, ↓	Move cursor up or down
Ctrl-→	Move cursor one word right
Ctrl-←	Move cursor to beginning of previous field
PgUp, PgDn	Move up or down one page (browse), one record (edit)
↵ or Tab	Move to next field
Shift-Tab	Move to previous field

Table 2.8: Editing Keys for the BROWSE and EDIT Commands (Continued)

Key	Action
End	Move to last column (browse) or end of current field (edit)
Home	Move to first column (browse) or first character of current field (edit)
Ctrl-End	Save changes and exit
Data (F2)	Toggle between browse and edit
Ins or Insert	Toggle insert mode on/off

CALCULATE

Performing Multiple Calculations

• SYNTAX

CALCULATE *(scope)* *(***AVG(***expression***))** *(***CNT()***)* *(***MAX(***expression***))** *(***MIN(***expression***))** *(***NPV(***rate*),(*flows*),(*initial* **))** *(***STD(***expression***))** *(***SUM(***expression***))** *(***VAR(***expression***))** *(***FOR** *condition)* *(***WHILE** *condition)* *(***TO** *memory variables/***TO ARRAY** *array name)*

• USAGE CALCULATE performs statistical and financial calculations on data in the currently selected database file. The types of calculations and options available are listed in Table 2.9.

If SET TALK is on, calculation results are displayed on the screen immediately. If SET TALK is off, you should store results to memory variables or an array using the TO or TO ARRAY option. Use ? or @ to display the results later.

Table 2.9: Calculations Available through the CALCULATE Command

Calculation	Option
Average	AVG()
Count	CNT()
Highest value	MAX()
Lowest value	MIN()
Net present value	NPV()
Standard deviation	STD()
Sum	SUM()
Variance	VAR()

• **EXAMPLE** Assuming the currently open database contains a numeric or float field named Score, the following commands calculate and display the highest and lowest score, as well as the variance and standard deviation of all scores, excluding scores that are less than or equal to 0:

```
SET TALK ON
CALCULATE MIN(Score), MAX(Score), STD(Score);
 VAR(Score), FOR Score > 0
```

Suppose the currently open database contains a date field named DateSold, and numeric fields named Qty and UnitPrice. The following commands calculate the earliest and latest dates, the highest, lowest, total, and average total sale (as calculated by Qty * UnitPrice), and the total number of sales. Only records for the month of August in 1994 are included in the calculation. Results are stored in memory variables and displayed with ? commands:

```
CALCULATE MIN(DateSold),MAX(DateSold), ;
   MAX(Qty*UnitPrice),MIN(Qty*UnitPrice), ;
   SUM(Qty*UnitPrice),AVG(Qty*UnitPrice), ;
   CNT() FOR CMONTH(DateSold)="August" .AND. ;
   YEAR(DateSold) = 1994 TO Earliest, Latest, ;
```

```
    HiSale, LowSale, TotSale, AvgSale, HowMany

? "Earliest sale = ", Earliest

? "Latest sale = ", Latest

? "Largest sale = ", HiSale

? "Smallest sale = ", LowSale

? "Total sales = ", TotSale

? "Average sale = ", AvgSale

? "Total transactions = ", HowMany
```

If you wanted to use an array named Results, rather than memory variables, you would need to use these commands:

```
DECLARE Results(7)

CALCULATE MIN(DateSold),MAX(DateSold),;
   MAX(Qty*UnitPrice),MIN(Qty*UnitPrice), ;
   SUM(Qty*UnitPrice),AVG(Qty*UnitPrice), ;
   CNT() FOR CMONTH(DateSold)="August" .AND. ;
   YEAR(DateSold) = 1994 TO ARRAY Results

? "Earliest sale = ", Results(1)

? "Latest sale = ", Results(2)

? "Largest sale = ", Results(3)

? "Smallest sale = ", Results(4)

? "Total sales = ", Results(5)

? "Average sale = ", Results(6)

? "Total transactions = ", Results(7)
```

Suppose a database includes a numeric field named Amount, each record of which contains a positive or negative cash flow amount. To calculate the net present value of the cash flows, given a discount rate of 6.0 percent and an initial investment of $15,000, use the commands:

```
SET TALK ON
CALCULATE NPV(.06,Amount,–15000)
```

Note that the interest rate is expressed as a decimal (.06 rather than 6.0), and the initial investment is expressed as a negative number, as this is cash outflow.

See Also AVERAGE, COUNT, MAX(), MIN(), SUM

CALL

Executing an Assembly Language Subroutine

• SYNTAX

CALL *module name* (**WITH** *expression list*)

• USAGE CALL executes an assembly language (binary) module that you have already loaded into RAM. The optional WITH portion of the CALL command can pass up to seven parameters to the assembly language subroutine. The parameters can be expressed as the names of existing memory variables, fields, or array elements of any data type.

The DISPLAY/LIST STATUS command shows the names of all assembly language modules currently loaded into RAM.

• EXAMPLE The following command calls a loaded binary module called MakeBar, passing to it a string containing the characters MTV01-0001:

```
PartNo = "MTV01-0001"
CALL MakeBar WITH PartNo
```

See Also CALL(), LOAD, RELEASE, RUN/!

CANCEL

Terminating a Command File

• SYNTAX

```
CANCEL
```

• USAGE CANCEL terminates program execution and returns control to the dot prompt. If a program is suspended, you can enter **CANCEL** at the dot prompt to cancel both the suspension and the program execution.

CANCEL does not close open procedure files or databases. It does, however, erase all memory variables and arrays that were private to the command file.

• EXAMPLE In the next routine, if the user presses ↵ without entering a name in response to the ACCEPT prompt, the IF clause terminates program execution:

```
ACCEPT "Enter your name " TO Name
IF LEN(TRIM(Name))=0
  CANCEL
ENDIF
```

See Also CLOSE PROCEDURE, RESUME, RETRY, RETURN, SET REPROCESS, SUSPEND

CHANGE

Displaying and Editing a Record

CHANGE is identical to EDIT; see the **EDIT** command.

CLEAR

Clearing Objects from Memory

• SYNTAX

CLEAR*(***ALL/FIELDS/GETS/MEMORY/MENUS/POPUPS/ SCREENS/TYPEAHEAD/WINDOWS***)*

• USAGE When used by itself, CLEAR clears the entire screen, but leaves intact all objects in memory. You can also use the CLEAR command with one option, as listed in Table 2.10, to erase objects from memory.

To remove individual menus, pop-ups, and windows from the screen, use the RELEASE command instead of CLEAR.

• EXAMPLE The following commands clear all currently defined menus and pop-ups from memory, but leave memory variables and other objects in memory intact:

```
CLEAR MENUS
CLEAR POPUPS
```

The CLEAR TYPEAHEAD command prevents extraneous keystrokes from prematurely terminating the INKEY() pause:

```
CLEAR TYPEAHEAD
X = INKEY(5)
```

Table 2.10: Options Used with the CLEAR Command

Option	Effects
ALL	Closes all open database, index, format, and low-level files, and the current catalog. CLEAR ALL also clears from the screen and memory all objects in this table, then selects work area 1.
FIELDS	Releases field restrictions placed by a SET FIELDS command.
GETS	Releases all @...GET commands on the screen from further READ access, but does not erase them from the screen.
MEMORY	Erases all memory variables (except system variables) and array elements from memory.
MENUS	Erases all defined horizontal bar menus from the screen and from memory.
POPUPS	Erases all defined pop-up menus from the screen and from memory.
SCREENS	Removes from memory screens saved as a memory variable with the SAVE SCREENS TO commands.
TYPEAHEAD	Flushes out any keystrokes in the typeahead buffer.
WINDOWS	Erases any defined windows from the screen and memory.

See Also CLOSE, ERASE, MEMORY(), RELEASE, SET FIELDS, SET FORM, SET TYPEAHEAD, SET VIEW

CLOSE

Closing a File

• SYNTAX

CLOSE ALL/ALTERNATE/DATABASES/FORMAT/INDEXES/ PRINTER/PROCEDURE

• USAGE The CLOSE command allows you to close files that you no longer need for immediate use. You can use CLOSE in conjunction with commands that will work only with closed files (such as ERASE, MODIFY, SELECT, and others) to close a particular file before issuing the command.

Note that the CLOSE DATABASES command closes database (.DBF), index (.NDX and .MDX), format (.FMO), and memo field (.DBT) files in all work areas, not just the selected work area. If you want to close a database in the selected work area only, issue the USE command with no file name or options.

When you close a file, any data in that file that was temporarily stored in memory is saved to disk.

CLOSE PRINTER closes the file opened with the SET PRINTER TO command.

• EXAMPLE The following command closes all open database files with their associated memo, index, and format files:

CLOSE DATABASES

See Also CLEAR, SELECT, SET ALTERNATE, SET FORMAT, SET PRINTER, SET PROCEDURE, USE

COMPILE

Preparing Source Code for Execution

• SYNTAX

COMPILE *file name* (**RUNTIME**)

• USAGE The COMPILE command reads a dBASE IV source-code file and creates an executable object-code file without executing the program. If the file has an extension other than .PRG, you must include the extension in the file name. Regardless of the extension of the source-code file, dBASE IV always creates an object file with the .DBO extension.

If SET DEVELOPMENT is on and you are using an external editor, dBASE IV checks the creation date and time before executing the program with a DO command. If the object file is older than the source-code file, the source-code file is automatically compiled before execution.

If SET DEVELOPMENT is off and you are using an external editor, you must compile the source code before executing with a DO command. If the compiled program is to be run on RunTime and you want to check for potential RunTime errors, use the RUNTIME option.

At compile time, you can specify conditional compiler directives to indicate which sections of the program you want compiled. The directives can appear anywhere in the program. If you are debugging a program and find errors in one small part, you can compile only that part and not take time to recompile error-free segments. The compiler directives are:

#define *name*	Defines a *name*
#undef *name*	Undefines *name*
#ifdef *name*	Branches if *name* was defined
#ifndef *name*	Branches if *name* was not defined

#else	Alternate branch that follows an #ifdef or #ifndef directive
#endif	Terminates #ifdef and #ifndef branching

The directive name may consist of up to 32 letters or numbers, the first of which must be a letter. Embedded spaces are not allowed. The names are not case-sensitive.

In addition to the built-in compiler, Borland also provides the dBASE Compiler for DOS that creates applications for end-use on systems without dBASE. This compiler compiles and links source files, including database forms, reports, and command files, into a single executable file (.exe). See Appendix D for more information.

• **EXAMPLE** The command that follows compiles a command file named EntCust.PRG for a RunTime application:

```
COMPILE EntCust RUNTIME
```

When you insert directives into your command file, COMPILE and DO compile selectively. The following example shows the effects of inserting compiler directives into a command file.

```
*----- MyProg.PRG
*----- Main program commands
...
...
*----- Insert definition directive
#define DoComp
#ifdef DoComp

*----- These commands are compiled

#else

*----- These command are not compiled

#endif
```

Then undefine the DoComp variable:

```
#undef DoComp
#ifdef DoComp
```

```
*----- These commands are not compiled
#else
*----- These commands are compiled
#endif
```

See Also DEBUG, DO, FUNCTION, MODIFY COMMAND, PROCEDURE, SET DEBUG, SET DEVELOPMENT, SET EXACT, SET PATH, SET TRAP

CONTINUE

Resuming a Search Operation

• SYNTAX

```
CONTINUE
```

• USAGE The CONTINUE command resumes the search specified in the most recent LOCATE command, starting with the current record. If no additional matching records are found, the FOUND() function returns .F., and EOF() returns .T.

CONTINUE finds records that are marked for deletion only if the SET DELETED command is off. CONTINUE will not find records hidden by a SET FILTER or QUERY condition.

• EXAMPLE The next command locates the first record in the current database with the last name Smith:

```
LOCATE FOR LastName = "Smith"
```

The following command locates the next record in the database with Smith in the LastName field:

```
CONTINUE
```

See Also EOF(), FIND, FOUND(), LOCATE, SEEK, SEEK()

CONVERT

Using Database Files on Networks

• SYNTAX

CONVERT *(***TO** *number)*

• USAGE The CONVERT command changes the extension of the active database file to .CVT, adds a character field (_dbaselock) to the structure, and copies the file to the new database structure.

The _dbaselock field stores information required for lock detection on a network. It can be 8, 16, or 24 characters long. The first eight characters are reserved for:

- Count: A two-byte number used by the CHANGE() function.
- Time: A three-byte number that records the time a lock was placed on the record.
- Date: A three-byte number that records the date a lock was placed on the record.

The default field length of 16 reserves the last 8 characters for the log-in name. If you convert to the maximum field length of 24, the last 16 characters are reserved for the log-in name.

When you use the CHANGE() function, dBASE IV reads the first two bytes of the field from the disk file and compares the results with the first two bytes in the active database record. If the two numbers are different, a change has been made to the record since it was retrieved from disk and CHANGE() returns a logical true (.T.).

The time, date, and log-in name are used by the LKSYS() function to return the log-in name (if available), date, and time the field was locked. If a file lock is placed on the file, the first record of the file contains the CHANGE() and LKSYS() information.

• **EXAMPLE** To convert the CustList database file for network use with a 24-character log-in name, enter

CONVERT CustList TO 24

See Also CHANGE(), FLOCK(), LKSYS(), LOCK(), NETWORK(), SET LOCK, SET REPROCESS, UNLOCK

COPY

Copying a Database File

• **SYNTAX**

COPY TO *file name ((***TYPE***) file type)/((***WITH***)* **PRODUCTION***) (***FIELDS** *field list) (scope) (***FOR** *condition) (***WHILE** *condition)*

• **USAGE** COPY copies records from the currently open database file to a new database file. You can use the TYPE option with one of the options listed in Table 2.11 to convert the dBASE IV data to different formats in the copied file.

The WITH PRODUCTION option copies the production (.MDX) file as well and gives it the same name as the new database file.

The FIELDS option allows you to specify specific fields and the order in which they will be listed in the copied file.

Records that are marked for deletion are copied to the new file unless SET DELETED is on.

The SET SAFETY setting determines whether dBASE asks for permission before overwriting a file during a COPY operation.

To add the data from one file to existing records in another file, use APPEND FROM instead of COPY.

Table 2.11: Options for Copying dBASE IV Database Data

TYPE Option	Produces
DELIMITED	ASCII text file with individual fields separated by commas, and records separated by carriage return and line feed (CRLF).
DELIMITED WITH *character*	ASCII text file with individual fields separated by the specified *character*, and records separated by a CRLF
DELIMITED WITH BLANK	ASCII text file with individual fields separated by a blank space, and records separated by a CRLF
SDF	ASCII text file with fixed field length, no delimiters between fields, and records separated by a CRLF
DBASEII	dBASE II database file with the extension .DB2.
DBMEMO3	dBASE III PLUS format with a memo field.
RPD	RapidFile data (.RPD) file.
FW2	Framework II (.FW2) file.
SYLK	Multiplan SYLK format, with no file name extension.
DIF	Visicalc Data Interchange Format with .DIF file name extension.
WKS	Lotus 1-2-3 spreadsheet (Version 1A) file with .WKS file name extension.

• **EXAMPLE** The next commands copy all fields and records from the Charges.DBF database to a database named ChrgBak.DBF:

```
USE Charges
COPY TO ChrgBak
```

These commands copy fields named CustNo, PartNo, and Qty from the Orders.DBF database to a Lotus 1-2-3 spreadsheet file named Ord123.WKS. Only records with OrdDate dates from the year 1994 are included in the copied file.

```
USE Orders TAG CustNo

COPY TO Ord123  TYPE WKS FIELDS ;
   CustNo,PartNo,Qty, ;
   FOR YEAR(OrdDate) = 1994
```

See Also APPEND FROM, COPY FILE, COPY INDEXES, COPY STRUCTURE, COPY TAG, EXPORT, IMPORT, SET DELETED, SET FIELDS, SET SAFETY

COPY FILE

Copying Any File

• SYNTAX

COPY FILE *file name* **TO** *file name*

• USAGE Unlike COPY TO, which copies only database, index, and memo field files, COPY FILE can copy any type of closed file. COPY FILE acts like the DOS COPY command, but does not support wildcards.

You must specify the file name and extension of both the file being copied and the name of the copy. If either the original or the copy is not stored on the current drive and directory, you must specify a path with the file name.

If you use COPY FILE to copy a database (.DBF) file, you must issue a separate command to copy index (.NDX and .MDX) files, and yet another command to copy the memo field (.DBT) file. The COPY TO command copies memo field files automatically and copies the production index file if you choose the WITH PRODUCTION option.

• **EXAMPLE** To store a copy of a program named YearEnd.PRG on the disk in drive A, assigning the name YearEnd.BAK to the copy, enter the command

COPY FILE YearEnd.PRG TO A:YearEnd.BAK

See Also COPY, COPY INDEXES, COPY MEMO, COPY TAG

COPY INDEXES

Combining Index Files into a Multiple Index File

• **SYNTAX**

COPY INDEXES *.ndx file list* (**TO** *.mdx file name*)

• **USAGE** The COPY INDEXES command combines up to ten dBASE III PLUS index files (.NDX) into a single dBASE IV multiple index file (.MDX). By default, the production index is used. The production index has the same name as the database, but with the extension .MDX. If there is no production index, COPY INDEXES creates one with the same name as the active database file and the file header is updated to show the existence of a production index file. Alternatively, you can use a different file name for the multiple index file by using the TO option.

If you are using the COPY INDEXES command on a network, you must have exclusive use of the database file.

• **EXAMPLE** The following commands copy three dBASE III PLUS index (.NDX) files into a multiple index file named CustList.MDX:

```
USE CustList INDEX CustNum, CustName, SalesRep
COPY INDEXES CustNum, CustName, SalesRep
```

See Also COPY TAG, INDEX, KEY(), MDX(), NDX(), SET INDEX, SET ORDER, TAG(), USE

COPY MEMO

Creating ASCII Text Files from Memo Fields

• SYNTAX

COPY MEMO *memo field name* **TO** *file name* (**ADDITIVE**)

• USAGE The COPY MEMO command creates an ASCII text file and copies to it the contents of the memo field of the active record. To give the file name an extension other than the default, .TXT, you must include the extension in the file name.

The file receiving the copy will be overwritten with new data, unless you use the ADDITIVE option, in which case the new memo field will be appended to the existing file.

• EXAMPLE Suppose a sample database named Referenc.DBF contains a memo field named Abstract. The commands here copy the contents of the Abstract fields in records number 3 and 5 to an ASCII file named HoldMemo.TXT:

```
USE Referenc
GOTO 3
COPY MEMO Abstract TO HoldMemo
GOTO 5
COPY MEMO Abstract TO HoldMemo ADDITIVE
```

To copy the combined memo fields in the HoldMemo file into the ABSTRACT field of a new record in Referenc, you could enter the commands:

```
APPEND BLANK
APPEND MEMO Abstract FROM HoldMemo.TXT
```

See Also APPEND MEMO, COPY, COPY FILE, SET SAFETY

COPY STRUCTURE

Copying the Structure of a Database

• SYNTAX

COPY STRUCTURE TO *file name* (**FIELDS** *field list*) ((**WITH**) **PRODUCTION**)

• USAGE Use COPY STRUCTURE to copy the structure of the currently selected database file, without copying any of the database records.

If the FIELDS option does not specify specific fields in the new database, the entire database structure is copied to the new file.

The WITH PRODUCTION option creates an empty production index file that includes all the tags from the original .MDX file. If you also specify the fields to copy, make sure you have included all the fields used in the .MDX tags.

• EXAMPLE To copy the field definitions for the CustNo, PartNo, Qty, UnitPrice, and OrdDate fields in the Orders database to a new database named OrdHist.DBF and create a replica .MDX file, enter these commands:

```
USE Orders

COPY STRUCTURE TO OrdHist FIELDS CustNo, ;
  PartNo, Qty, UnitPrice, OrdDate WITH PRODUCTION
```

See Also APPEND, APPEND FROM, COPY STRUCTURE EXTENDED, DISPLAY STRUCTURE, REPLACE, SET SAFETY

COPY STRUCTURE EXTENDED

Converting Fields to Records

• SYNTAX

COPY TO *file name* **STRUCTURE EXTENDED**

• USAGE COPY STRUCTURE EXTENDED creates a database file with five fields that are named FIELD_NAME, FIELD_TYPE, FIELD_LEN, FIELD_DEC, and FIELD_IDX. Each record in the new database represents a field definition from the original database.

This command is generally used in applications, in conjunction with the CREATE FROM command, to allow users to modify a database structure without using the MODIFY STRUCTURE command.

• EXAMPLE Suppose the Orders database contains the following fields:

Field Name	Type	Width	Dec	Index
PartNo	Character	5		Y
Qty	Numeric	3	0	N
UnitPrice	Numeric	9	2	N
Taxable	Logical	1		N
Date	Date	8		N

Entering the following commands creates a structure-extended file named Temp.DBF:

```
USE Orders
COPY TO Temp STRUCTURE EXTENDED
```

To view the contents of the Temp database file, enter the commands:

```
USE Temp
LIST
```

The results of the previous command are as follows:

Record #	FIELD_NAME	FIELD_TYPE	FIELD_LEN	FIELD_DEC	FIELD_IDX
1	PARTNO	C	5	0	Y
2	QTY	N	3	0	N
3	UNITPRICE	N	9	2	N
4	TAXABLE	L	1	0	N
5	DATE	D	8	0	N

See Also APPEND FROM, CREATE FROM, LIST/DISPLAY STRUCTURE

COPY TAG

Creating an Index from a Production File

• SYNTAX

COPY TAG *tag name* (**OF** *.mdx file name)* **TO** *.ndx file name*

• USAGE The COPY TAG command creates a single index (.NDX) file from the contents of a dBASE IV multiple index (.MDX) file tag. The multiple index file must be open and you can create only one index file at a time.

COPY TAG assumes that the index to be copied is stored in the production index file, which has the same name as the database file and the extension .MDX. To copy an index from a different multiple index file, use the OF option followed by the name of the multiple index file.

• EXAMPLE The following commands copy an index named CustNum from the production index file (CustList.MDX) to a single index (.NDX) file named CustNum.NDX:

```
USE CustList
COPY TAG CustNum to CustNum
```

See Also COPY INDEXES, INDEX, MDX(), NDX(), SET INDEX, SET ORDER, TAG()

COPY TO ARRAY

Copying Data to an Array

• SYNTAX

COPY TO ARRAY *array name* (**FIELDS** *fields list*) (*scope*)
(**FOR** *condition*) (**WHILE** *condition*)

• USAGE The COPY TO ARRAY command copies data from the active database file to a previously declared array.

dBASE IV begins copying the fields in the first record in the database file into the first elements of the row in the array and continues until there are either no more records to copy or no more array rows to fill. To select records to copy to the array, specify a scope and/or use the FOR and WHILE options.

If there are fewer columns in the array than there are fields in the database, the extra fields are ignored. Similarly, if there are more columns in the array than there are fields in the database, the extra array columns are ignored.

To copy selected fields to the array, use the FIELDS option.

• EXAMPLE The following routine creates an array named Sold with 30 elements (ten rows and three columns). The array contains the customer number, sales representative number, and total sale price of the first ten records from the Sales.DBF database, where the total sale is greater than $1000.

```
DECLARE Sold(10,3)
USE Sales
COPY TO ARRAY Sold FIELDS ;
  CustNum, SlsRep, TotSale FOR TotSale > 1000
```

See Also APPEND FROM ARRAY, COPY FILE, COPY STRUCTURE, DECLARE, DO WHILE, EXPORT, PUBLIC, SET DELETED, SET FIELDS, SET SAFETY

COUNT

Counting Records

• SYNTAX

COUNT *(***TO** *memory variable) (scope) (***FOR** *condition)* *(***WHILE** *condition)*

• USAGE The COUNT command tallies the number of records in the database field that match a search criterion. If SET TALK is off, the results are not displayed, and must be stored in a memory variable with the TO option to be accessible. Records hidden by SET FILTER, MODIFY QUERY, or SET DELETED ON are not included in the tally.

• EXAMPLE The command

```
COUNT TO HowMany FOR MONTH(DateSold) = 12
```

counts the number of records in the database that have a December date in the DateSold field. The result is stored in a memory variable named HowMany.

See Also AVERAGE, CALCULATE, RECCOUNT(), SUM

CREATE

Creating a New Database File

• SYNTAX

CREATE *file name* (**FROM** *structure-extended file*)

• USAGE The CREATE command takes you to the database design screen and allows you to create a new database structure. To modify an existing database structure, open the existing database with **USE** and enter the **MODIFY STRUCTURE** command.

A database file name can be up to eight characters long, excluding the extension. Each database field name can be up to ten characters long. Field names must begin with a letter and should not be the same as any command or even a valid abbreviation of a command. Technically, dBASE allows field names that are the same as a command, but it sometimes handles them incorrectly, making your program behave unpredictably. The only punctuation allowed in field names is the underscore (_) character. Table 2.12 shows examples of valid and invalid field names.

Each field must be assigned one of the six data types: character, numeric, float, date, logical, or memo. Date, logical, and memo fields are assigned widths automatically. You must assign widths to the other data types. You also must assign a number of decimal places to the numeric data types.

A single record can contain a maximum of 255 fields or a total width of 4,000 bytes, whichever comes first.

The rightmost column on the database design screen, labeled Index, determines whether the field is indexed. If you mark a field as **Y** in this column, an index tag (name) and index are created for the field in the production index file. You can also create more complex indexes using options on the Organize pull-down menu. By default, all indexes are stored in a *production index file* that has the same name as the database, but the .MDX extension.

Table 2.12: Keys Used in the Database Design Screen

Valid Field Name	Invalid Field Name
FirstName	1stName (begins with a number)
Last_Name	Last Name (contains a space)
Restaurant	Rest (name of a scope condition)
F_Other	Record (name of a scope condition)
Is_Ready	Is:Ready (colon not acceptable punctuation)

Table 2.13 lists the keys for managing the cursor in the database design screen. To save a new or modified database structure, press Ctrl-End or select Save Changes and Exit from the Exit pull-down menu.

The CREATE FROM command copies a structure-extended file back to a standard database structure. See **COPY** for a definition and example of a structure-extended file.

• **EXAMPLE** The following command lets you define a new database file named MyData.DBF on the currently logged disk drive and directory.

```
CREATE MyData
```

See Also APPEND, COPY STRUCTURE, COPY STRUCTURE EXTENDED, DISPLAY STRUCTURE, SET BLOCKSIZE, SET SAFETY

Table 2.13: Keys Used in the Database Design Screen

Key	Alternate Key	Effect
↵		Completes entry and moves to the next column or row
↑	Ctrl-E or Ctrl-K	Moves the cursor up one row
↓	Ctrl-X or Ctrl-J	Moves the cursor down one row
→	Ctrl-D or Ctrl-L	Moves the cursor right one character
←	Ctrl-S	Moves the cursor left one character
Tab or F4	Ctrl-M or Ctrl-I	Moves the cursor right one column
Shift-Tab or F3	Ctrl-A or Ctrl-H	Moves the cursor left one column or to the beginning of the previous row, depending on the cursor position
Home	Ctrl-Z	Moves to the Field Name column
End	Ctrl-B	Moves to the Index column
Ctrl-F		Moves to the end of the word or column, or the beginning of next column, depending on the cursor position
PgDn	Ctrl-C	Moves to the last row on the screen
PgUp	Ctrl-R	Moves to the first row on the screen

Table 2.13: Keys Used in the Database Design Screen (Continued)

Key	Alternate Key	Effect
Ctrl-N		Inserts a new field at the cursor position
Ins	Ctrl-V	Toggles Insert key
Ctrl-U		Deletes the row at the cursor position
Del		Deletes the character at the cursor position
Ctrl-T		Deletes the column entry at the cursor position
Ctrl-End	Ctrl-W	Saves all changes and leaves the database design screen
Esc	Ctrl-Q	Abandons current changes and leaves the database design screen
F10		Accesses the pull-down menus
F1		Provides Help (Esc leaves the help screen)

CREATE/MODIFY APPLICATION

Accessing the Applications Generator

• SYNTAX

CREATE/MODIFY APPLICATION *file name*/**?**

• USAGE CREATE APPLICATION and MODIFY APPLICATION are identical commands for accessing the Applications Generator. In the Applications Generator, you can have dBASE IV generate the code necessary to tie objects (databases, queries, custom screens, and reports) together in a single application consisting of a bar menu, pull-down menus, pop-up menus, and windows.

You must use the file name in the command. If a catalog is open, entering **?** in lieu of a file name displays the names of all applications in the catalog.

After you complete the initial application definition screen, you'll see the applications design screen. Now you can select options from the Design pull-down menu to create horizontal bar menus, pop-up menus, files lists, structure lists, and values lists. Keys used for sizing and moving these objects appear at the bottom of the screen. You can also press **F1** (Help) for instructions while using the Applications Generator.

To save the new or modified application design after generating the code, select **Save Changes and Exit** from the Exit pull-down menu. From the dot prompt, use the DO command to run the application.

• EXAMPLE The following command allows you to design a new application named MyApp, or modify an existing application named MyApp.

```
MODIFY APPLICATION MyApp
```

After you generate the code for the application and save the application design, you can enter the following command at the dot prompt to run the application:

```
DO MyApp
```

See Also MODIFY COMMAND

CREATE/MODIFY LABEL

Formatting Labels

• SYNTAX

CREATE LABEL *file name*/**?**

or

MODIFY LABEL *file name*/**?**

• USAGE You use the CREATE or MODIFY LABEL command to access the labels design screen, where you can create a new label format or modify an existing format for the currently open database or view. This is equivalent to selecting **<create>** or highlighting a file name and pressing **Shift-F2** in the Labels panel of the Control Center.

If a catalog is open, the ? option displays a list of the label form files in the catalog.

Pressing **F1** (Help) provides instructions for designing a label format. Table 2.14 lists the functions of various editing keys in the labels design screen and Table 2.15 describes the mouse operations

When you save a label design and use the LABEL FORM command to print the labels, dBASE IV generates three files with the name you specified in the CREATE LABEL or MODIFY LABEL commands and the following extensions:

.LBL Used only by the labels design screen

.LBG Generated code for printing labels

.LBO Compiled code for printing labels

Neither CREATE LABEL nor MODIFY LABEL is available if the SET DESIGN option is off.

• EXAMPLE The commands

```
USE Customer
MODIFY LABEL ThreeCol
```

allow you to create a mailing label format file named ThreeCol for the Customer.DBF database.

See Also LABEL FORM, SET CATALOG, SET SAFETY, SET VIEW

Table 2.14: Keys Used in Object Design Screen

Key	Effect
↑,↓,→,←	Moves cursor in direction indicated by arrow
PgUp	Moves cursor to top of screen
PgDn	Moves cursor to bottom of screen
Home	Moves cursor to beginning of line
End	Moves cursor to end of line or text
Tab	Moves cursor to next tab stop
Shift-Tab	Moves cursor to previous tab stop
Ins	Toggles insert mode on and off
Del	Deletes character over cursor or selected field or block
F1	Displays help
F5	Adds or modifies a field template
F6	Selects a field template or area to move
F7	Moves selected template or area
Shift-F7	Sizes the selected template
F8	Copies selected template or area
F10	Accesses pull-down menus
Ctrl-N	Inserts blank line
Ctrl-Y	Deletes line at cursor
Esc	Abandons changes and exits design screen
Ctrl-End	Saves changes and exits design screen

Table 2.15: Mouse Operations for Label and Report Design Screens

Action	Operation
Position cursor	Click left mouse button.
Add a field	Position mouse pointer and double-click on Add Field.
Modify a field	Double click field template.
Highlight (select) item	Click on template, or click and drag to highlight block.
Unhighlight item	Click outside item, or, if field was moved, press **Esc**.
Move a field	Highlight field or block, click Select:F6 in navigation line, click Move:F7, move mouse pointer to new position and click.
Copy a field	Highlight field or block, click Select:F6 in navigation line, click Copy:F8, move mouse pointer to desired position and click.
Change field template size	Click template, click Size:Shift-F7 in navigation line, move mouse pointer to desired size and click.

CREATE/MODIFY QUERY/VIEW

Building a Filter Condition

• SYNTAX

CREATE/MODIFY QUERY *file name*/**?**

or

CREATE/MODIFY VIEW *file name*/**?** (**FROM ENVIRONMENT**)

• **USAGE** CREATE QUERY, MODIFY QUERY, CREATE VIEW, and MODIFY VIEW are identical commands that call up the dBASE IV queries design screen. With the queries design screen, you can build a filter condition to isolate specific records, link multiple database files into a view, and perform update operations. You can also use the queries design screen to perform calculations and sort the results of the query.

The FROM ENVIRONMENT option is included in dBASE IV to retain compatibility with dBASE III PLUS. The .VUE file also cannot save sort orders in the query. The option creates a view from the current environment instead of accessing the query design screen. The resulting .VUE file is compatible with dBASE III PLUS. When you save a .VUE file from the query design screen, a new .QBE file is created instead of .VUE. .VUE files cannot save GROUP BY clauses, aggregate operators (SUM, MIN, MAX), or UNIQUE or FIND queries, since they must retain compatibility with dBASE III PLUS.

When constructing queries, be sure to enclose in proper delimiters the value being searched for, as in the following examples:

Data Type	**Example**
Character field:	"Smith"
Numeric/Float field:	123.45
Date field:	{12/30/89}
Logical field:	.T.

The queries design screen can search memo fields only through a condition box. For example, to search a memo field named Abstract for the character string "Avocado," first select **Add a Condition Box** from the Condition pull-down menu. Within the condition box, enter the expression **"Avocado" $ Abstract**.

When you use the queries design screen to link two or more files into a view, the key field that links the file must have the same name, data type, and width in both database files. The key field also should be indexed in both database files. Note that all files in the view will be read-only, and therefore the data can be viewed but not modified.

If you save a query or view, the source code generated by the queries design screen is stored in a file with the name that you specified in the CREATE/MODIFY QUERY or CREATE/MODIFY VIEW command, with the extension .QBE. However, queries that involve an update operator (such as REPLACE, APPEND, MARK, or UNMARK) are stored in the specified file, but with the extension .UPD.

If a catalog is open, using the ? option in lieu of a file name displays existing queries in the current catalog. For help while using the queries design screen, press **F1** (Help).

- **EXAMPLE** The commands

```
CLOSE DATABASES
USE Orders ORDER PartNo IN 1
USE Master ORDER PartNo IN 2
SELECT 1
MODIFY QUERY OrdMast
```

call up the queries design screen with file skeletons for the Orders.DBF and Master.DBF databases.

Figure 2.3 shows a sample query for the two databases on the screen. You must select **Include Indexes** from the Fields pull-down menu to activate the index. Fields marked with the ↓ symbol are included in the view skeleton, and hence will be displayed when the query is executed. Pressing **F5** places and removes fields from the view skeleton.

The LINK1 example element relates the two database files by the common field PartNo. The expression >=100 is a filter condition that limits the results to records with a value of 100 or more in the Unit Price field.

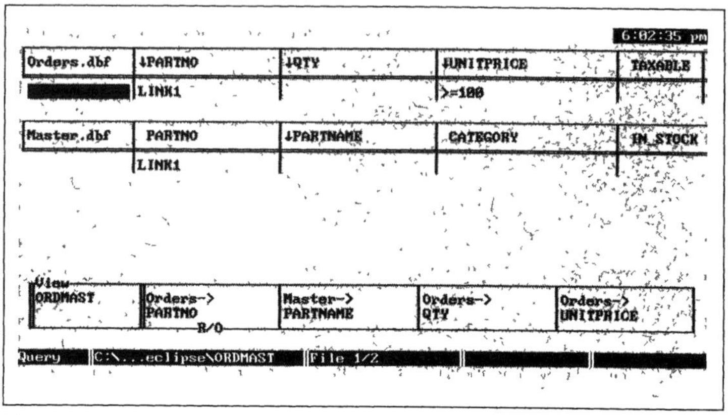

Figure 2.3: A Sample Query on the Queries Design Screen

See Also REPLACE, SET CATALOG, SET FILTER, SET RELATION, SET VIEW

CREATE/MODIFY REPORT

Designing a Report Format

• SYNTAX

CREATE MODIFY REPORT *file name/* **?**

• USAGE CREATE/MODIFY REPORT activates the dBASE IV reports design screen, through which you can design a report to be printed by the REPORT FORM command. This is equivalent to selecting **<create>**, or to highlighting a file name and pressing **Shift-F2** in the Reports panel of the Control Center. You should open the appropriate database or view before issuing the CREATE/MODIFY REPORT command. The ? option displays a list of existing report form files in the current catalog.

The Quick Layouts option on the Layout pull-down menu lets you select one of the following initial formats for the report:

Column layout	Data will be spaced in even columns, perhaps involving totals and subtotals.
Form layout	Data will use a free-form, noncolumnar layout, as when each record requires several lines of printing.
Mailmerge layout	Used for designing form letters.

Table 2.14 (shown earlier) lists the editing keys available in the reports design screen and Table 2.15 describes the mouse operations.

As you create, save, and print a report format, dBASE IV creates three files, each with the name specified in the CREATE/MODIFY REPORT command, but with the following different extensions:

.FRM	File used by the reports design screen
.FRG	Source code generated by the reports design screen
.FRO	Compiled code for printing the report

You can make changes directly to the .FRG command file by using MODIFY COMMAND, but if you open the report design screen later, your changes will be overwritten when the new .FRG file is created.

You cannot access the reports design screen when SET DESIGN is set to off.

- **EXAMPLE** The commands

```
USE Orders
MODIFY REPORT TotSales
```

allow you to create or edit a report format named TotSales.FRM. Figure 2.4 shows a sample report format that includes subtotals for individual part numbers within the Orders.DBF database.

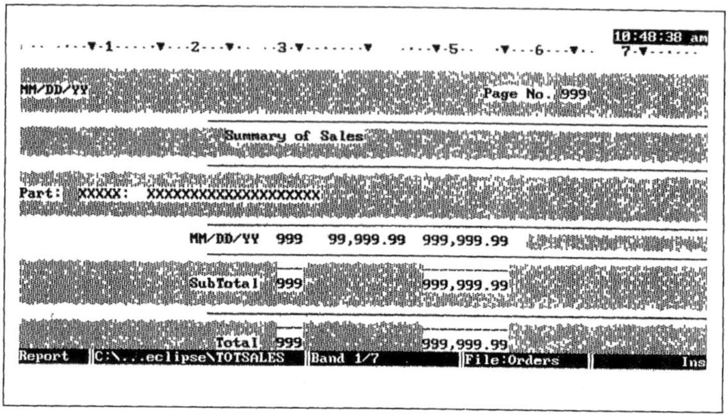

Figure 2.4: Sample Report Format with Subtotals

In the example, the Group Band is based on a field named PartNo. Subtotals are displayed via calculated fields in the Group 1 Summary Band. These fields use PartNo as the Reset Every value. Totals in the Report Summary band are also summary fields, using REPORT as the Reset Every value.

Because this report uses PartNo as the grouping (subtotal) value, the database must be indexed on the PartNo field. That index must control the sort order while the report is being printed. For example, assuming you've created and saved the report shown in Figure 2.4, if you have already created an index of the PartNo field at the database design screen, you would enter the following commands to print the report:

```
USE Orders TAG PartNo
REPORT FORM TotSales TO PRINT
```

Figure 2.5 shows some sample data printed by the TotSales report format.

See Also REPORT FORM, SET CATALOG, SET DESIGN, SET SAFETY, SET VIEW

```
08/01/94                                                    Page No.    1
                              Summary of Sales

Part:  A-111:  Solar Calculator

                    06/01/94     2        $50.00       $100.00
                    06/02/94     3        $50.00       $150.00
                    06/05/94     4        $50.00       $200.00
                               ---                  ----------
                    SubTotal     9                      450.00

Part:  B-222:  Mouse

                    06/01/94     2       $100.00       $200.00
                    06/01/94     1       $100.00       $100.00
                    06/15/94     1       $100.00       $100.00
                               ---                  ----------
                    SubTotal     4                      400.00

Part:  C-333:  Portable Computer

                    06/15/94     2       $500.00     $1,000.00
                    06/15/94     1       $500.00       $500.00
                    07/01/94     2       $500.00     $1,000.00
                    06/01/94     1       $500.00       $500.00
                               ---                  ----------
                    SubTotal     6                    3,000.00

                               ---                  ----------
                       Total    19                    3,850.00
```

Figure 2.5: Sample Data Printed by the TotSales Report Format

CREATE/MODIFY SCREEN

Drawing Custom Screens

• SYNTAX

CREATE/MODIFY SCREEN *file name*/**?**

• USAGE CREATE SCREEN and MODIFY SCREEN both provide access to the dBASE IV forms design screen. Either command allows you to create a new custom screen or modify an existing one. You can also access the forms design screen by selecting **<create>** from the Forms panel of the Control Center. If you are designing a screen for a particular database or view, you should open that database or view before entering the CREATE SCREEN or MODIFY SCREEN command. When you reach the forms design screen, you can use the keys presented in Table 2.13 to design a form and the mouse operations described in Table 2.14. Note that to add or change a field template, you use the **F5** (Field) key. If you wish to move or copy a field template, you must first select the area to move or copy using the **F6** (Select) key. Then, use either the **F7** (Move) or **F8** (Copy) key to move or copy. Instructions to help with these operations appear in the navigation line at the bottom of the screen.

You can draw lines and boxes on the custom form by selecting **Box** or **Line** from the Layout pull-down menu. To change the foreground and background colors of text on the screen, first select the area to be colored using the **F6** key. Then select **Display** from the Words pull-down menu, and select colors from the palette that appears. Color changes will not be apparent until you remove the selection highlight by pressing **Esc**.

The center of the status bar near the bottom of the screen always displays the current row and column position of the cursor. When designing your form, keep in mind that row 0 is reserved for the dBASE IV scoreboard messages, and rows 22 through 24 are used for the status bar, navigation line, and messages, unless you remove these with the SET SCOREBOARD and SET STATUS commands. Therefore, the first page of a custom screen should fit between rows 1 and 21, the second page between rows 23 and 43, the third page between rows 45 and 65, and so forth. A single form can consist of up to 32,767 rows or 32 screen pages.

To save a completed custom screen, select **Save Changes and Exit** from the Exit pull-down menu. dBASE will generate three files, each with the file name you provided in the CREATE SCREEN or MODIFY SCREEN command, but with different extensions

.SCR	File used by the forms design screen
.FMT	Source code for the generated custom screen, containing mostly @...SAY...GET commands
.FMO	Compiled screen code used by the SET FORMAT command

To activate a completed custom screen from the dot prompt or from within a command file, enter the **SET FORMAT TO** command followed by the name of the custom form file. The next READ, APPEND, EDIT, or INSERT command will automatically display the form on the screen. To use picture templates, functions, and validation options from a custom form in the browse screen, use the **BROWSE** command with the **FORMAT** option.

The format file that dBASE generates from the forms design screen uses double quotes (") as delimiters. Therefore, you should avoid using double quotes while designing a custom form.

Tip: To change the template, picture function, or edit option for a field on the forms design screen, move the cursor to the field template and press **F5** (Field). The options presented on the submenus are the same as those described in the discussion of the @...SAY...GET commands earlier in this chapter.

To use the @...SAY...GET commands that the labels design screen generates in a command file, you can read a copy of the .FMT file into the command file using the program editor (see **MODIFY COMMAND**).

You can also make changes directly to the .FMT file with the program editor (MODIFY COMMAND) but if you open the forms design screen again, your changes will be overwritten.

• **EXAMPLE** The following commands open a database file named Orders.DBF, and then take you to the forms design screen where you design a custom form named MyForm:

```
USE Orders
MODIFY SCREEN MyForm
```

See Also @...SAY...GET, APPEND, BROWSE, EDIT, INSERT, SET CATALOG, SET FORMAT, SET SAFETY, SET VIEW

DEACTIVATE MENU

Removing a Menu from the Screen

• SYNTAX

DEACTIVATE MENU

• USAGE DEACTIVATE MENU deactivates the current horizontal bar menu and removes it from the screen. The menu definition is retained in memory, and you can reactivate it with an ACTIVATE MENU command. Pressing **Esc** does the same thing as DEACTIVATE MENU.

If you have assigned pull-down menus to bar menu options with the ON PAD command, DEACTIVATE MENU also deactivates those menus and clears them from the screen. After DEACTIVATE MENU executes, it passes control to the first command line in the program beneath the ACTIVATE MENU command that activated the menu.

You cannot use the DEACTIVATE MENU command from the dot prompt. You should use it in a procedure or as the command option of an ON SELECTION command.

To remove a horizontal bar menu definition from memory, use the RELEASE MENUS *menu names* command. To clear all horizontal bar menu definitions from memory, use the CLEAR MENUS command. When the menu definition is removed from memory, you need to define it again before you can activate it.

The DISPLAY MEMORY command lists the names of all menus that are currently stored in memory.

• EXAMPLE See the **DEFINE MENU** command.

See Also ACTIVATE MENU, CLEAR, DEFINE MENU, ON SELECTION PAD, RELEASE

DEACTIVATE POPUP

Removing a Pop-Up Menu from the Screen

• SYNTAX

DEACTIVATE POPUP

• USAGE DEACTIVATE POPUP deactives a pop-up menu and removes it from the screen. Any text that was hidden by the pop-up menu reappears. The menu definition is maintained in memory, and you can reactivate it with an ACTIVATE POPUP command.

To remove a pop-up menu definition from the screen and from memory, use the RELEASE POPUPS *popup names* command. To release all current pop-up definitions from the screen and from memory, use the CLEAR POPUPS command. Once released, a pop-up menu cannot be activated.

The DISPLAY MEMORY command lists the names of pop-up menus currently stored in memory.

• EXAMPLE See the **DEFINE POPUP** command.

See Also ACTIVATE POPUP, CLEAR, DEFINE POPUP, ON SELECTION POPUP, RELEASE

DEACTIVATE WINDOW

Removing Windows from the Screen

• SYNTAX

DEACTIVATE WINDOW *window name list*/**ALL**

• USAGE DEACTIVATE WINDOW erases active windows from the screen. You can list one or more window names, separated by commas, to deactivate specific windows. The previously active window becomes active again. Use the ALL option to deactivate all windows currently on the screen and return to full screen mode. The window definitions remain in memory and can be reactivated at any time with an ACTIVATE WINDOW command.

To remove a window from both the screen and memory, use the RELEASE WINDOW *window name* command. To clear all windows from the screen and from memory, use the CLEAR WINDOWS command. The DISPLAY MEMORY command displays the names and screen coordinates of all windows currently stored in memory.

• EXAMPLE The routine that follows displays the progress of the PACK command in a window named ShowProg, and then removes the window from the screen:

```
USE AnyFile

*-- Show PACK progress in a window.
DEFINE WINDOW ShowProg FROM 15,5 TO 21,75
ACTIVATE WINDOW ShowProg

  SET TALK ON
  PACK
  SET TALK OFF
DEACTIVATE WINDOW ShowProg
```

The next command removes from the screen the windows named HelpScr, ErrMsg, and BrowScr:

```
DEACTIVATE WINDOW HelpScr,ErrMsg,BrowScr
```

See Also ACTIVATE SCREEN, ACTIVATE WINDOW, DEFINE WINDOW, MOVE WINDOW, RELEASE, RESTORE WINDOW, SAVE WINDOW

DEBUG

Using the Interactive Debugger

• SYNTAX

DEBUG *file name/procedure name* (**WITH** *parameter list)*

• USAGE DEBUG executes a command file or procedure file, simultaneously activating the full-screen interactive debugger. As it does in the DO command, the WITH option allows you to pass parameters to a PARAMETERS command within the program or procedure. The parameters list can contain up to ten constants and an unlimited number of variables. Make sure the left-to-right order and data types of passed parameters match the order and data types specified in the PARAMETERS command.

Proper delimiters are required when passing literal data. For example

DO AnyProc WITH "Smith",{12/1/89},.F.,123.45}

passes a character, date, logical, and numeric value to a procedure named AnyProc.

Within the debugger, you can enter up to four breakpoint expressions. Each breakpoint expression must evaluate to either .T. or .F. (for example, Counter >= 10). Press **Ctrl-End** after entering breakpoint expressions, and press **R** to begin program execution. When any of the breakpoint expressions evaluates to .T., program execution is halted and the debugging window reappears.

You can also view the current values of memory variables or expressions in the display window. Press **D** to enter the display window, enter up to four variable names or expressions, and press **Ctrl-End**.

You can run only one DEBUG session at a time. If you suspend a debugging session to return to the dot prompt, you must enter **RESUME** to return to the debugger and press **Q** to exit the debugger before starting a new debugging session.

Keys and options available in the debugger are listed in Table 2.16

Table 2.16: Keys Used in the Debugger

Option	Key
Add/Change breakpoint expressions	B
Add/Change display expressions	D
Edit command file	E
Continue processing from selected line	L
Execute next [n] command(s) at same or above level	*[n]*N
Show program traceback information	P
Quit the debugger	Q
Run until next error or breakpoint	R
Execute next statements	*[n]*S
Step through commands individually	S
Suspend debugger and return to dot prompt	U
Execute current command(s)	[*n*]<F128><159><F255>
Display/Remove help screen	F1
Display/Remove debugger screen	F9 (Zoom)
Show previous line(s)	[*n*]↑
Show next line(s)	[*n*]↓
Scroll one screen up	PgUp
Scroll one screen down	PgDn
Move to beginning of file	Ctrl-PgUp
Move to end of file	Ctrl-PgDn
Set current line as breakpoint	Ctrl-T
Invoke highlighted command	Ctrl-L

• **EXAMPLE** Suppose a procedure file named MyProcs.PRG contains a procedure named PropCase. PropCase includes the command PARAMETERS AnyString, where AnyString receives character data. To run the PropCase procedure through the debugger, enter these commands:

```
SET PROCEDURE TO MyProcs
DEBUG PropCase WITH "This is a Test"
```

See Also CANCEL, COMPILE, DO, LINENO(), MODIFY COMMAND/FILE, PROGRAM(), RESUME, SET DEBUG, SET ECHO, SET PROCEDURE, SET STEP, SET TALK, SET TRAP

DECLARE

Creating an Array

• **SYNTAX**

DECLARE *array name 1* **[***number of rows {,number of columns}* **]**
{,array name 2...}

Note that as indicated by the boldface type in which they appear, the square brackets ([]) shown here are required, literal parts of this command syntax. The curly braces ({}) are used here to indicate optional items.

• **USAGE** The DECLARE command creates one- or two-dimensional arrays of memory variables. Each memory variable within the array is referred to as an *element* of the array. Each element is described by its name and subscript. For example, a programmer might refer to Day[7] as "day sub-seven".

Each element in an array is initially a logical variable containing the value .F. When a new value is assigned to an array element, the element takes on the new data type.

An array definition consists of the array name (up to ten characters) and one or two numbers (subscripts) enclosed in square brackets ([]). If you declare one subscript, the array is one-dimensional. For example, here is an array created by the command DECLARE Day[5]:

Day[1]

Day[2]

Day[3]

Day[4]

Day[5]

If you declare two subscripts, the array is two-dimensional. The first subscript represents rows and the second subscript represents columns. For example, the command DECLARE Item[5,3] produces the following array elements:

Item[1,1]	Item[1,2]	Item[1,3]
Item[2,1]	Item[2,2]	Item[2,3]
Item[3,1]	Item[3,2]	Item[3,3]
Item[4,1]	Item[4,2]	Item[4,3]
Item[5,1]	Item[5,2]	Item[5,3]

An array can have as many elements as your virtual memory will hold, as long as one dimension does not exceed 65,535 elements. Regardless of the number of elements in an array, the array uses only one slot from the pool of available memory variables. The elements of the array are stored separately in memory.

You can specify an array subscript as a number, an expression that results in a number, or the name of a memory variable that contains a number. For example, if Counter = 5, the command

```
? Day(Counter-1)
```

displays the contents of the array element Day[4].

By default, an array is considered private (local) to the procedure or command file in which it was created. To create an array of public memory variables, use the PUBLIC ARRAY command. Declaring memory variables PUBLIC speeds up processing.

You can view the contents of an existing array with a DISPLAY MEMORY or LIST MEMORY command. Remember, however, that declared arrays are local to the command file that created them. For instance, if a command file creates the array, ends, and returns to the dot prompt, the array no longer exists. (An array that you created with the PUBLIC ARRAY command, however, would not be erased.)

• **EXAMPLE** Suppose that a database named Orders.DBF contains the fields shown here:

Field	Field Name	Type	Width	Dec	Index
1	Invoice	Numeric	6		Y
2	CustNo	Numeric	4		N
3	PartNo	Character	6		Y
4	QtyOrdered	Numeric	3		N
5	OrdDate	Date	8		N
6	SelPrice	Numeric	9	2	N

The following routine creates an array named Order that contains ten rows and five columns. The DO WHILE loop then assigns initial values to each element in the array and displays each element on the screen using @...GET. Next, the READ command allows the user to enter values into the array.

```
*************************** Sample array manipulation.
SET TALK OFF
DECLARE Order(10,5)

CLEAR
@ 4,1 SAY "Invoice Customer  Part     Qty     Paid"

*----- Display fields on screen.
Counter = 1
DO WHILE Counter <= 10
  STORE 0 TO Order(Counter,1),Order(Counter,2), ;
      Order(Counter,4)
  Order(Counter,3) = SPACE(6)
  @ Counter+5,1 GET Order(Counter,1) PICTURE "99999"
  @ ROW(),10 GET Order(Counter,2) PICTURE "9999"
```

```
  @ ROW(),20 GET Order(Counter,3) PICTURE "!!!!!!"
  @ ROW(),30 GET Order(Counter,4) PICTURE "999"
  @ ROW(),40 GET Order(Counter,5) PICTURE "Y"
  Counter = Counter + 1
ENDDO
RELEASE Counter
READ

*--- Append array elements to end of Orders.DBF.
USE Orders
APPEND FROM ARRAY Order FOR Invoice > 0
```

When the user is finished entering values, the APPEND FROM ARRAY command copies the elements from the array to the first (leftmost) five fields in the Orders database. The Date field will be filled in with the current date.

The next command creates an array named MemMemo that contains as many elements as there are lines in the memo field named Abstract:

```
DECLARE MemMemo(MEMLINES(Abstract))
```

See Also APPEND, CALCULATE, CLEAR, COPY TO ARRAY, COUNT, LIST MEMORY, MEMLINES(), PUBLIC, RECCOUNT(), RELEASE, RESTORE, SAVE, SUM

DEFINE BAR

Defining the Options of a Pop-Up Menu

• SYNTAX

DEFINE BAR *line number* **OF** *popup menu* **PROMPT** *text* (**MESSAGE** *text*) (**SKIP** (**FOR** *condition*))

• USAGE DEFINE BAR defines one option on a pop-up menu. You must have already named the pop-up menu using a DEFINE POPUP command. You cannot use DEFINE BAR if the pop-up was defined with the PROMPT FIELD, PROMPT FILES, or PROMPT STRUCTURE options.

The *line numbers* must be positive whole numbers. The specified number is the one returned by the BAR() function when the user selects the option.

The PROMPT defines the text displayed as the menu option. This is also the value returned by the PROMPT() function after the user makes a selection.

The MESSAGE text is a character string of up to 79 characters that is displayed at the bottom of the screen when the user highlights the menu option.

Use the SKIP option to include in the pop-up menu a shaded option that cannot be selected. You can use SKIP FOR to specify a condition that determines whether the option is to be shaded. When the condition returns .T., the option is shaded.

• **EXAMPLE** In the following routine, the *Edit records* prompt is shaded and cannot be selected if the currently selected database contains no records. (The currently selected database is the one that is open when the ACTIVATE POPUP ModRec command is executed):

```
DEFINE POPUP ModRec FROM 2,2 TO 6,17

DEFINE BAR 1 OF ModRec PROMPT "Add records"
DEFINE BAR 2 OF ModRec PROMPT "Edit records" ;
   SKIP FOR RECCOUNT()=0
DEFINE BAR 3 OF ModRec PROMPT "Exit"

ON SELECTION POPUP ModRec DEACTIVATE POPUP

USE AnyFile
ACTIVATE POPUP ModRec
```

See Also ACTIVATE POPUP, BAR(), BARCOUNT(), BARPROMPT(), DEACTIVATE POPUP, DEFINE MENU/PAD/POPUP, ON BAR, ON EXIT BAR/MENU/PAD/POPUP, ON SELECTION POPUP, PADPROMPT(), POPUP(), PROMPT(), RECCOUNT(), SHOW POPUP

DEFINE BOX

Printing Boxes

• SYNTAX

DEFINE BOX FROM *print column* **TO** *print column* **HEIGHT** *number* [**AT LINE** *print line*] [**SINGLE/DOUBLE/***border definition string*]

• USAGE The DEFINE BOX command defines a box for printed output. The definition must include the left column (FROM *print column*), the right column (TO *print column*), and the height of the box. The height of the box is expressed in numbers of rows, including the rows used by the upper and lower borders of the box itself.

If you do not use the AT LINE option in the definition, the box begins printing at the current line position.

The box can be a single or double line, or a custom border defined by the border definition string. The border definition string follows the same rules as the SET BORDER command.

Text output to the printer takes precedence over a defined box. If your defined box is too small to completely outline your printed text, the text characters will be printed instead of the border.

Boxes will only be printed if the _box system memory variable is set to .T.

• EXAMPLE The following command defines a box 50 columns wide and three lines tall, to be printed starting at the second line of every page during a print job:

```
DEFINE BOX FROM 5 TO 55 HEIGHT 3 AT LINE 2
```

See Also @...TO, SET BORDER

DEFINE MENU

Creating Horizontal Bar Menus

• SYNTAX

DEFINE MENU *menu name* (**MESSAGE** *text*)

• USAGE DEFINE MENU assigns a name, and optionally a message, to a horizontal bar menu. The message can be up to 79 characters and is centered at the bottom of the screen whenever the bar menu is active.

To define a horizontal bar menu completely, you need to follow DEFINE MENU with a series of DEFINE PAD commands, which define the menu options, and ON SELECTION PAD or ON PAD commands, which assign an action to each menu option.

• EXAMPLE The routine that follows demonstrates a complete horizontal bar menu definition using DEFINE MENU, DEFINE PAD, ON SELECTION PAD, and ON PAD commands. These commands, together with those found in the DEFINE POPUP and DEFINE WINDOW sections, were used to create the screen shown in Figure 2.6. You can enter the routine as shown here, and run it, to try out the menu.

```
*----- Clear scoreboard line to make room for menu.
SET SCOREBOARD OFF
*----- Create message line.
BarMsg = "Move highlight: "+CHR(27)+CHR(26)+ ;
   "  Select: "+CHR(17)+CHR(196)+CHR(217)

*----- Assign a menu name.
DEFINE MENU MainMenu MESSAGE BarMsg

*----- Define the bar menu options (pads).
DEFINE PAD Option1 OF MainMenu PROMPT "Add" AT 1,1
DEFINE PAD Option2 OF MainMenu PROMPT "Edit" AT 1,7
DEFINE PAD Option3 OF MainMenu PROMPT "Print" AT 1,14
```

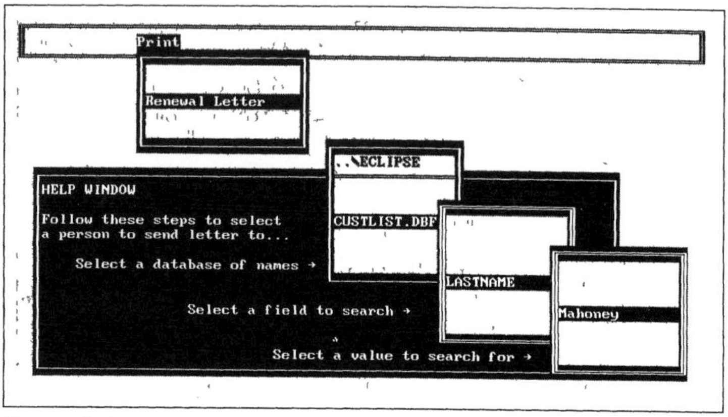

Figure 2.6: A Horizontal Bar Menu, Window, and Pop-Ups

```
DEFINE PAD Option4 OF MainMenu PROMPT "Tools";
  AT 1,21
DEFINE PAD Option5 OF MainMenu PROMPT "Exit" AT 1,28

*----- Assign an action to each bar menu option (pad).
ON SELECTION PAD Option1 OF MainMenu DO ShowIt
ON SELECTION PAD Option2 OF MainMenu DO ShowIt
*----- Assign pop-up menu to display when Option3 is
*----- highlighted.
ON PAD Option3 OF MainMenu;
  ACTIVATE POPUP PrinMenu
ON SELECTION Option4 OF MainMenu DO ShowIt
*----- Deactivate menu when Exit is selected.
ON SELECTION PAD Option5 OF MainMenu;
  DEACTIVATE MENU

*----- Activate the menu.
CLEAR
ACTIVATE MENU MainMenu

*----- This is reached only after a DEACTIVATE MENU
*----- command.
```

```
@ 18,5 SAY "Now the menu is deactivated"
@ 19,5 SAY "because you selected "+PAD()+;
  " "+PROMPT()

*----- Called by Option1, Option 2 and Option 4.
PROCEDURE ShowIt
  @ 11,1 CLEAR
  @ 11,20 SAY "You selected "+PAD()+" "+PROMPT()
  @ 13,20 SAY "Horizontal bar menu is still active"
RETURN
```

See Also BARCOUNT(), BARPROMPT(), DEFINE BAR/PAD/POPUP, MENU(), ON BAR/MENU/PAD/POPUP, ON EXIT BAR/MENU/PAD/POPUP, ON SELECTION BAR/MENU/PAD/POPUP, PAD(), PADPROMPT()

DEFINE PAD

Creating the Horizontal Bar Menu Options

• SYNTAX

DEFINE PAD *pad name* **OF** *menu name* **PROMPT** *text* (**AT** *row,col*) (**MESSAGE** *text*)

• USAGE DEFINE PAD defines one menu option in a horizontal bar menu. The *pad name* can be any variable name. As such, it may contain up to ten characters, must begin with a letter, may not contain spaces, and may contain numbers and underscores after the first letter. The *pad name* is returned by the PAD() function when the menu is activated and the user selects that option. The *menu name* is a menu already defined with DEFINE MENU.

The PROMPT is the text of the menu option (such as *Add* or *Exit*), as displayed in the menu. The PROMPT is also the value returned in the PROMPT() function after the user selects the option when the menu is active.

By default, the menu options are displayed horizontally at the top of the screen, starting at row 0, column 0, when the menu is activated. You can use the AT option in the DEFINE PAD command to place menu options somewhere besides the top of the screen. The options need not be displayed horizontally if you use the AT option.

If SET STATUS is on, the message text is displayed at the bottom of the screen. If SET STATUS is off, the message is positioned by the SET MESSAGE TO *text* AT *location*. You should also turn off SET SCOREBOARD to prevent scoreboard information from overwriting the menu options.

● **EXAMPLE** See **DEFINE MENU** and **ON PAD** commands.

See Also BARCOUNT(), BARPROMPT(), DEFINE BAR/MENU/PAD/POPUP, ON BAR/MENU/PAD/POPUP, ON EXIT BAR/MENU/PAD/POPUP, ON SELECTION BAR/MENU/PAD POPUP, PAD(), PADPROMPT(), SET SCOREBOARD

DEFINE POPUP

Creating Pop-Up Menus

● **SYNTAX**

DEFINE POPUP *popup name* **FROM** *row1,col1* [**TO** *row2,col2*] [**PROMPT FIELD** *field name*/**PROMPT FILES** [**LIKE** *skeleton*]/**PROMPT STRUCTURE**] [**MESSAGE** *text*]

● **USAGE** DEFINE POPUP defines a pop-up or pull-down menu with options arranged vertically. You must specify the upper-left row and column position in the FROM portion of the command. The TO coordinates define the lower-right corner of the window. If you omit the TO row and column coordinates, dBASE IV automatically adjusts the width and length of the window to accommodate the largest prompt.

If you omit a PROMPT option, the pop-up menu displays custom options that you define with the DEFINE BAR command. You can also display a list by using one of the PROMPT options described next.

PROMPT FIELD displays a values list that shows the contents of a field in an open database. If you want the fields to display in sorted order, use an index before activating the pop-up. If you wish to display only unique values from the field, use an index defined as UNIQUE before activating the pop-up.

The value that the user selects from the values list is stored in the PROMPT() function, but the record pointer is not moved to the record. If the field is indexed, use the command

```
SEEK PROMPT()
```

to position the record pointer. If the field is not indexed, you can use the command

LOCATE FOR *field name* **= PROMPT()**

(where *field name* is the name of the field being searched) to position the record pointer.

You may precede the field name with an alias to display fields from an unselected database. A values list cannot display the contents of memo fields.

If you want the values list to display an undetermined field, you can use macro substitution for the field name. For example, if the user selects a field from a structure list, your program can store that field name in a memory variable, using a command such as

```
FldName = PROMPT()
```

Then substitute **&FldName** for a literal field name in the DEFINE POPUP command. For example,

```
DEFINE POPUP ValList FROM 10,10 ;
  PROMPT FIELD &FldName
```

PROMPT FILES displays a files list—a menu of the file names in the current catalog. If you use the optional LIKE *skeleton* parameter, the displayed files must match the skeleton before they are displayed. For example, displaying files LIKE *.DBF displays only dBASE IV database files. The name of the file that the user selects is stored in the PROMPT() function.

PROMPT STRUCTURE displays a structure list—a menu of field names in the current database file. If a previous SET FIELDS command has defined a list of fields, only those fields are displayed when SET FIELDS is on. When the user selects a field from the structure list, the field name is stored in the PROMPT() function.

The MESSAGE is a character string of up to 79 characters displayed at the bottom of the screen when the pop-up menu is displayed and SET STATUS is on. If SET STATUS is off, you can put the message anywhere with the SET MESSAGE TO...AT command.

To convert a pop-up menu to a pull-down menu (one that is displayed when the option is highlighted), use the ON PAD command when assigning actions to horizontal menu bar options, instead of the ON SELECTION PAD command, which waits for the option to be selected. To attach a pop-up menu or list to a function key, use the ON KEY command. To attach a pop-up menu to a custom form, store the ACTIVATE POPUP command in a procedure that is called by an ON READERROR command, or in a user-defined function that is called by an @...VALID command.

• **EXAMPLE** The pull-down menu shown earlier in Figure 2.6 was defined using these commands:

```
DEFINE POPUP PrinMenu FROM 2,14 TO 8,33 ;
  MESSAGE "Highlight a letter type, and press ENTER"

DEFINE BAR 1 OF PrinMenu PROMPT "Roster"
DEFINE BAR 2 OF PrinMenu PROMPT "New Member Letter"
DEFINE BAR 3 OF PrinMenu PROMPT "Renewal Letter"
DEFINE BAR 4 OF PrinMenu PROMPT "Dunning Letter"
DEFINE BAR 5 OF PrinMenu PROMPT "Mailing Labels"
```

The pop-up was activated by the command

```
ON PAD Option3 OF MainMenu ACTIVATE POPUP ;
  PrinMenu
```

See **DEFINE MENU** for more information.

The files list shown earlier in Figure 2.6 was defined and activated with these commands:

```
SET BORDER TO DOUBLE
DEFINE POPUP FileList FROM 8,36 TO 17,51 ;
  PROMPT FILES LIKE *.DBF
ON SELECTION POPUP PrinMenu ACTIVATE POPUP FileList
```

The structure list shown in Figure 2.6 was defined and activated in the following procedure:

```
PROCEDURE StruDisp

*----- Get the database file name from the prompt text
*-----  of the PrinMenu pop-up.
USE PROMPT()
DEFINE POPUP StruList FROM 12,49 TO 21,64 ;
  PROMPT STRUCTURE

*----- Assign the values list procedure to the structure list
*----- menu.
ON SELECTION POPUP StruList DO ValDisp
ACTIVATE POPUP StruList
RETURN
```

The values list and message at the bottom of the screen in Figure 2.6 were defined and activated by the next procedure, which also shows how to position the record pointer to the user's selection and display that record:

```
PROCEDURE ValDisp
*----- Assign prompt text (field name) to memory
*----- variable.
FldName = PROMPT()

*----- Define the values list pop-up.
DEFINE POPUP ValList FROM 15,62 to 23,77 ;
  PROMPT FIELD &FldName MESSAGE MenuMsg
*----- Clear menu after selection is made.
ON SELECTION POPUP ValList DEACTIVATE POPUP

*----- Show the values list.
ACTIVATE POPUP ValList
```

```
*----- Display selected record.
SelValue = PROMPT()

*----- Use LOCATE instead of SEEK
*----- since the file may not be indexed on this field.
LOCATE FOR UPPER(&FldName) = UPPER("&SelValue")

DISPLAY

?
RETURN
```

See Also ACTIVATE POPUP, BAR(), BARCOUNT(), BARPROMPT(), DEFINE BAR/MENU/PAD, ON BAR/MENU/BAR/MENU/PAD/POPUP, POPUP(), PAD PROMPT(), PROMPT()

DEFINE WINDOW

Creating Windows

• SYNTAX

DEFINE WINDOW *window name* **FROM** *row1,col1* **TO** *row2,col2* (**DOUBLE/PANEL/NONE**/*border definition string*) (**COLOR** (*standard*) (*,enhanced*) (*,frame*))

• USAGE DEFINE WINDOW creates a window and defines its border and color attributes. The FROM and TO coordinates define the upper-left and lower-right corners of the window.

By default, the border is the same as the current SET BORDER definition. You can define the border to be a double-line box, reverse-video box, or a different border definition string. Alternatively, you can suppress the border altogether. See the **SET BORDER** command for a description of the *border definition string*.

If you change the SET BORDER definition after you create the window, the window border does not change, but retains the definition that was in effect when you defined it.

The COLOR option defines colors for standard and enhanced text and the frame border. See **SET COLOR** for a list of color codes.

A maximum of 20 windows can be defined and resident in memory at once. Use the LIST/DISPLAY MEMORY command to view the currently defined windows. Use the RELEASE WINDOWS *window name(s)* command to remove window definitions from memory, or CLEAR WINDOWS to release all windows from memory.

- **EXAMPLE** The Help window shown earlier in Figure 2.6 was defined and displayed with the following commands:

```
*----- Define the help (text) window.
SET BORDER TO SINGLE
SET STATUS OFF
DEFINE WINDOW TextWind FROM 10,2 TO 23, 69 ;
  COLOR N/W

*----- Activate the window and display text.
ACTIVATE WINDOW TextWind

@ 0,0  SAY "HELP WINDOW"
@ 2,0  SAY "Follow these steps to select"
@ 3,0  SAY "a person to send letter to..."
@ 5,4  SAY "Select a database of names "+CHR(26)
@ 8,17 SAY "Select a field to search "+CHR(26)
@ 11,27 SAY "Select a value to search for "+CHR(26)

SET BORDER TO DOUBLE
ACTIVATE SCREEN
```

See Also ACTIVATE WINDOW, DEACTIVATE WINDOW, MOVE WINDOW, RELEASE, RESTORE WINDOW, SAVE WINDOW, SET BORDER TO, SET COLOR, SET WINDOW OF MENU

DELETE

Marking Records for Deletion

• SYNTAX

DELETE *(scope)* **(For** *condition)* **(WHILE** *condition)*

• USAGE DELETE marks records for deletion in the currently selected database file. Unless you specify a scope, WHILE, or FOR clause, only the current record is marked. You can then use the SET DELETED ON command to hide these records from access, or you can remove them permanently with the PACK command. You can unmark such records with the RECALL command. The DELETED() function returns true (.T.) when the current record is marked for deletion.

The LIST and DISPLAY commands display an asterisk to the left of records marked for deletion. If SET STATUS is on, the APPEND, EDIT, CHANGE, and BROWSE commands display *Del*—either at the top of the screen or on the status bar—for records marked for deletion.

If the record pointer is at the end of the file (EOF()) when you execute DELETE, the command has no effect.

• EXAMPLE The following commands attempt to find the database record with 1002 in the indexed field. If the appropriate record is found, it is marked for deletion.

```
USE Master ORDER Master
FindIt = 1002
SEEK FindIt
DELETE
```

See Also DELETED(), PACK, RECALL, SET DELETED, ZAP

DELETE FILE

Deleting a File from a Disk

DELETE FILE is identical to ERASE. See **ERASE**.

DELETE TAG

Deleting Index Tags from .MDX Files

• SYNTAX

DELETE TAG *tag name 1* (**OF** *.mdx file name*) (*,tag name 2* (**OF** *.mdx file name*)...)

• USAGE The DELETE TAG command deletes the specified indexes from an active multiple index (.MDX) file or closes specified index (.NDX) files. All tags and indexes must be associated with the databse file in the current work area.

If the tag name is in a multiple index file other than the production .MDX file, you must include the OF *.mdx file name* option.

If the tag name specified is the name of an .NDX file, that file is closed rather than deleted. If the tag was the controlling index, the database file reverts to its natural record number order.

The tag is removed from the active catalog and if all the tags in an .MDX file are deleted, the .MDX file is also deleted.

To delete a tag in a multiuser environment, the database file must be in exclusive use.

• EXAMPLE The following example uses the database file CustList and automatically opens the production .MDX file. It then deletes the index named CustNum from the production index file.

```
USE CustList
DELETE TAG CustNum
```

See Also COPY INDEXES, COPY TAG, INDEX, MDX(), NDX(), ORDER(), SET ORDER, TAG(), USE

DEXPORT

Creating a Binary Named List File

• SYNTAX

DEXPORT SCREEN/REPORT/LABEL *filename* [**TO** *BNL filename*]

• USAGE DEXPORT creates a Binary Named List (BNL) file from a screen, report, or label design. These files are passed to the Template Language Interpreter, which generates template programs from design objects.

The root name of the design object is used for the BNL File unless otherwise specified. The BNL file extension depends on the type of design object:

Screen	.SNL
Report	.FNL
Label	.LNL

See dBASE IV Template Language references for more information.

• EXAMPLE The command

```
DEXPORT REPORT TotSales
```

creates a BNL file named TotSales with the file extension, .FNL.

DIRECTORY

Displaying File Names

• SYNTAX

DIRECTORY/DIR *(***(ON***) drive:) (***(LIKE***) (path) skeleton)*

• USAGE DIRECTORY and DIR are different names for a single command. As in DOS, DIR displays the names of files on a directory. By default, DIR displays only the names of database (.DBF) files. Use a wildcard in the DIR command to display non-database files.

For .DBF files, dBASE displays the file name, number of records, date of the most recent update, file size, total number of files, total number of bytes used by these files, and the number of bytes remaining on the disk. For other types of files, DIR displays only the file names.

The current drive and directory are assumed, unless a path is provided.

The functions FDATE(), FTIME(), and FSIZE() return the date and time of the most recent update and the file size. See dBASE Functions in Part 4.

• EXAMPLE The command

DIR C:\MyProgs*.PRG

displays the names of all program (.PRG) files on the MyProgs directory of drive C.

See Also FDATE(), FSIZE(), FTIME(), LIST FILES, SET AUTOSAVE, SET DEFAULT, SET DIRECTORY

DISPLAY

Displaying Data

• SYNTAX See **LIST**.

• USAGE The DISPLAY command is virtually identical to the LIST command, except that DISPLAY pauses for a key press after each 20 lines of text.

If a database is in use, the DISPLAY command, with no options, displays the contents of the current database record. The contents of a memo field are not displayed unless the name of the field is specifically requested in the *field names/expressions* list.

See Also LIST

DO

Executing a Command File

• SYNTAX

DO *program name/procedure name* (**WITH** *parameters*)

• USAGE The DO command executes all commands in a command file or procedure. If the command file or procedure has not been compiled since the last revision, DO first compiles the source code and creates a compiled (.DBO) version of the file.

If you enter DO at the dot prompt, the dot prompt reappears when the command file or procedure has finished running. If you use DO in a command file to execute another program or procedure, control is returned to the main program when the called program is finished or when RETURN is encountered. The next command to be executed is the one just below the DO command that called the subordinate program or procedure.

If the program or procedure being executed includes a PARAMETERS command, use the WITH option to pass up to 50 parameters. Make sure the left-to-right order and data types of passed parameters match the order and data types specified in the PARAMETERS command in the called program or procedure.

Proper delimiters are required when passing literal data. For example,

DO AnyProc WITH "Smith",{12/1/94},.F.,123.45}

passes a character, date, logical, and numeric value to a procedure named AnyProc.

Each DO counts as an open file. A maximum of 99 simultaneously open files is allowed of which up to 32 may be .DBO files. If you nest programs too deeply within calling programs, you may exceed the number of allowed open files. The resulting error message will normally be *Too many files are open*. Modify the Config.SYS file with the MODIFY COMMAND to increase the number of files to 99. Remember to restart dBASE with the new parameter.

The order in which DO searches for a program or procedure to execute is summarized here:

- A procedure in the current command file
- A procedure in the current procedure file
- A procedure in other open command files
- A compiled (.DBO) command file on disk
- An uncompiled (.PRG) command file on disk
- An SQL (.PRS) command file on disk

If DO does not find the named procedure or file in the search, it returns the error message *File does not exist*.

To terminate program execution prematurely, press **Esc**. If windows remain on the screen when the dot prompt reappears, you can remove these by entering the **CLEAR WINDOWS** command.

• **EXAMPLE** To execute a command file named MyProg.PRG, or a procedure named MyProg that does not contain a PARAMETERS command, enter the command

DO MyProg

See Also CANCEL, COMPILE, DEBUG, FUNCTION, MODIFY COMMAND, PARAMETERS, PROCEDURE, PRIVATE, PUBLIC, REPORT FORM, RETURN, SET DEVELOPMENT, SET FORMAT, SET PROCEDURE

DO CASE...ENDCASE

Selecting One Option among Alternatives

• **SYNTAX**

```
DO CASE
  CASE condition
    commands...
  (CASE condition
    commands...)
  (OTHERWISE
    commands...)
ENDCASE
```

• **USAGE** Use the DO CASE clause when only one option out of several alternatives is to be selected. As soon as a single CASE statement evaluates to true, dBASE performs all commands between that CASE statement and the next one in the clause. All other CASE statements are then ignored whether or not they evaluate to true, and processing resumes at the first command after the ENDCASE command.

If none of the CASE statements in a DO CASE clause evaluates to true, the commands listed after the optional OTHERWISE command are executed. If there is no OTHERWISE command and none of the CASE statements evaluates to true, all commands between DO CASE and ENDCASE are ignored.

Like the DO WHILE...ENDDO and IF...ENDIF constructs, DO CASE clauses can be nested inside one another as long as each clause begins with a DO CASE command and ends with an ENDCASE command.

The DO CASE clause differs from a series of stacked IF clauses, in that the alternatives in a DO CASE clause are always mutually exclusive.

• **EXAMPLE** The following sample routine displays a pop-up menu and then executes a procedure or program based on the user's selection:

```
*----- Define menu.
DEFINE POPUP MainMenu FROM 5,28 TO 11,49
DEFINE BAR 1 OF MainMenu PROMPT "Add members"
DEFINE BAR 2 OF MainMenu PROMPT "Browse members"
DEFINE BAR 3 OF MainMenu PROMPT "Print Letters"
DEFINE BAR 4 OF MainMenu PROMPT "Exit"
*----- Deactivate menu when user makes a selection.
ON SELECTION POPUP MainMenu DEACTIVATE POPUP

*----- Keep displaying menu until user exits.
Exiting = .F.

DO WHILE .NOT. Exiting
  CLEAR
 *----- Display the menu.
   ACTIVATE POPUP MainMenu

 *----- Respond to user's selection.
  DO CASE
    CASE BAR() = 1
       DO AddMemb

    CASE BAR() = 2
       DO BrowMemb

    CASE BAR() = 3
```

```
        DO PrintLet

      OTHERWISE
        Exiting = .T.

    ENDCASE
  ENDDO
  RETURN
```

See Also DO, DO WHILE, IF...ELSE...ENDIF, IIF()

DO WHILE...ENDDO

Constructing Iterative Loops

• SYNTAX

DO WHILE *condition*
  commands...
  *(***LOOP***)*
  *(***EXIT***)*
  commands...
ENDDO

• USAGE A DO WHILE loop tells dBASE to repeat a series of commands as long as a certain condition exists. The DO WHILE command marks the start of the loop and the ENDDO command marks the end of the loop. Every DO WHILE command must have one, and only one, ENDDO command associated with it. If the DO WHILE condition is not true when the loop is entered, the loop will not be processed at all. Be sure to include a command within the loop that changes with each time through the loop and affects the DO WHILE condition (for example, incrementing a counter), or you will never meet the exit condition.

You can use the LOOP and EXIT options to control the flow of program logic. EXIT forces the DO loop to terminate, and control then passes to the command right after the ENDDO command. LOOP passes control back to the first command in the loop.

● **EXAMPLE** The DO WHILE loop that follows prints all of the nonblank elements from an existing array called Names, which contains ten elements:

```
*---- Print nonblank array elements.
SET TALK OFF
Counter = 1

DO WHILE Names(Counter) # " ".AND.Counter <= 10
  ? Names(Counter)
  Counter = Counter + 1
ENDDO
```

See Also DECLARE, DO CASE, EXIT, IF...ELSE...ENDIF, LOOP, RETURN, SCAN...ENDSCAN

EDIT

Displaying and Editing a Record

● **SYNTAX**

EDIT *(***NOINIT***)* *(***NOFOLLOW***)* *(***NOAPPEND***)* *(***NOMENU***)* *(***NOORGANIZE***)* *(***NOEDIT***)* *(***NODELETE***)* *(***NOCLEAR***)* *(record number)* *(***FIELDS** *field names)* *(scope)* *(***FOR** *condition)* *(***WHILE** *condition)*

● **USAGE** EDIT displays the contents of a single record and allows you to change the contents of any field. If a format file is not activated with a SET FORMAT command, EDIT will create a simple screen for editing data. The cursor-control keys that EDIT supports are similar to those used by the BROWSE command. See Table 2.8 for more information.

The command options NOINIT...NOCLEAR have the same effect as they do in the Browse screen (see Table 2.7). The *record number* option displays that record for editing. The FIELDS option allows you to limit the display to the fields listed.

• EXAMPLE The commands

```
USE Orders
SET FORMAT TO OrdForm
EDIT 22
```

let you edit records on the Orders database, starting at record number 22, using the custom screen named OrdForm. Note that the similar command

```
EDIT RECORD 22
```

allows you to edit *only* record number 22.

See Also BROWSE, READ, SET AUTOSAVE, SET DESIGN, SET FIELDS, SET FORMAT, SET LOCK, SET REFRESH, SET WINDOW

EJECT

Ejecting the Current Page from the Printer

• SYNTAX

```
EJECT [PAGE]
```

• USAGE The EJECT command ejects the current page from the printer, aligning the print head at the top of the next page to be printed. PROW() and PCOL() are reset to 0. For proper operation, you must physically set the print head to the top of a new page before the printer is turned on, or use the printer's top-of-form (TOF) button with the printer on. Manually removing paper from the printer will misalign the print head with the top of the page.

The PAGE option with the PRINTJOB...ENDPRINTJOB commands advances output to an ON PAGE routine. Typically, the routine will print a page header or footer. After the page footer is printed, you should issue an EJECT PAGE command to eject the printed page, increment the _pageno system memory variable by one, and reset the _plineno system variable to 0.

• EXAMPLE See the sample program included with the **PRINTJOB...ENDPRINTJOB** command.

See Also ???, ON PAGE, PCOL(), PRINTJOB...ENDPRINTJOB, PRINTSTATUS(), PROW(), SET ALTERNATE, SET CONSOLE, SET PRINTER

ERASE

Deleting a File

• SYNTAX

ERASE *file name*/**?**

• USAGE ERASE permanently deletes a file from the disk. The *filename* must contain the file extension and you can erase only one file at a time. Unless you specify otherwise, ERASE searches only the currently logged drive and directory for the file to erase. Furthermore, ERASE does not search the path defined in a dBASE SET PATH or DOS PATH command.

An open file cannot be erased. Use the appropriate CLOSE command to close the file before erasing it.

If the name of the file to be erased is stored in a memory variable, surround the memory variable name with parentheses in the ERASE command.

Unlike DOS, dBASE does not support wildcard characters in file names used with the ERASE command. To use wildcard characters in an ERASE command, use the RUN or ! command to access the

DOS ERASE command. Use the ? option to select from a list of files in the current catalog.

The DELETE FILE command is identical to the ERASE command.

• EXAMPLE The following commands erase the Mail.DBF database and its index and memo field files from the disk in drive B:

```
ERASE B:Mail.DBF
ERASE B:Mail.DBT
ERASE B:Mail.MDX
```

The next commands erase the file named Temp.DBF from the currently logged drive and directory:

```
FileName = "Temp.DBF"
ERASE (FileName)
```

See Also CLOSE, DELETE, FILE(), USE

EXIT

Terminating a Loop Prematurely

• SYNTAX

```
EXIT
```

• USAGE EXIT forces termination of a DO WHILE or SCAN loop, regardless of the condition that controls the loop. Whereas the LOOP command passes control back to the top of the loop, the EXIT command passes control to the first command below the ENDDO or ENDSCAN command.

• EXAMPLE The following routine displays on the screen the message *Press the space bar to stop printing* and then prints records from the currently open database using a SCAN...ENDSCAN loop. If the user presses the spacebar (ASCII 32) while the program is running, however, the enclosed EXIT command passes control to the SET PRINT OFF command beneath ENDDO, and stops printing.

```
@ 5,5 SAY "Press the space bar to stop printing"
USE AnyFile

SET PRINT ON
SCAN ALL
  ? Name, Address, City, State, Zip
  IF INKEY() = 32
    EXIT
  ENDIF
ENDSCAN
SET PRINT OFF
```

See Also DO WHILE...ENDDO, LOOP, SCAN...ENDSCAN

EXPORT

Copying a Database to Another File Format

• SYNTAX

EXPORT TO *file name* (**TYPE**) *file type* (**FIELDS** *field list*) *(scope)*
(**FOR** *condition*) (**WHILE** *condition*)

• USAGE Like the COPY TO command, EXPORT can copy dBASE IV data to several other formats. EXPORT can copy files into more formats than COPY TO, including the PFS:FILE format. The IMPORT command can read files from the same foreign formats and convert them to dBASE format. See Table 2.17 for a list of foreign file options for exporting from and importing to dBASE IV data.

To copy data and a custom screen to PFS:FILE format, open the database file and the dBASE IV custom screen using the SET FORMAT command before issuing the EXPORT command.

Table 2.17: File Types Used with EXPORT and IMPORT

TYPE Option	File Format
PFS	PFS:FILE file
DBASEII	dBASE II database file with .DB2 file extension
FW2	Framework II (.FW2) file
FW3	Framework III (.FW3) file
FW4	Framework IV (.FW4) file
RPD	RapidFile data (.RPD) file
WKS	Lotus 1-2-3 spreadsheet (Version 1A) file with .WKS file extension
WK1	Lotus 1-2-3 spreadsheet (Version 2 and later) file with .WK1 file extension

• **EXAMPLE** The following commands export a copy of a database named Mail.DBF and an associated MailScr.FMT format file to a PFS:FILE file named PFSMail:

```
USE Mail
SET FORMAT TO MailScr
EXPORT TO PFSMail. TYPE PFS
```

See Also APPEND FROM, COPY TO, IMPORT, SET FORMAT, SET SAFETY

FIND

Finding a Value in an Index File

• **SYNTAX**

FIND *literal*

• **USAGE** FIND searches an indexed database file for the first record whose controlling index key matches the *literal* string. The controlling index is the one specified by the ORDER option in the USE command, or by the most recent SET ORDER command.

If SET NEAR is off (the default setting), FIND attempts to locate a value that exactly matches the value being searched for. If SET NEAR is on, FIND positions the record pointer to the record that most closely matches the value being searched for.

Besides positioning the record pointer at the appropriate record, FIND changes the values stored in the FOUND() and EOF() functions. The relationships between the FIND and SET NEAR commands and the FOUND() and EOF() functions are summarized here:

When SET NEAR is off:

If an exact match is found:

FOUND() returns .T.

EOF() returns .F.

If an exact match cannot be found:

FOUND() returns .F.

EOF() returns .T.

When SET NEAR is on:

If an exact match is found:

FOUND() returns .T.

EOF() returns .F.

If a near match is found:

FOUND() returns .F.

EOF() returns .F.

If SET EXACT is off, only the leftmost characters need to match for the search to be successful. If SET EXACT is on, only a character-for-character match will be successful.

FIND will locate a record marked for deletion only if the SET DELETED parameter is off. FIND will not find a record hidden by a SET FILTER or MODIFY QUERY condition.

If the index file contains several keys, the field widths and formats of both the data being searched for and the key expression of the index file must match exactly. FIND cannot locate characters embedded within the index expression.

If the search value is stored in a memory variable, use SEEK rather than FIND. If the field you are searching is not the first-listed key in the controlling index key expression, use LOCATE.

The function SEEK() is faster than FIND for locating data in a file. FIND must be interpreted as a macro expansion of the key expression, while SEEK() simply uses the expression as an argument.

• **EXAMPLE** If the CustDate index was created with the command

```
INDEX ON STR(CustNo,4)+DTOC(DateSold) TAG ;
  CustDate
```

the following commands attempt to locate the first record with 1001 as the customer number (CustNo):

```
USE AnyFile ORDER CustDate
SET EXACT OFF
SET NEAR OFF
FIND 1001
```

See Also EOF(), FOUND(), INDEX, KEY(), LOCATE(), LOOKUP(), SEEK, SEEK(), SET DELETED, SET EXACT, SET FILTER, SET NEAR, SET ORDER, TAG(), USE

FUNCTION

Creating User-Defined Functions

• SYNTAX

FUNCTION *function name*
PARAMETERS *parameter list*
commands...
RETURN *returned value*

• USAGE The FUNCTION command identifies a user-defined function in either a command file or a procedure file. The name of the function can be up to ten characters long, must begin with a letter, may not contain spaces or punctuation other than the underscore, and may not be the same as any built-in dBASE command or function.

When the function is called from a command, the parameters passed to it must match the number, order, and data types of parameters defined in the PARAMETERS command.

A function must end with a RETURN command. The RETURN command must include an expression (or variable name) that specifies the value returned from the function. If the user-defined function is called from an @...VALID, @...WHEN, or other command that expects a .T. or .F. result, the RETURN expression should return .T. or .F..

A function must be compiled before it can be called. The SET PROCEDURE and DO commands will automatically compile user-defined functions if SET DEVELOPMENT is on. You can use the COMPILE command to compile the file in which the user-defined function is stored.

Like the built-in dBASE IV functions, user-defined functions must operate on a specific item of data, or several data items, and not on databases or files as a whole. Therefore, there are some restrictions on the dBASE commands you can include in a UDF. A UDF may not:

- CLOSE, CONVERT, PACK, MODIFY STRUCTURE, USE, or ZAP a database file that was open and active when the function began.
- CLEAR or RELEASE an active window.
- Use BROWSE, EDIT, CHANGE, INSERT, or APPEND to access the same database file recursively.
- Use LIST or DISPLAY recursively.

You may use macro substitution (the & symbol) in a user-defined function.

You can relax some of these restrictions and allow for a more experienced user who presents less risk of damaging the database files by using SET DBTRAP OFF.

Tip: Using UDFs in an index expression or a SET FIELDS list will slow down your processing, since dBASE must evaluate the UDF for each record.

• EXAMPLE Suppose you need to convert to proper case names that were originally entered in all uppercase letters (DR. JOHN L. SMITH to Dr. John L. Smith). Since dBASE does not have a built-in function to perform the conversion, you need to create your own function.

First, enter the following command at the dot prompt to create or modify the MyProcs.PRG procedure file:

```
MODIFY COMMAND MyProcs
```

Next, type in the PropCase user-defined function, as here:

```
******************************** MyProcs.PRG

*** Capitalize first letter of every word.
FUNCTION PropCase
PARAMETERS String
```

```
   String = UPPER(LEFT(String,1)) + ;
     LOWER(RIGHT(String,LEN(String)-1))

   STORE 1 TO BlankSpot, CapSpot
   DO WHILE BlankSpot > 0
  BlankSpot = AT(" ",,;
  SUBSTR(String,CapSpot,;
     LEN(TRIM(String))-CapSpot))
     IF BlankSpot > 0
        CapSpot = BlankSpot + CapSpot
        String = STUFF(String,CapSpot,1,;
        UPPER(SUBSTR(String,CapSpot,1)))
     ENDIF
   ENDDO
 RETURN String
```

Save the completed user-defined function by pressing **Ctrl-End**. When the dot prompt appears, enter the command

```
SET PROCEDURE TO MyProcs
```

so that the user-defined function will be compiled and accessible. As a compiled procedure, it evaluates faster than as a function, especially in loops.

Next, open the database that contains the uppercase names and enter this command (assuming the field containing data to be converted is called Name):

```
REPLACE ALL Name WITH PropCase(Name)
```

Remember to execute the SET TALK OFF command before calling this user-defined function, to prevent extraneous data from appearing on the screen.

See Also DO, PARAMETERS, PROCEDURE, RETURN, SET PROCEDURE, SET DBTRAP

GO/GOTO

Moving the Record Pointer

• SYNTAX

GO/GOTO TOP/BOTTOM/[[**RECORD**] *record number/expression*] [**IN** *alias*]

or

record number/expression [**IN** *alias*]

• USAGE You can use GO and GOTO interchangeably. The TOP and BOTTOM options move the record pointer to the first or last record in the database file, or to the first and last records as determined by the controlling index. The GO or GOTO commands used with a specified number always send the record pointer to the record with that number, regardless of the index.

The IN option lets you specify a database outside the current work area. The record pointer in the currently selected work area does not change, nor does the specified work area become the current work area. The record number can be calculated in an expression.

The GO and GOTO commands can position the record pointer at a record that is marked for deletion, even if the SET DELETED parameter is on.

Whenever you issue a SET FILTER command, always issue GO TOP next to reposition the record pointer and activate the filter.

• **EXAMPLE** The commands

```
USE Charges ORDER PartNo IN 1
USE Master IN 2

SELECT 1
GO TOP
GOTO 5 IN Master
```

position the record pointer to the first record in the Charges database as defined by the PartNo index order, and to record number 5 in the Master database file. Work area 1, which contains the Charges database, remains the current work area.

The command

```
GOTO RECNO()+5
```

moves the record pointer five records beneath the current record.

See Also ON ERROR, RECNO(), SET DELETED, SET FILTER, SET RELATION, SKIP

HELP

Displaying Help Screens

• **SYNTAX**

HELP *(command/function)*

• **USAGE** The help system provides general help with dBASE IV concepts and design screens, and help with the syntax and options for a specific command or function.

If you enter **HELP** without any optional command or function (or press **F1**) at the dot prompt, dBASE displays a general table of contents for the help system. Note that you can scroll to more general or more specific tables of contents. To get help with a particular topic, use the arrow keys to highlight the appropriate topic and press ↵.

To get help with a particular command or function, type **HELP** at the dot prompt, followed by the command or function you need help with, and press ↵.

To leave help, press **Esc**.

Tip: To get help with a particular command or function while using the dBASE IV program editor, press **F1** and then press ↵ to select CONTENTS. Press **F3** twice for a more general table of contents, and then select **Dot Prompt Commands and Functions**. From the displayed menu, select Commands, Set Commands, Functions, System Memory Variables, or the alphabetically or numerically listed Error Messages.

When the command or function list appears on the screen, you can type the first letter of the command you need help with. Then highlight the specific command or function that you need help with and press ↵. Press **Esc** to return to the program editor.

• EXAMPLE To get help with the syntax and options available with the LIST command, type

```
HELP LIST
```

at the dot prompt and press ↵. Press **Esc** to return to the dot prompt.

See Also ASSIST, MODIFY COMMAND, SET HELP, SET INSTRUCT

IF...ELSE...ENDIF

Making Decisions

• SYNTAX

```
IF condition
  commands...
(ELSE
  commands...)
ENDIF
```

• USAGE IF...ELSE...ENDIF sets up a decision-making clause in a program. The condition used in the IF command must evaluate to either true (.T.) or false (.F.) as the command file is being executed.

Each IF command must have one, and only one, ENDIF command associated with it. The ELSE command is optional.

If the condition evaluates to .T., all commands between the IF and ELSE commands are executed. If ELSE is not specified in the command and the condition evaluates to .T., all commands between IF and ENDIF are executed.

If the condition evaluates to .F., all commands between ELSE and ENDIF are executed, and commands between IF and ELSE are ignored. If no ELSE is specified and the condition evaluates to .F., all commands in the loop are ignored.

• EXAMPLE In the next routine, if the user types Y in response to the WAIT command, the IF clause sets the printer on. If the user types any letter other than Y, the printer is not set on.

```
*----- Ask about printer.
WAIT "Send results to printer? (Y/N) " TO YesNo

*----- If user enters Y or y, set the printer on.

IF UPPER(YesNo) = "Y"
```

```
  SET PRINT ON
ENDIF
```

In the IF clause that follows, the extended price is calculated either with or without tax, depending on whether the field named Taxable contains .F. or .T.:

```
IF .NOT. Taxable
  ExtPrice = Qty*UnitPrice
ELSE
  ExtPrice = 1.06*Qty*UnitPrice
ENDIF
```

Tip: If you are setting a single variable to one of only two values, it is faster to use the IIF() function instead of an IF...ELSE...ENDIF loop. For example, the five commands above would be replaced by the single command

```
ExtPrice = ;
  IIF(Taxable=".F.",Qty*UnitPrice,1.06*Qty*UnitPrice)
```

See Also DO CASE, DO WHILE, IIF()

IMPORT

Creating a Database from External Data Files

• SYNTAX

IMPORT FROM *file name* (**TYPE**) *file type*

• USAGE The IMPORT command is similar to the APPEND FROM...TYPE command, in that it reads data from an external format into a dBASE database file. Unlike APPEND FROM, which imports data into an existing database file, IMPORT actually creates a new database file, using the structure of the data being imported to determine data types and field widths.

The file types that can be imported into dBASE IV are the same as those to which you can export from dBASE. See Table 2.17 with the EXPORT command) for a description of the allowed file types.

Unlike APPEND FROM, the IMPORT command also allows you to import data from a PFS:FILE database. Imported PFS files are converted into three separate dBASE files: .DBF (the database file), .FMT (a format file), and .FMO (a compiled format file). All three files have the same file name as the imported file.

• **EXAMPLE** The command below copies data from a PFS:FILE database and custom screen named MailData into three dBASE IV files, which will be named MailData.DBF, MailData.FMT, and MailData.FMO.

```
IMPORT FROM MailData TYPE PFS
```

See Also APPEND FROM, COPY, EXPORT, SET FORMAT

INDEX

Creating an Index File

• **SYNTAX**

INDEX *(***ON** *key expression)* **TO** *.NDX file name (***UNIQUE***)*

or

INDEX *(***ON** *key expression) (***TAG** *tag name (***OF** *.MDX file name)(***FOR** *condition) (***DESCENDING***)) (***UNIQUE***)*

• **USAGE** INDEX ON creates an index for the currently selected database, using the field name or expression you specify. If you use the TO option, the index is stored as a separate file with the extension .NDX (as in earlier versions of dBASE). If you use the TAG option, the index is stored in a dBASE IV multiple (.MDX) index file.

The TAG option stores the index in the production multiple index file, which has the same name as the database file but the .MDX extension. To specify a different multiple index file name, use the OF option with a valid DOS file name.

Only the production index file (the one with the same name as the database) is opened automatically when you issue a USE command. Like any multiple index file, the production index file may contain up to 47 tags or indexes. All indexes in the production index file are updated automatically when you add, change, or delete data. Only one index at a time may be the *controlling* index that determines the sort order. Use the SET ORDER command, or the ORDER option with the USE command, to select the controlling index.

The FOR option limits the number of entries in an .MDX file to those that match the indicated condition. This results in faster searching.

Indexes sort into ascending order unless you use the DESCENDING option.

The UNIQUE option hides all but the first occurrence of repetitive data. For example, if the State field of records 3, 5, and 10 contains CA, and you create a unique index of the State field, only record 3 is displayed when the index is active.

When using multiple fields in an index expression to create a sort-within-a-sort order, always convert all fields to the character data type to ensure proper sorting. Here are some functions for converting data types:

DTOS()	Converts date to character in yyyymmdd format
VAL()	Converts character to numeric
STR()	Converts numeric and float to character

To sort character data in *dictionary* instead of ASCII order, use the UPPER() function to convert all letters to uppercase.

Whenever you convert data types to create an index, you must use the same conversions when searching the index with the SEEK and FIND commands or SEEK() and FIND() functions.

You can use any dBASE functions in an index expression. However, avoid using TRIM(), LTRIM(), or RTRIM() in an index key expression. Doing so produces key expressions of varying widths which disrupt the sort order.

The maximum length of the combined fields in a complex index expression is 100 characters. The actual expression formula used in the INDEX command cannot exceed 220 characters.

• **EXAMPLE** Since both LastName and FirstName are character fields, the following INDEX command creates a dictionary sort that displays names in last name and then first name order (for example, Ann Smith precedes Bob Smith):

```
INDEX ON UPPER(LastName+FirstName) TAG Names
```

The next command creates an index named DateQty based on a date field named DateSold and a numeric field named Qty. Records will be displayed in DateSold order, with records sorted by Qty within each date.

```
INDEX ON DTOS(DateSold)+STR(Qty,3,0) TAG DateQty
```

To display dates in ascending order, but quantities in descending order within each date, subtract the value of the Qty field from a large constant, as in this example:

```
INDEX ON DTOS(DateSold)+STR(9999–Qty,3,0);
  TAG DateQty
```

The next command creates a sort order based on a logical field named Paid, placing the .T. values above the .F. values:

```
INDEX ON IIF(Paid,"T","F") TAG Paid DESCENDING
```

The following command sorts records by floor and room number, assuming that both of these fields are numeric or float data types:

```
INDEX ON STR(Floor)+STR(RoomNum) TAG Rooms
```

Suppose a database named Employes.DBF includes a record for each employee in a company, and the record includes the employee's department. You want to send a memo to each department, *not* to each employee. To limit the record display to unique departments only, create a unique index as follows:

```
USE Employes
INDEX ON Department TAG UniqDept UNIQUE
SET ORDER TO UniqDept
```

See Also COPY INDEXES, COPY TAG, DELETE TAG, DESCENDING(), FIND, FOR(), KEY(), MDX(), NDX(), ORDER(), REINDEX, SEEK, SEEK(), SET INDEX, SET NEAR, SET ORDER, SET UNIQUE, TAG(), TAGCOUNT(), UNIQUE(), USE

INPUT

Accepting Numeric Input

• SYNTAX

INPUT *(prompt)* **TO** *memory variable*

• USAGE Use INPUT to request numeric or character data from the user. You can enclose the optional prompt in double quotation marks, apostrophes, or brackets. After the user types in a response and presses ↵, the entry is stored in the named memory variable.

• EXAMPLE The following commands request the user's name and age. The first INPUT command displays the prompt *What is your name?* and waits for a response, which is then stored in the memory variable UserName. After the user types in the name and presses ↵, the second INPUT command displays the prompt *How old are you?* and waits for that response. The user's response is stored in the memory variable named UserAge.

```
INPUT "What is your name?" TO UserName
INPUT "How old are you? " TO UserAge
```

See Also @...READ, ACCEPT, PRIVATE, PUBLIC, STORE, WAIT

INSERT

Inserting Records into a Database

• SYNTAX

INSERT *[***BLANK***]* *[***BEFORE***]* / *[***NOORGANIZE***]*

• USAGE INSERT is identical to APPEND, except that it places the new record immediately after the current record rather than at the bottom of the database. With no options, INSERT clears the screen, displays the field list, and opens the full-screen editor.

INSERT allows you to enter data into only a single record, unless the record is inserted at the bottom of the file. In this case, INSERT allows you, as in APPEND, to add multiple records.

The optional BEFORE clause inserts the new record ahead of the current pointer position. The INSERT BLANK command inserts a blank record into the database but does not activate full-screen mode for entering data. A REPLACE command or a READ command with a custom screen allows you to enter data into the newly inserted record.

By disabling the Organize menu, the NOORGANIZE option prevents the user from changing the index or sorting the database file during an application.

The SET CARRY and SET FORMAT commands work with INSERT as they do with APPEND. Command keys used in APPEND work similarly in INSERT. INSERT automatically updates all currently active index files. Any custom screen activated by SET FORMAT will be used by INSERT.

• EXAMPLE The following commands insert a record into the appropriate alphabetical position for the last name Miller, assuming that the Mail database is already indexed on the LName field, and that LName contains last names. You can then enter data through the MailScr custom format screen.

```
USE Mail
SET FORMAT TO MailScr
LOCATE FOR LName >= "Miller"
INSERT BEFORE
CLOSE FORMAT
```

See Also APPEND, EDIT

JOIN

Merging Two Databases

• SYNTAX

JOIN WITH *alias* **TO** *file name* **FOR** *condition* *(***FIELDS** *field list)*

• USAGE Before using JOIN to merge two files into a third new file, you must open both files. If you do not include the FIELDS option, all fields from both database files are included in the newly created file (up to the 255 fields per record limit). You can include any type of field, other than a memo field, from both files in the *Field* list.

Using SET RELATION to link two files is faster than using JOIN.

• EXAMPLE The following commands create a database file named BigFile consisting of the FName and LName fields from the Customer database and the Amount and Date fields from the Charges database:

```
USE Customer IN 1
USE Charges IN 2

SELECT 1
JOIN WITH Charges TO BigFile FOR;
  CustNo = B->CustNo ;
  FIELDS FName, LName, B->Amount, B->Date
```

See Also SET FIELDS, SET RELATION

KEYBOARD

Entering Characters into the Type ahead Buffer

• SYNTAX

KEYBOARD *character* *(***CLEAR***)*

• USAGE KEYBOARD is used to place characters in the type ahead buffer, just as if the operator had entered them via a command such as ACCEPT, INPUT, INKEY(), or READ. It simulates user input much like PLAY MACRO does, by automatically entering keystrokes when a command looks for keyboard input.

The CLEAR option empties the type ahead buffer before the characters are inserted.

This command can be useful when writing self-running demonstration programs or entering repetitious data.

• EXAMPLE The command below retrieves the company name from the type ahead buffer whenever the user presses **Ctrl-F7**.

```
ON KEY Ctrl-F7 KEYBOARD "Computer Intelligence, Inc."
```

The following commands prompt the user to enter the letter category for the part number to place on order. The letter is entered into the type ahead buffer with a dash. When the Orders database file is opened, a blank record is appended and the letter and dash are entered automatically into the PartNo field. The user then completes the order.

```
SET STATUS OFF
mmodel = SPACE(1)
@22,0 SAY "Order for model A, B, or C?";
  GET mmodel PICTURE "!"
READ
```

```
KEYBOARD mmodel+CHR(45) CLEAR

*----- When the Orders database file is opened...

USE Orders
APPEND
mpartno = SPACE(5)
@22,0 GET mpartno
READ
REPLACE PartNo WITH mpartno
SET STATUS ON
```

See Also CLEAR, INKEY(), ON KEY, PLAY MACRO, READKEY(), RESTORE MACROS, RESTORE SCREEN, SAVE MACRO, SET TYPEAHEAD

LABEL FORM

Printing Labels

• SYNTAX

LABEL FORM *file name*/**?** *(scope)* (**FOR** *condition)* (**WHILE** *condition)* (**SAMPLE**) (**TO PRINTER/TO FILE** *file name)*

• USAGE Using the format designed in the dBASE IV labels design screen, LABEL FORM prints, writes to a file, or displays mailing labels from the database currently in use.

The optional WHILE and FOR commands specify records to be printed. The TO PRINTER option sends the labels to the printer. If you use SAMPLE with TO PRINTER, dummy labels are printed to help align the labels in the printer.

The TO FILE option sends mailing labels to an ASCII disk file. The disk file is assigned the extension .TXT unless another is provided in the command line.

• EXAMPLE The commands

USE MailList
LABEL FORM ThreeUp SAMPLE TO PRINT

display all records from the MailList database using the format specified in the ThreeUp label format file. Labels are sent to the printer, and you can print several dummy labels to help align them.

See Also CREATE/MODIFY LABEL, SET PRINTER TO

LIST

Displaying the Contents of Database Records

• SYNTAX

LIST/DISPLAY *(***(FIELDS***) field names/expressions)* **(OFF***)*
(scope) *(***FOR** *condition)* *(***WHILE** *condition)* *(***TO**
PRINTER/TO FILE *file name)*

or

LIST/DISPLAY FILES *(***(LIKE***) skeleton)* *(***TO PRINTER/TO FILE**
file name)

or

LIST/DISPLAY HISTORY *(***LAST** *number)* *(***TO PRINTER/TO FILE**
file name)

or

LIST/DISPLAY MEMORY *(***TO PRINTER/TO FILE** *file name)*

or

LIST/DISPLAY STATUS *(***TO PRINTER/TO FILE** *file name)*

or

LIST/DISPLAY STRUCTURE (**IN** *alias*) (**TO PRINTER/TO FILE** *file name*)

or

LIST/DISPLAY USERS

• USAGE When used without any options, LIST displays every record in the currently open database file. If you include a scope option, the display is limited to the number of records specified in the scope condition. The FOR and WHILE options limit the display to records that match a search criterion. The OFF option suppresses the display of the database record numbers. The TO PRINTER option directs output to the printer. The TO FILE option directs output to an ASCII text file. You must specify a file name for the output. If you do not include an extension in the file name, dBASE adds the .TXT extension.

LIST and DISPLAY are virtually identical, but LIST displays all output without pausing, while DISPLAY pauses for a keypress after each screenful of output. With no options, DISPLAY displays only the current record in the open database file. Use DISPLAY ALL to see all the database records, one screen at a time.

The contents of memo fields are not displayed by the LIST/DISPLAY commands unless specifically requested in the *field names/expressions* list. The width of the memo field display is determined by the SET MEMOWIDTH command.

Field names or expressions are displayed above the data if the SET HEADINGS parameter is on. If SET HEADINGS is off, only the data is displayed.

Other options for the LIST/DISPLAY options are summarized here:

FILES	Displays the names and other information about files on a directory.

HISTORY	Displays a list of the last commands typed at the dot prompt. The maximum number stored in the history buffer is 20, unless set higher with SET HISTORY. The LAST option specifies the number of commands from the buffer to display.
MEMORY	Displays a summary of memory use and the amount of available memory. It lists the number of memory variables, their names, type, size, status, and contents. It also displays menu, pad, and pop-up definitions.
STATUS	Displays the current status of open files, SET commands, and programmable function keys.
STRUCTURE	Displays the filename, number of records, date of last change, field definitions, and record size of the active database file. If SET FIELDS is on, a ">" symbol appears to the left of each field listed with SET FIELDS TO.
USERS	Displays the names of all workstations currently logged into dBASE on the network.

• **EXAMPLE** The following command prints the CustNo, Qty, and UnitPrice fields, and the product of the UnitPrice field multiplied by the Qty field, adding 6 percent tax if the Tax field is .T.. Only records that have 1001 in the CustNo field are included in the display. Record numbers are not included in the display.

```
USE Sales

LIST CustNo, Qty, UnitPrice, ;
  IIF(Tax,(Qty*UnitPrice)*1.06,Qty*UnitPrice) ;
  FOR CustNo = 1001 OFF TO PRINT
```

The next command creates an ASCII file named FilNames.TXT that contains the names of all files on the current directory:

```
LIST FILES LIKE *.* TO FILE FilNames
```

The following command displays the current status of dBASE IV on the screen, pausing for a keypress after each screenful of data:

```
DISPLAY STATUS
```

See Also MODIFY REPORT, NETWORK(), REPORT FORM, SET HEADINGS, SET MARGIN

LOAD

Loading an Assembly Language Subroutine

• SYNTAX

LOAD *binary file name*

• USAGE LOAD copies an assembly language subroutine into RAM, where you can execute it with a CALL command or CALL() function. LOAD assumes that the assembly language subroutine has been converted to a binary file with the DOS EXE2BIN program, which produces a file with the .BIN extension.

You can load up to 16 assembly language subroutines into RAM at once, each with a maximum length of 65,500 bytes. Each loaded binary file must have a unique name.

• EXAMPLE The following commands load into memory two assembly language subroutines, MyMod1.BIN and MyMod2.BIN:

```
LOAD MyMod1
LOAD MyMod2
```

See Also CALL, CALL(), LIST STATUS, RELEASE, RUN/!

LOCATE

Finding a Record Matching a Search Criterion

• SYNTAX

LOCATE (**FOR** *condition*) (*scope*) (**WHILE** *condition*)

• USAGE LOCATE searches the disk file directly rather than an index file, so you can use it with any field or combination of fields. LOCATE supports all dBASE functions and operators.

If LOCATE fails to find a matching record, the EOF() function is set to .T. and the FOUND() function is set to .F. If the SET TALK parameter is on and LOCATE fails to find a matching record, the screen will display the message *End of LOCATE scope*. LOCATE will find records marked for deletion only if the SET DELETED command is off. LOCATE will not find records hidden by a SET FILTER or QUERY condition.

If SET EXACT is off, only the leftmost characters need to match for the search operation to be successful. If SET EXACT is on, only a character-for-character match will be successful.

You can use the CONTINUE command with LOCATE to find the next record that matches the search condition.

• EXAMPLE The command

```
LOCATE FOR UPPER(LastName) = "SMITH" .AND. ;
  Amount > 1000 .AND. OrdDate = {12/31/94}
```

will locate the first record in the database that has Smith in the LastName field, an amount greater than 1000 in the Amount field, and the date 12/31/94 in the OrdDate field.

The command

```
LOCATE FOR MONTH(OrdDate) = "12" NEXT 5
```

will locate the next five records of orders in December.

See Also CONTINUE, EOF(), FIND, FOUND(), SEEK

LOGOUT

Logging the User Out of the Network

• SYNTAX

```
LOGOUT
```

• USAGE LOGOUT forces a user to log out of a system if you have set up a protection scheme with PROTECT. After one user has logged out, LOGOUT presents the log-in screen so a new user can log onto the same workstation. If no protection scheme has been devised, LOGOUT simply returns control to the dot prompt.

LOGOUT closes all open database and related files, and program files at the current workstation.

• EXAMPLE The following routine asks the current user to confirm his or her request to log out. Answering **Y** logs this user out and presents the log-in screen to a new user. Answering **N** keeps the current user logged in:

```
LeaveNow = .F.
@ 5,2 SAY "Are you sure? (Y/N) ";
GET LeaveNow PICTURE "Y"
READ
IF LeaveNow
  LOGOUT
ENDIF
```

See Also PROTECT

LOOP

Returning to the Top of a Loop

• SYNTAX

LOOP

• USAGE LOOP is an optional command you use to pass control back to the beginning of a DO WHILE or SCAN loop. The command then evaluates the condition and determines whether to repeat or terminate the loop.

• EXAMPLE In the following routine, the READ command waits for the user to enter a person's last name and then stores that entry in a variable named Search. If the user enters a name, the SEEK command attempts to find the name and the IF clause that follows responds accordingly. However, if the user presses ↵ without typing a last name, the LOOP command passes control back to the top of the DO WHILE loop, ignoring the SEEK command and IF clause altogether, and repeating the request for a last name.

```
USE CustList ORDER LastName

Search = SPACE(10)

DO WHILE Search # " "

  @ 5,5 SAY "Search for what last name? " ;
    GET Search
  READ
*----- If no name entered, ignore commands below.
  IF Search = " "
    LOOP
  ENDIF

*----- Attempt to find name and edit.
  SEEK UPPER(Search)
```

```
IF FOUND()
  EDIT RECNO()
ELSE
  @ 22,1 SAY "Can't find "+Search
ENDIF

ENDDO

RETURN
```

See Also DO WHILE...ENDDO, EXIT, IF...ENDIF, SCAN...ENDSCAN

MODIFY COMMAND/FILE

Creating or Modifying Command Files

• SYNTAX

MODIFY COMMAND/FILE *file name* (**WINDOW** *window name*)

• USAGE MODIFY COMMAND accesses the dBASE IV full-screen text editor, where you can write or edit programs and format files. By default, the file you create is assigned the .PRG extension. The MODIFY FILE command also calls up the text editor, but does not assume the .PRG extension and does not add an extension to the file you create.

The program editor provides automatic indentation to help you structure your programs better. To unindent a line, press **Shift-Tab**. To disable automatic indenting, select **Enable Automatic Indent** from the Words pull-down menu and press the spacebar to change its setting from **Yes** to **No**.

To use a smaller portion of the screen for editing or creating a command file, use the WINDOW option with the name of an existing window that is not the currently active window.

Table 2.18 lists the keys that you can use in the program editor.

Table 2.18: Keys Used in the dBASE IV Program Editor

Action	Key
Abandon changes and exit	Esc or Escape
Access help screens	F1
Access pull-down menus	F10
Delete character at cursor	Del or Delete
Delete to end of word	Ctrl-T
Delete previous character	Backspace
Delete previous word	Ctrl-Backspace
Delete current line	Ctrl-Y
Disable automatic indent	Shift-Tab
End line and move to next	↵
Insert a blank line	Ctrl-N or ↵
Insert/Overwrite mode (toggle)	Ins or Insert
Move left one character	← or Ctrl-S
Move right one character	→ or Ctrl-D
Move up or down one line	↑, ↓
Move to beginning of line	Home
Move to end of line	End
Move to next word	Ctrl-→ or Ctrl-F
Move to previous word	Ctrl-← or Ctrl-A
Move to end of file	Ctrl-PgDn
Move to beginning of file	Ctrl-PgUp
Move to next tab stop	Tab
Read in another file	Ctrl-K R
Save changes and exit	Ctrl-End or Ctrl-W
Save changes and stay in editor	Ctrl-↵

Table 2.18: Keys Used in the dBASE IV Program Editor (Continued)

Action	Key
Scroll down one screen	PgDn
Scroll up one screen	PgUp
Search for specific string	Shift-F5
Search for previous occurrence of string	Shift-F3
Search for next occurrence of string	Shift-F4
Search and replace string	Shift-F6
Select a block of text	F6
Copy selected block	F8
Delete selected block	Del or Delete
Move selected block	F7
Unselect selected block	Esc
Write selected block to file	Ctrl-K W

• EXAMPLE To create a command file named MyProg.PRG, enter the following command at the dot prompt:

```
MODIFY COMMAND MyProg
```

To use only a small portion of the screen to edit the command file, define a window and specify it in the MODIFY COMMAND command:

```
DEFINE WINDOW PeekaBoo FROM 12,2 TO 20,78
*----- The next command activates the window
  PeekaBoo
MODIFY COMMAND MyProg WINDOW PeekaBoo
```

When you finish editing the program and press Crtl-End to save the file, the window automatically deactivates.

See Also COMPILE, CREATE FROM, CREATE/MODIFY APPLICATION, DO, NOTE/*/&&, PROCEDURE, RENAME, SET DEVELOPMENT, SET PROCEDURE, TYPE, UPDATE

MODIFY STRUCTURE

Restructuring an Existing Database File

• SYNTAX

MODIFY STRUCTURE

• USAGE The MODIFY STRUCTURE command takes you to the database design screen, where you can change the structure of the currently open database file. You can use MODIFY STRUCTURE to:

- add or delete fields
- change a field name, data type, or width
- add a tag

The editing keys used in MODIFY STRUCTURE are identical to those used with the CREATE command. Press **Ctrl-N** to insert a new field between existing fields. Press **Ctrl-U** to delete a field.

Take care not to change both the name of a field and its width during a single MODIFY STRUCTURE session. Doing so will probably lead to data loss. Instead, use MODIFY STRUCTURE to change the name of the field and save the new database structure immediately. Then use MODIFY STRUCTURE again to change the width of the field and to save the new structure.

• EXAMPLE Use these commands to modify the structure of the Mail.DBF database:

```
USE Mail
MODIFY STRUCTURE
```

See Also APPEND FROM, COPY STRUCTURE, CREATE FROM

MOVE WINDOW

Moving Windows

• SYNTAX

MOVE WINDOW *window name* **TO** *row, col*/**BY** *row offset,col offset*

• USAGE MOVE WINDOW repositions a window on the screen. You can specify the new position of the window as either a set of coordinates or as a relative offset from the current position. The coordinates specify the new position of the upper-left corner of the window.

If you specify the new position of the window by using the BY option, the entire window must fit on the screen; otherwise, an error message is displayed and the MOVE WINDOW command is ignored.

• EXAMPLE The following routine defines and activates a window named MoveIt, pauses for two seconds, moves the window to the upper-left corner of the screen, pauses for two more seconds, and then moves the window down 10 rows and across 48 columns:

```
SET TALK OFF
SET STATUS OFF

DEFINE WINDOW MoveIt FROM 6,25 TO 18,55;
  COLOR GR+/B,,W+/R
ACTIVATE WINDOW MoveIt

@5,12 SAY "Hello"
Holder = INKEY(2)

MOVE WINDOW MoveIt TO 0,0
```

```
Holder = INKEY(2)

MOVE WINDOW MoveIt BY 10,48
ACTIVATE SCREEN
DEACTIVATE WINDOW MoveIt
```

See Also ACTIVATE WINDOW, CLEAR, DEACTIVATE WINDOW, DEFINE WINDOW, RELEASE, RESTORE WINDOW, SAVE WINDOW, SET WINDOW

ON BAR/ON POPUP

Assigning an Action to a Pop-Up Menu Option

• SYNTAX

ON BAR *bar number* **OF** *popup name* **(***command***)**

or

ON POPUP *popup name* **(***command***)**

• USAGE The ON BAR and ON POPUP commands assign an action to a pop-up menu option. ON BAR specifies the menu option to which the action is assigned. ON POPUP assigns an action to the options not specified with an ON BAR command and serves as a default action.

The specified *command* is executed when the cursor moves onto the option and it becomes highlighted. You may assign any valid dBASE command except those that change the flow of control, such as IF...ELSE or DO WHILE. If you do not include the *command*, no action is taken and the previously assigned action is disabled.

The ON SELECTION BAR and POPUP commands also assign actions to pop-up menu options, but the command is not executed until the option is selected by highlighting and pressing ↵ or by double-clicking the mouse.

If you have activated a window or other temporary display with the ON command, use the ON EXIT command to remove it when the cursor moves off the menu option.

You cannot use ON BAR if you have already assigned an action to that menu option with the ON SELECTION BAR command. You may, however, mix the ON BAR and ON SELECTION BAR commands within a single menu definition.

When a bar associated with an ON BAR command is highlighted, BAR() returns the bar number and PROMPT() returns the text of the bar prompt.

• EXAMPLE The commands below define a horizontal bar menu named MainMenu with three options that allow the user to look up file names, display a custom help screen, or exit. A pop-up menu is associated with the pad, LookUp, for the user to select the type of file names to display. Some of the actions take place when the option is highlighted and others not until the option is selected.

```
CLEAR
*----- Define the main menu
DEFINE MENU MainMenu
DEFINE PAD LookUp OF MainMenu ;
  PROMPT "Look up files" AT 1,1
DEFINE PAD HelpMe OF MainMenu ;
  PROMPT "Help!" AT 1,15
DEFINE PAD Quit OF MainMenu ;
  PROMPT "Quit" AT 1,25

*----- Attach a pop-up menu to the first option.
ON SELECTION PAD LookUp ;
  OF MainMenu ACTIVATE POPUP FileList
*----- Call the Helper procedure when the Help pad is
*----- highlighted
ON PAD HelpMe OF MainMenu DO Helper
*----- Exit the program when Quit is selected.
ON SELECTION PAD Quit OF MainMenu ;
  DEACTIVATE MENU
ON EXIT PAD Help Me OF Main Menu DO CkrHelp

*----- Define the pop-up menu for file lookup
```

```
DEFINE POPUP FileList FROM 2,1 TO 10,20
DEFINE BAR 1 OF FileList PROMPT "Databases"
DEFINE BAR 2 OF FileList PROMPT "Queries"
DEFINE BAR 3 OF FileList PROMPT "Reports"
DEFINE BAR 4 OF FileList PROMPT "Forms"
DEFINE BAR 5 OF FileList PROMPT "Programs"

ON SELECTION BAR 1 OF FileList ;
    DO ShowList WITH PROMPT()
ON BAR 2 OF FileList DO ShowList WITH PROMPT()
*----- Do nothing (for now) when bars 3-5 are highlighted
ON POPUP FileList

*----- Activate the main menu
ACTIVATE MENU MainMenu

*----- The following procedure displays the list of file
*----- names.
PROCEDURE ShowList
PARAMETERS FileType
DEFINE WINDOW Wind1 FROM 10,0 TO 20,79
ACTIVATE WINDOW Wind1
DO CASE
    CASE FileType = "Databases"
        DISPLAY FILES LIKE *.DBF
        WAIT
    CASE FileType = "Queries"
        DISPLAY FILES LIKE *.QBE
        WAIT
ENDCASE
DEACTIVATE WINDOW Wind1
RETURN
```

Additional CASE statements display the names of the .FRM, .FMT, and .PRG files. The procedure Helper can display a window containing custom help messages and ClrHelp can remove the Window and Help option and unhighlight it.

See Also BAR(), BARCOUNT(), BARPROMPT(), DEFINE BAR/POPUP/PAD/MENU, MENU(), ON EXITBAR/POPUP/PAD/MENU, ON MENU/ON PAD, ON SELECTION BAR/POPUP/PAD/MENU, PAD(), POPUP(), PROMPT()

ON ERROR

Trapping an Error during Program Execution

• SYNTAX

ON ERROR *(command)*

• USAGE The ON ERROR command specifies a command or procedure to be executed as soon as an error occurs while a program is running. Typically, this command calls a custom error-handling procedure to handle common run-time errors such as *printer not ready* or *disk full* without having the application or command file "crash" back to the dot prompt. If you do not specify a command, dBASE displays its own error message and prompts you to choose among a number of options, depending on the type of error.

As soon as an ON ERROR command is triggered, the ERROR() function receives a numeric value representing the error, and the MESSAGE() function receives a character string describing the error. For more information regarding any of these error messages, press **F1** (Help) from the dot prompt. Then select **Error Messages** from the table of contents and type the first letter of the desired error message. Use the ↓ key to scroll to a specific error message and then press ↵. Appendix A of the *dBASE IV Language Reference* manual that came with your dBASE IV package lists all error messages and ERROR() numbers.

When using ON ERROR to trap errors and a DO CASE clause to respond to them, always include an OTHERWISE option to display the number and message of any errors that do not match any of those included in the CASE statements. Otherwise, it will be very difficult to track and correct program bugs that are not detected by the DO CASE clause.

The ON ERROR command, without any additional command on the line, deactivates any previous ON ERROR command and resets the dBASE error routine to the default setting.

A procedure that is called by an ON command must be compiled before being called. Therefore, the same rules that apply to user-defined functions apply to procedures that are called by an ON ERROR command. The procedure must not contain any macros and cannot use the same commands as user-defined functions. See **FUNCTION** for information about prohibited commands.

• EXAMPLE In the following example, the ON ERROR DO ErrTrap command passes control to a procedure named ErrTrap as soon as an error occurs during program execution. A DO CASE clause then determines how to handle the error on the basis of the contents of the ERROR() function.

```
*----- Main program.
DEFINE WINDOW ErrWind FROM 5,20 TO 19,60

*----- Activate error handling.
ON ERROR DO ErrTrap

*----- (Rest of main program follows)
*-----Before ending program, deactivate error handler.
 ON ERROR
RETURN

*----- End of main program.

*----- Error-handling procedure.
PROCEDURE ErrTrap
 ACTIVATE WINDOW ErrWind
 DO CASE

*----- Too many files open.
   CASE ERROR() = 6
   TEXT
    Program cannot run because
    FILES setting in Config.sys
    is less than 40
   ENDTEXT
   WAIT "Press any key to end..."
   CLOSE ALL
   CLEAR ALL
```

```
    CANCEL

  *----- Fix bad index.
    CASE ERROR ()=114
      ? "Need to fix index, please wait..."
      SET TALK ON
      REINDEX
      SET TALK OFF

  *----- More CASEs for other errors can be added

  *----- Handle errors not accounted for above.
    OTHERWISE
    ? "This error not accounted for: "
    ? ERROR(), MESSAGE()
    WAIT "Press any key..."

   ENDCASE
   DEACTIVATE WINDOW ErrWind

  RETURN
```

See Also ERROR(), INKEY(), LASTKEY(), MESSAGE(), ON READERROR, PROCEDURE, RETRY, RETURN, SET ESCAPE, SET PROCEDURE, SET TYPEAHEAD

ON ESCAPE/KEY

Responding to a Keypress

• SYNTAX

ON ESCAPE *(command)*

or

ON KEY (LABEL *key label name) (command)*

• USAGE Usually as a command file is running, the user can press **Esc** to interrupt execution immediately and return to the dot prompt or Control Center. The ON ESCAPE command allows you to perform some other command or a procedure as soon as the user presses **Esc**. The SET ESCAPE parameter must be set on for the ON ESCAPE command to function.

ON KEY LABEL *key label name* tells dBASE to perform a specific command or procedure as soon as the user presses a specific key (other than **Esc**). For printable characters (A–Z, 0–9, and punctuation symbols), the *key label name* is identical to the key pad character. For example

ON KEY LABEL Z DO HoldIt

activates the HoldIt procedure only when the user types **Z** or **z.** ON KEY is not case-sensitive.

If you use ON ESCAPE or ON KEY with no command, the key is reset to its default function.

To use a nonprintable character such as a function key, Ctrl-key combination, or arrow key in an ON KEY LABEL command, use the appropriate *key label name* listed in Table 2.19. For example, the command

ON KEY LABEL Shift-F1 DO HoldIt

executes the HoldIt procedure when the user presses **Shift-F1**.

Table 2.19: Key Label Names Used with the ON KEY LABEL Command

Key	Key Label Name
←	LEFTARROW
→	RIGHTARROW
↑	UPARROW
↓	DOWNARROW
Alt-0 to Alt-9	Alt-0, Alt-1...Alt-9
Alt-A to Alt-Z	Alt-A, Alt-B...Alt-Z

Table 2.19: Key Label Names Used with the ON KEY LABEL Command (Continued)

Key	Key Label Name
Backspace	BACKSPACE
Ctrl-←	Ctrl-LEFTARROW
Ctrl-→	Ctrl-RIGHTARROW
Ctrl-A to Ctrl-Z	Ctrl-A, Ctrl-B...Ctrl-Z
Ctrl-End	Ctrl-END
Ctrl-F1 to Ctrl-F10	Ctrl-F1, Ctrl-F2...Ctrl-F10
Ctrl-Home	Ctrl-HOME
Ctrl-PgDn	Ctrl-PGDN
Ctrl-PgUp	Ctrl-PGUP
Del (or Delete)	DEL
End	END
F1 to F10	F1, F2...F10
Home	HOME
Ins (or Insert)	INS
PgDn	PGDN
PgUp	PGUP
Shift-F1 to Shift-F9	Shift-F1, Shift-F2...Shift-F9
Shift-Tab	BACKTAB
Tab	TAB

If you omit the LABEL option and a key label name in the ON KEY command, dBASE executes the specified command or procedure as soon as the user presses any key on the keyboard. However, if a SET ESCAPE command is also active, and SET ESCAPE is on, ON ESCAPE takes precedence over ON KEY.

dBASE always processes an ON ESCAPE command immediately, even in the middle of a time-consuming task such as INDEX ON or

REPORT FORM. By contrast, the command procedure called by ON KEY is not executed until the current command is finished performing its job. For example, if an active ON KEY command calls a procedure named HoldIt, and the user presses a key during a time-consuming REPORT FORM command, the HoldIt procedure is not executed until the entire report has been printed. The exception to this rule are the EDIT, BROWSE, READ, APPEND, and ACTIVATE commands. These commands cause an immediate "trigger" when you press a key specified in an ON KEY command. This allows you to display custom windows, pop-ups, and help screens as the user is adding or editing data or using a custom menu.

To create keystroke interruptions for time-consuming commands such as REPORT FORM or LIST, use the INKEY() function with a WHILE option in the command. See **INKEY().**

The keystroke that triggers the ON KEY command stays in the keyboard buffer until it is explicitly removed by another command or stored in a memory variable. This can cause an ON KEY call to be repeated indefinitely. Therefore, if an ON KEY command calls a procedure, the procedure should include a command such as

```
X = INKEY()
```

to store the keystroke in a memory variable, thereby removing it from the type-ahead buffer.

A procedure that is called by an ON command must be compiled before being called. Therefore, the same rules that apply to user-defined functions apply to procedures that are called by an ON ESCAPE, ON KEY, or ON KEY LABEL command. The procedure must not contain any macros, and cannot use the same commands as user-defined functions. See **FUNCTION** for information about the prohibited commands.

When a SET FUNCTION and ON KEY LABEL command are both sensitive to the same key, the ON KEY LABEL command takes precedence.

If a WAIT command is executed, the key pressed to interrupt the WAIT will not trigger an ON KEY command. However, when a pending GET is on the screen and the user presses a key specified in an ON KEY command, the ON KEY is triggered and the keystroke is not passed to the GET variable.

• **EXAMPLE** The ON KEY LABEL command here tells dBASE to execute a procedure named CustHelp as soon as the user presses **F1**. The CustHelp procedure, in turn, displays a custom help screen, depending on which command file in an application is currently running.

```
*----- Define help window.
DEFINE WINDOW HelpWind FROM 5,5 TO 20,75

*----- Set up F1 key for custom help.
ON KEY LABEL F1 DO CustHelp

*----- <any other commands may follow>.

*----- Before exiting application,return to normal F1 key.
ON KEY LABEL F1
RETURN

*----- end of main program.

*----- CustHelp procedure.
PROCEDURE CustHelp
ACTIVATE WINDOW HelpWind

 DO CASE
  CASE PROGRAM( ) = "ADDDATE"
  TEXT
   This program lets you add new data.
   (additional help text...)
  ENDTEXT

  CASE PROGRAM( ) = "EDITDATA"
  TEXT
   This program lets you edit data.
   (additional help text...)
  ENDTEXT

 ENDCASE
 WAIT"Press any key to return..." TO GoBack
 DEACTIVATE WINDOW HelpWind
RETURN
```

See Also DO, FUNCTION, INKEY(), LASTKEY(), ON READ-ERROR, PROCEDURE, PROGRAM(), READKEY(), SET ESCAPE, SET PROCEDURE, SET TYPEAHEAD

ON EXIT BAR/POPUP/PAD/MENU

Assigning an Action to Leaving a Menu Option

• SYNTAX

ON EXIT BAR *bar number* **OF** *popup name* (*command*)

or

ON EXIT POPUP *popup name* (*command*)

or

ON EXIT PAD *pad name* **OF** *menu name* (*command*)

or

ON EXIT MENU *menu name* (*command*)

• USAGE The ON EXIT set of commands assign an action to be taken when the cursor moves off the menu option. As with the corresponding set of ON commands, ON EXIT BAR or PAD applies to a specific option in a popup or horizontal bar menu while the ON EXIT POPUP or MENU can be used to apply to the remaining unassigned options.

You can assign any valid dBASE command except one that changes the program flow, such as DO WHILE or IF...ELSE. In all cases, if you omit the *command*, no action takes place and the previously assigned action is disabled.

• **EXAMPLE** See **ON BAR** for an example of **ON EXIT**.

ON MENU/ON PAD

Assigning an Action to a Horizontal Bar Menu

• **SYNTAX**

ON MENU *menu name (command)*

or

ON PAD *pad name* **OF** *menu name* **(ACTIVATE POPUP** *popup name/command)*

• **USAGE** The ON MENU and ON PAD commands assign an action to a horizontal bar menu option. ON PAD specifies the menu option to which the action is assigned. ON MENU assigns an action to the options not covered by an ON PAD command and serves as a default action.

The specified *command* is executed when the cursor moves onto the option and it becomes highlighted. You can use any valid dBASE command except one that changes the flow of control, such as IF...ELSE or DO WHILE. If you do not include a command, the previously assigned action is disabled.

Use the ON SELECTION MENU or PAD to delay the action until the option is actually selected. Use ON EXIT MENU or PAD to assign an action to when the option is unhighlighted.

The ACTIVATE POPUP option of the ON PAD command allows you to attach a previously defined pop-up menu to a horizontal bar menu option. The pop-up menu is displayed when that menu pad is highlighted. It is automatically deactivated when the cursor moves off the pad.

You cannot use the ON PAD command if you have already assigned an action to that option with an ON SELECTION PAD command. You can, however, mix the ON PAD and ON SELECTION PAD commands within a single menu definition.

When a pad associated with an ON PAD command is highlighted, PAD() returns the pad name and PROMPT() returns the text of the menu option.

• EXAMPLE See **ON BAR** for an example of ON MENU and ON PAD.

ON MOUSE

Assigning an Action to the Mouse Button

• SYNTAX

ON MOUSE *(command)*

• USAGE The ON MOUSE command assigns an action to a mouse button click. It senses when you click the left mouse button and executes a command when the button is released. ON MOUSE can be used only in the following specified areas:

- Outside of all pop-up menus and outside of all pads.
- On the left and right borders of active user-defined menus and pop-ups.
- Outside of all @...GET areas during READ or EDIT.
- Outside of an active window.
- On a window border if the window does not contain a BROWSE screen.

ON MOUSE is not active in the following situations:

- In an active internal dBASE menu system as indicated by the highlighting.
- In user-defined menu pads.
- On a BROWSE screen or design surface.
- Inside @...GET regions.

ON MOUSE will not work if SET MOUSE is set off. The mouse pointer must be in an available location when the button is clicked as well as when it is released.

• EXAMPLE The commands

```
CLEAR
SET TALK OFF
ON MOUSE DO WherMous
mclick = "Click the mouse anywhere!"
@ 5,10 GET mclick
READ
RETURN

PROCEDURE WherMous
@ 10,10 SAY "You clicked the mouse at row "+ ;
    LTRIM(STR(MROW()))+" and column "+ ;
    LTRIM(STR(MCOL()))
RETURN
```

prompt you to move the mouse pointer anywhere on the screen and click the left button. When you do so, the message tells you the location where you released the button.

See Also ISMOUSE(), MCOL(), MROW(), SET(), SET MOUSE

ON PAD

See **ON MENU** for information on ON PAD.

ON PAGE

Managing Headers and Footers in a Print Job

• SYNTAX

ON PAGE *(***AT LINE** *number command)*

• USAGE The ON PAGE command tells dBASE to execute a command or procedure when a ?, ??, or EJECT PAGE command increments the _plineno system variable past a specified line number. Typically, the command is a call to a procedure that prints a page heading or footer or issues a page eject.

You must already have compiled the procedure called by the ON PAGE command with either the COMPILE or SET PROCEDURE command, or by including the procedure in the same command file as the ON PAGE command. Commands that you cannot use in the FUNCTION command are also prohibited in the ON PAGE command. Using the ON PAGE command without the AT LINE or *command* option deactivates the most recent ON PAGE command.

• EXAMPLE See the sample program in the **PRINTJOB...ENDPRINTJOB** section of this chapter.

See Also ?/??/???, PRINTJOB...ENDPRINTJOB, PROCEDURE, REPORT FORM, SET PRINTER

ON POPUP

See **ON BAR** for information about ON POPUP.

ON READERROR

Trapping Errors during Full-Screen Operations

• SYNTAX

ON READERROR *(command)*

• USAGE The ON READERROR command traps errors caused by invalid dates, exceeded RANGE specifications, and unmet VALID conditions during full-screen operations such as APPEND, EDIT, BROWSE, and READ.

Typically, the command performed by the ON READERROR command will execute a procedure designed to handle specific errors. The procedure can use a DO CASE clause with VARREAD() functions to respond to errors in particular fields.

A procedure that is called by an ON command must be compiled before being called. Therefore, the same rules that apply to user-defined functions apply to procedures that are called by an ON READERROR command. The procedure must not contain any macros, or commands that are prohibited in user-defined functions. See **FUNCTIONS** for more information.

To deactivate an ON READERROR trap, execute an ON READERROR command with no command.

• EXAMPLE The main program here tells dBASE to execute a procedure named BadEntry as soon as an input or editing error occurs while the user is entering records via the custom screen named AddData.

```
*----- Main program.
DEFINE WINDOW ShowProb FROM 9,30 TO 15,50

ON READERROR DO BadEntry
SET FORMAT TO AddData
APPEND

*----- Deactivate error handler after data entry.
CLOSE FORMAT
ON READERROR
RETURN

*----- End of main program

*-----Handle data-entry errors.
PROCEDURE BadEntry
  ACTIVATE WINDOW ShowProb
  DO CASE
*----- Error in PartNo field.
    CASE VARREAD( ) = "PARTNO"
      ? "No such part number"
*----- Can activate popup to show valid entries.
      ACTIVATE SCREEN
      ACTIVATE POPUP ShowParts

*----- Error in OrdDate field.
    CASE VARREAD ( ) = "ORDDATE"
      ? "Dates must be in MM/DD/YY format"
      WAIT "Press a key to try again"

  ENDCASE
  DEACTIVATE WINDOW ShowProb

RETURN
```

See Also @, APPEND, EDIT, INSERT, ON ERROR, READ, VARREAD()

ON SELECTION BAR/POPUP/PAD/MENU

Assigning an Action to a Menu Option

• SYNTAX

ON SELECTION BAR *bar number* **OF** *popup name* *(command)*

or

ON SELECTION POPUP *popup name*/**ALL (BLANK)** *(command)*

or

ON SELECTION PAD *pad name* **OF** *menu name* *(command)*

or

ON SELECTION MENU *menu name (command)*

• USAGE The ON SELECTION command assigns an action to be executed when the user selects an option from a horizontal bar or pop-up menu. This command differs from the ON command set that executes the action as soon as the option is highlighted. You can assign any valid dBASE command to the option except those such as IF...ELSE which change the flow of control.

ON SELECTION BAR assigns a command to the specified bar number of the named pop-up menu. When the bar is selected, the command is executed.

The ON SELECTION POPUP command assigns an action to any bars in the pop-up that are not already associated with a command with ON SELECTION BAR.

Using the ALL option with ON SELECTION POPUP instead of naming a pop-up menu, the action applies to any selection from any active pop-up menu. The BLANK option clears the pop-up from the screen before the command is executed.

The ON SELECTION PAD command is commonly used to specify one of the following commands:

- **DO**: To call a procedure that contains the commands to be performed when the user selects the menu option.
- **ACTIVATE POPUP**: To display a pop-up menu or list.
- **DEACTIVATE MENU**: To deactivate and remove the menu, as when the user selects **Exit**.

Unless the command, procedure, or program deactivates the menu, the menu is available for another selection after the action is finished.

If you do not include a command, the previously assigned action is disabled.

When the user makes a selection from the pop-up menu, the BAR() function contains the row number of the selection, and PROMPT() contains the text of the menu option. Similarly, when a pad is selected from a bar menu, PAD() returns the pad name and PROMPT() returns the text of the menu option.

• EXAMPLE See **ON BAR** for an example of using the **ON SELECTION** commands.

See Also BAR(), BARCOUNT(), BARPROMPT(), DEACTIVATE MENU/POPUP, DEFINE BAR/POPUP/PAD/MENU, MENU(), ON EXIT BAR/POPUP/PAD/MENU, POPUP(), PROMPT()

PACK

Permanently Deleting Database Records

• SYNTAX

PACK

• USAGE The PACK command removes records that are marked for deletion, compresses the remaining records into the space the deleted records occupied, and reclaims the disk space occupied by the deleted records. Records deleted with PACK cannot be recovered.

PACK affects only the currently selected database file. Any related database files in use are unaffected by the PACK command.

To check that you know exactly which records are going to be removed during a PACK command, you can USE the database file and enter the commands **SET DELETED OFF** and **DISPLAY FOR DELETED()** to view the marked records.

• EXAMPLE The commands

```
DEFINE WINDOW ShowProg ;
  FROM 17,3 TO 20,30 DOUBLE
ACTIVATE WINDOW ShowProg

USE Orders
SET TALK ON
PACK
SET TALK OFF
DEACTIVATE WINDOW ShowProg
```

permanently remove all records marked for deletion from the Orders database, displaying the progress odometer in a small window named ShowProg.

See Also COPY, DELETE, DELETED(), RECALL, REINDEX, SET AUTOSAVE, ZAP

PARAMETERS

Assigning Local Variable Names

• SYNTAX

PARAMETERS *parameter list*

• USAGE The PARAMETERS command assigns up to 50 private (local) memory variable names to data passed to a command file, procedure, or user-defined function. PARAMETERS must be the first executable command in a command file, or the first executable command beneath the PROCEDURE or FUNCTION command in a procedure or user-defined function. Only programmer comments are nonexecutable commands.

When calling a command file or procedure that contains a PARAMETERS command, you must use the WITH option in the DO command to pass the appropriate parameters. When calling a user-defined function that contains a PARAMETERS command, you must include the appropriate values, enclosed in parentheses and separated by a comma, to the right of the function name. In each case, the parameters must appear in the same order and be of the same data type in both the PARAMETERS command and the procedure or function call.

The variable names listed in the PARAMETERS command exist only while the procedure or user-defined function is being executed. Any other variables with the same name as those listed in the PARAMETERS command remain unchanged.

• EXAMPLE Suppose a command file, procedure, or user-defined function contains the command

PARAMETERS Amount, Today, Name, IsPaid

where Amount is numeric or float data, Today is a date, Name is character data, and IsPaid is a logical data value. If you stored the command in a command file or procedure, you would call that command file or procedure as follows:

DO *file/procedure name* **WITH 123.45,{12/01/94},"Joe",.T.**

If you stored the sample PARAMETERS command in a user-defined function, you could call that function with the following syntax:

@ 1,2 SAY *function name* **(123.45,{12/01/94},"Joe",.T.)**

See Also DO, PCOUNT(), PRIVATE, PROCEDURE, PUBLIC, SET PROCEDURE, STORE

PLAY MACRO

Using Recorded Keystroke Macros

• SYNTAX

PLAY MACRO *macro name*

• USAGE The PLAY MACRO command executes a prerecorded keystroke macro. Macro recording is available at the Control Center and various design screens by pressing **Shift-F10**. Macros can be identified either by name or by a key.

If a program includes a series of PLAY MACRO commands, the macros are first stacked in memory in a LIFO (last-in-first-out) basis, and played back in that manner.

In a command file, recorded keystrokes are not played back until an opportunity for simulating input occurs. For example, to use a macro to enter data into a new database record, you must first issue the **PLAY MACRO** command and then the **APPEND** command so that the keystrokes are typed onto the Edit/Browse screen.

Rather than using PLAY MACRO to execute a macro, you can use any of the following techniques:

- If the macro is assigned to a function key F1 through F9, hold down **Alt** and press the macro key.
- If the macro is assigned a single-letter key name (A through Z), press **Alt-F10** and the macro key name.
- From the Control Center, select **Macros**, **Play**, and the macro key name from the Tools pull-down.

• EXAMPLE Suppose you use MODIFY SCREEN to call up the forms design screen to develop a tutorial for a particular database, then record keystroke macros named X and F1. In a command file that plays back the keystrokes, you need to open the database file, play back the macros in reverse order, and enter the forms design screen, as follows:

```
USE AnyFile

PLAY MACRO F1        && will be played second.
PLAY MACRO X         && will be played first.

*----- Now play the macros on the forms design screen.
MODIFY SCREEN Temp
```

See Also RESTORE MACROS/SCREEN, SAVE MACROS

PRINTJOB...ENDPRINTJOB

Controlling a Print Job

• SYNTAX

```
PRINTJOB
  commands
ENDPRINTJOB
```

• USAGE You use PRINTJOB...ENDPRINTJOB to control the printer, via the system memory variables, as a report is being printed. Table 2.20 lists the system memory variables. The DISPLAY MEMORY command displays the current status of system memory variables. For quick on-screen reminders of system memory variable options, enter **HELP** at the dot prompt, press ↵, and select **System Memvars** from the Table of Contents that appears.

Table 2.20: System Memory Variables

Variable	Function and Settings
_alignment	Specifies alignment of text output by ? and ?? commands when _wrap is set to .T. Acceptable values are "LEFT", "CENTER", and "RIGHT."
_box	Determines whether boxes defined with the DEFINE BOX command are displayed (.T.) or not (.F.).
_indent	Sets the level of indentation for the first line of each printed paragraph when _wrap is set to .T. The default is 0, but you can set this variable to any number up to the right margin setting.
_lmargin	Specifies the left margin for the ? command when _wrap is set to .T. _lmargin can have any value in the range of 0 to 254, and affects both the screen and printer.
_padvance	Specifies how the printer ejects a page; either as "FORMFEED" (the default value), or "LINEFEEDS." The "FORMFEED" setting ejects as many lines as necessary to eject the page, as determined by the printer's page length setting. The "LINEFEEDS" setting ejects the page according to the page length defined by the _plength system variable.
_pageno	Specifies or returns the current page number, between 1 and 32767.

Table 2.20: System Memory Variables (Continued)

Variable	Function and Settings
_pbpage	Specifies the page number at which to begin printing, using a default value of 1 (the first page) up to 32767.
_pcolno	Specifies the starting column number for printed output, in the range of 0 to 255.
_pcopies	Sets the number of copies to be printed in a print job, between 1 and 32767.
_pdriver	Loads the specified printer driver (assumes the .PR2 file name extension, but can be any valid DOS file name).
_pecode	Specifies printer control codes to be sent to the printer when the ENDPRINTJOB command is executed and printing is complete (less than 255 characters).
_peject	Determines when the page is ejected during a print job. Options are "BEFORE," "AFTER," "BOTH," and "NONE."
_pepage	Specifies the ending page for a print job. For example, if _pbpage = 3 and _pepage = 7, only pages 3 through 7 will be printed during a print job.
_pform	Activates a print form (.PRF) file, or returns the name of the active print form file.
_plength	Specifies or returns the length of the printed page in number of lines, in the range of 1 to 32,767 (66 is the default).
_plineno	Keeps track of the line number currently being printed.
_ploffset	Sets the left margin for printed output, but does not affect screen output (between 0 and 254).
_ppitch	Sets the printer pitch to "PICA," "ELITE," "CONDENSED," "DEFAULT."

Table 2.20: System Memory Variables (Continued)

Variable	Function and Settings
_pquality	Sets the print quality to letter-quality (.T.) or draft (.F.).
_pscode	Sends control codes to the printer as soon as the PRINTJOB command is executed (less than 255 characters).
_pspacing	Sets printed output spacing to single space (1), double space (2), or triple space (3).
_pwait	Determines whether the printer pauses after each printed page (.T.) or prints continuously (.F.).
_rmargin	Defines the right margin for ? and ?? output when _wrap is set to .T. (between 0 and 255).
_tabs	Determines tab stops for printing the {TAB} character. Default tab stops are "8," "16," "24," "48," and so on.
_wrap	Determines whether printed text that extends past the right margin setting (_rmargin) is word wrapped (.T.) or extended beyond the right margin (.F.).

You can change the contents of system memory variables with the same techniques that you use to change any other dBASE IV memory variable. You can use either the STORE command or the = operator.

• EXAMPLE The command file shown next illustrates a program for printing a report as a print job. First, system memory variables are set up to print the report using the Hewlett-Packard LaserJet compressed landscape mode (small sideways print).

Within the command file, the ON PAGE command tells dBASE to activate the procedure named NewPage as soon as the printed line number is three lines away from the bottom of the page (_plength–3). Note that the NewPage procedure called by the ON LINE command prints the page footer, ejects the printed page, and then prints the page header at the top of the new page.

Note also that the Footer procedure begins with a ? command. This is necessary to replace the linefeed preempted by the ON PAGE command. The Footer procedure also demonstrates how you can use the _pageno system memory variable to print the current page number.

```
**************************************** PJob.PRG
SET TALK OFF

*----- Set up system variables for HP
*----- LaserJet compressed landscape mode.
_pscode = "{ESC}E{ESC}&l10{ESC}&k2S"
_pecode = "{ESC}E"  && reset printer after job.
_Peject = "AFTER"
_ploffset = 20
_plength = 50
_plineno = 0
_pcopies = 1

USE Orders ORDER Part No
SET PRINTER ON

*----- Start the print job.
PRINTJOB
*----- Set line number for page breaks.
  ON PAGE AT LINE (_plength-3) DO NewPage

*----- Print heading on first page.
  DO Header

*----- Print database records.
  SCAN FOR .NOT. Printed
    ? CustNo,CustName,PartNo,PartName, ;
      Qty,UnitPrice PICTURE "99,999.99", ;
      Qty*UnitPrice FUNCTION "$" ;
      PICTURE "99,999.99"
  ENDSCAN
ENDPRINTJOB
```

```
SET PRINTER OFF
ON PAGE         && Deactivate the page handler

*----- Reset system variables back to normal.
STORE "" TO _pscode,_pecode
_peject = "BEFORE"
_ploffset = 0
_plength = 66
_plineno = 0

RETURN
**** End of main program: Procedures follow.

*----- Print footer, eject page, then print header.
PROCEDURE NewPage
  DO Footer
  EJECT PAGE
  DO Header
RETURN
*----- Procedure to print page headings.
PROCEDURE Header
  ?
  ? "Current Orders" AT 60 STYLE "B"
  ?
RETURN

PROCEDURE Footer
  ?  && Always start a page footer with ?.
  ?
  ? _pageno PICTURE "999" STYLE "B" ;
    AT 60
RETURN
```

See Also ON PAGE, PROCEDURE, REPORT FORM, RETURN, SET PRINTER TO, SET TALK

PRIVATE

Protecting Memory Variable Values

• SYNTAX

PRIVATE *variable list*/**ALL** (**LIKE/EXCEPT** *skeleton)*

• USAGE

The PRIVATE command temporarily hides the current value of a public memory variable so that a lower-level command file or procedure can use a variable with the same name without altering the contents of the existing public variable.

Use PRIVATE in general-purpose procedures and programs to keep local variable names from interfering with existing public or higher-level variables with the same names. Once a variable is declared private, the public or higher-level variable retains its value, but is temporarily hidden. Any new operations affect only the private variable.

When you are creating skeletons for use with the optional LIKE and EXCEPT components, the wildcard * stands for any combination of characters and ? stands for any single character.

• EXAMPLE

The command

PRIVATE ALL

declares all variable names used in the current procedure as private (local) to the procedure. The command

PRIVATE ALL LIKE C*

declares as private all memory variables with names that begin with the letter C.

The following procedure includes a memory variable named Counter declared as private. Any variable named Counter that existed before the procedure was called will resume its original value when the procedure returns control to the calling program.

```
PROCEDURE Tunes

*----- Don't disrupt an existing variable named Counter.
PRIVATE Counter

  SET TALK OFF
  Counter = 1

*----- Play a tune.    DOWHILE Counter <= 6
    SET BELL TO Counter*100,1
    ?? CHR(7)
    Counter = Counter + 1
  ENDDO

RETURN
```

See Also DECLARE, DO, PARAMETERS, PROCEDURE, PUBLIC, STORE

PROCEDURE

Naming a Procedure

• SYNTAX

PROCEDURE *procedure name*
(**PARAMETERS** *parameter list)*
  commands
RETURN

• USAGE Each individual procedure within a procedure file or command file must begin with the PROCEDURE command followed by the name of the procedure. The procedure name may start with a letter or a number and may be any length, but only the last nine characters are recognized. You can use numbers and underscores after the first character.

Every procedure must end with a RETURN command, which passes control back to the calling command file or procedure. You cannot include an expression in the RETURN command that ends a procedure; only user-defined functions permit this. You can also end a procedure with RETURN TO MASTER to pass control back to the highest-level calling program. RETURN TO with a procedure name passes control to the named procedure.

If you store the procedure in a procedure file, you must open the procedure file with the SET PROCEDURE command before you can access it with the DO command. If the procedure is stored in the current command file or a command file that called the current command file, SET PROCEDURE is not required.

Any procedure can call any other procedure with a DO command.

A single procedure file can contain up to 963 procedures, or as many as RAM permits.

• **EXAMPLE** The command file that follows contains a single procedure named Center that prints any character string centered within the specified margins. Within the main body of the program, the SCAN...ENDSCAN loop calls the Center procedure twice to center two character fields named Name and Address from the currently open database file.

```
*------------------- Main program.
SET TALK OFF USE AnyFile ORDER AnyOrd

RightMargn = 80

SCAN ALL
  DO Center WITH Name,RightMargn
  DO Center WITH Address,RightMargn
  ?
ENDSCAN

RETURN
*----- End main program, procedure(s) follow.

PROCEDURE Center
```

```
PARAMETERS String,ColWidth
  Padding = (ColWidth-LEN(TRIM(String)))/2
  ? SPACE(Padding)+TRIM(String)
RETURN
```

See Also DO, COMPILE, DEBUG, PARAMETERS, RETRY, RETURN, SET LIBRARY, SET PROCEDURE

PROTECT

Providing a Protection Scheme

• SYNTAX

```
PROTECT
```

• USAGE PROTECT allows you to define a protection scheme for applications that run on either a single-user system or a network. Once you initiate a protection scheme, all files are controlled through the scheme and are accessible only to users who know the appropriate passwords.

PROTECT presents a full-screen menu-driven program that allows you to set up protection at three different levels:

1. Log-in Security: Defines users who can access dBASE IV.
2. File and Field Access: Defines the files and fields each authorized user may access.
3. Data Encryption: Encrypts dBASE files so that only authorized users may view their contents.

PROTECT builds and maintains an encrypted password file named DbSystem.DB. The person in charge of the protection scheme should keep a printed hard copy of this file in a safe place to help users who have forgotten their log-in names or passwords.

See Also ACCESS(), LOGOUT, NETWORK(), SET ENCRYPTION

PUBLIC

Making a Memory Variable Globally Accessibie

• SYNTAX

PUBLIC *memvar list*/(**ARRAY** *array definition*)

• USAGE By default, all dBASE memory variables, including arrays, are private. That is, they are accessible only to the command files that created them and to programs at a lower level. A RETURN command erases all variables created in the current program. Memory variables created in the highest-level program are erased as soon as control is returned to the dot prompt.

Public memory variables speed up processing by being available to programs and procedures at all levels, as well as at the dot prompt. Variables you create at the dot prompt are public by default. To create public variables within a command file, you must use the PUBLIC command. To create one or more arrays of public memory variables, use the PUBLIC ARRAY command followed by array definitions.

In the command file, the PUBLIC command must come *before* the variable is assigned a value. Typically, all variables that are to be public in a given application are declared at the beginning of the highest-level program in the application, usually the main menu program.

• EXAMPLE The following commands create a public array named PubArray and public variables named UserName and UserAcct:

```
PUBLIC ARRAY PubArray(5,4)
PUBLIC UserName, UserAcct
```

See Also DECLARE, DO, PARAMETERS, PRIVATE, RELEASE, SAVE, STORE

QUIT

Returning to DOS

• SYNTAX

QUIT *(***WITH** *number)*

• USAGE QUIT terminates a dBASE IV session and closes all open files, including database files with their associated indexes and memo files. Any open program files are also closed. Control is returned to the operating system.

If dBASE was invoked from a batch file or other program, you can include an exit code by using the WITH option. The exit code can let the calling program know that the dBASE session ran successfully and quit normally. Numbers 0 through 255 can used directly; numbers less than 0 or more than 255 will be modulated by 256.

• EXAMPLE The command

QUIT WITH 73

returns control to the calling program and passes the exit code 73.

THE READ COMMAND

Activating GET Commands

• SYNTAX

READ *(***SAVE***)*

• USAGE Use READ to enter or edit memory variables or fields in a single database record. READ can be used in conjunction with APPEND BLANK to append a single record to a database file. You can use READ either with an open format file or in a command file containing GET commands. You can also use READ to separate individual pages within a format file.

The READ command allows the user to move the cursor about freely to edit the data displayed on the screen. The cursor-control keys used with other full-screen operations also operate when the READ command is issued and active GET commands are on the screen.

Only the GET commands displayed since the last CLEAR, CLEAR GETS, CLEAR ALL, or READ command are activated by READ. After the user cycles through all of the GET commands on the screen, they are cleared from further access. Unlike READ, the optional READ SAVE command does not automatically clear the GET commands that were just cycled through. Therefore, if you use READ SAVE instead of READ to edit a database record, the next READ SAVE or READ command accesses the same fields.

Note that the number of GET commands per READ command is limited. The default limit is 128 GET commands per READ, though this value can be changed to any value from 35 to 2000 through the Config.DB GETS setting. The CLEAR GETS command also frees GET space between READ SAVE commands. Use the CLOSE FORMAT command to close a format file after entering data or editing to prevent the format file from reappearing when it is not needed.

• **EXAMPLE** The following commands add a blank record to the currently open database file, open a custom format file named AScreen.FMT, and let the user enter new values into the blank record through the format file:

```
APPEND BLANK
SET FORMAT TO AScreen
READ
CLOSE FORMAT
```

See Also @...SAY...GET, CLEAR, SET FORMAT, MODIFY SCREEN, REPLACE, SET DEVICE, STORE

RECALL

Reinstating a Record Marked for Deletion

• SYNTAX

RECALL *(scope)* (**FOR** *condition)* (**WHILE** *condition)*

• USAGE RECALL removes the deletion mark from a record. This prevents the record from being hidden when SET DELETED is on and from being removed by a PACK command.

RECALL cannot reclaim records that have been removed with a ZAP or PACK command. If SET DELETED is on, you can only recall records using the syntax RECALL RECORD record number. A RECALL ALL, RECALL FOR, or RECALL WHILE command will not recall records when SET DELETED is on.

Even if multiple related database files are in use, RECALL affects only the currently selected database file.

• EXAMPLE The following command reinstates records marked for deletion that have February 1995 dates in the Exp_Date field and .T. in the Renewed field:

```
USE AnyFile
SET DELETED OFF
RECALL ALL FOR MONTH(Exp_Date) = 2 .AND. ;
  YEAR(Exp_Date) = 1995 .AND. Renewed
```

See Also DELETE, DELETED(), PACK, SET DELETED, ZAP

REINDEX

Rebuilding Corrupted Index Files

• SYNTAX

REINDEX

• USAGE REINDEX rebuilds all of the indexes in the current production index (.MDX) file, and any additional index (.NDX or .MDX) files that are in use. Use it to repair indexes that have been corrupted by a power failure or by a change in the database (such as adding, editing, or deleting records) that did not update the index.

In a network, you must have exclusive use of the database for REINDEX to work.

• EXAMPLE The following commands rebuild all indexes in the production index file named CustList.MDX:

```
USE CustList
REINDEX
```

See Also INDEX, KEY(), MDX(), NDX(), SET INDEX, SET UNIQUE

RELEASE

Removing Objects from Memory

• SYNTAX

RELEASE *memvar/array list*/**ALL** (**LIKE/EXCEPT** *skeleton*)

or

> **RELEASE MODULE** *(module name list)*
> / **MENUS** *(menu name list)*
> / **POPUPS** *(popup name list)*
> / **WINDOWS** *(window name list)*
> / **SCREENS** *(screen image list)*

• USAGE The RELEASE command removes objects from memory, reclaiming the space they occupied. When entered at the dot prompt, RELEASE ALL erases all memory variables except system memory variables. When executed in a command file, RELEASE ALL erases only private memory variables that you created in the current or lower level command files.

If you specify the name of an array in the RELEASE command, the entire array is removed from memory.

The RELEASE command has the following options:

MODULE	Erases from memory a loaded assembly language module.
MENUS	Removes defined menus from memory and disables ON SELECTION and ON PAD commands. (You cannot release an active menu.) If you do not include the names of menus to be released, all menus are released.
POPUPS	Deactivates, if necessary, and removes defined pop-ups from the screen and from memory, canceling the associated ON SELECTION commands. If you do not provide a list of pop-up menus, all pop-ups are released.
SCREENS	Removes from memory the listed screen images that were saved with SAVE SCREEN. If no list is supplied, all the screen images are released.
WINDOWS	Removes defined windows from the screen and memory. Any text that was hidden reappears on the screen. You cannot release an active window.

• **EXAMPLE** This command removes the memory variables or arrays named Choice, X, and Day:

RELEASE Choice, X, Day

The next command erases all memory variables and arrays whose names begin with the letters "MO":

RELEASE ALL LIKE MO*

The following command clears pop-up menus named FileMenu, FldMenu, and ValMenu from the screen and from memory:

RELEASE POPUPS FileMenu, FldMenu, ValMenu

See Also CLEAR, RESTORE, RETURN, SAVE, STORE

RENAME

Renaming a File

• **SYNTAX**

RENAME *old file name* **TO** *new file name*

• **USAGE** RENAME changes the name of an existing disk file. It requires that you use file name extensions in both the original and new file names. The current disk drive and directory are assumed in both file names, unless you specify otherwise. The RENAME command does not search paths specified in the DOS PATH or dBASE SET PATH commands.

You must rename the associated memo (.DBT) and production index (.MDX) files separately.

The new file name must be unique to the currently logged drive and directory. If another file with the specified new file name already exists, an error message is displayed and both files remain as they were.

An open file cannot be renamed. Use the appropriate version of the CLOSE command to close an open file before renaming it.

Unlike the DOS RENAME command, the RENAME command in dBASE does not support the wildcard characters * or ? Use RUN or ! to execute the DOS RENAME command if you need to use wildcards.

Tip: When you rename a database file that has a production index file, the header for the renamed file retains a reference to the production index file with the old name. This causes the error message *Production .MDX file not found* to be displayed when you try to open the new file. You must remove the reference to the index file from the header and reconstruct the production index after renaming the database file.

• EXAMPLE The following command changes the name of the MyProg.CMD file to MyProg.PRG:

```
RENAME MyProg.CMD TO MyProg.PRG
```

See Also CLOSE, COPY, COPY FILE, USECCE

REPLACE

Placing New Data in a Field

• SYNTAX

REPLACE *field* **WITH** *new value/expression*
  *(***ADDITIVE***) (,***field***...) (scope) (***REINDEX***) (***FOR** *condition)*
  *(***WHILE** *condition)*

• USAGE You can use REPLACE to change the contents of fields in records of a database file. The new value being placed into the field must be of the same data type as the field.

Avoid using REPLACE with scope or FOR/WHILE options to change the contents of a key field in the controlling index, because dBASE will re-sort the database after each field, move the record pointer, and probably miss a few records.

Use the REINDEX option to delay updating the active noncontrolling indexes until after all changes have been made.

Use the ADDITIVE option to add the new text to a memo field, rather than replacing the contents of the memo field.

• EXAMPLE The following commands increase the UnitPrice field by ten percent for all part numbers that begin with the letter A in a database file named Master.DBF. The active noncontrolling indexes are updated after changes are completed.

```
USE Master   && Don't use an index with replace.
SET EXACT OFF

REPLACE ALL UnitPrice WITH UnitPrice * 1.10 ;
  FOR PartNo = "A" REINDEX
```

The following example shows a single REPLACE command that replaces the values in four different fields named PartNo, Rec_Date, Vend_Code, and Notes (a memo field). Note successive WITH expressions are separated by commas. The M-> alias refers to data stored in memory variables.

```
REPLACE PartNo WITH M->PartNo, ;
  Rec_Date WITH DATE(), ;
  Vend_Code WITH M->VendCode, ;
  Notes WITH "Revised on "+DTOC(DATE()) ADDITIVE
```

See Also ORDER, REINDEX, SET INDEX, SET ORDER, STORE

REPLACE FROM ARRAY

Update Fields from Array

• SYNTAX

REPLACE FROM ARRAY *array name (scope)* (**FIELDS** *field list)* (**REINDEX**) (**FOR** *condition)* (**WHILE** *condition)*

• USAGE The REPLACE FROM ARRAY command copies data from a previously declared and filled array to the active database file.

dBASE IV begins copying the first array row into the first database record, one element into each field, and continues until there are no more rows in the array or until all the records have been replaced. To select rows (records) to copy from the array, specify a scope and/or use the FOR and WHILE options.

If there are fewer columns in the array than there are fields in the database, the extra fields are left blank. Similarly, if there are more columns in the array than there are fields in the database, the extra array columns are ignored.

To copy only to selected fields, use the FIELDS option. The order of the field names in the list determines which array elements will replace them.

REINDEX delays updating the active noncontrolling indexes until all replacements have been made.

• EXAMPLE The following routine indicates an array named Sold, which has previously been filled with appropriate data by the COPY TO ARRAY command. The array contains the customer number, sales representative number, and total sale price. These values are copied to those Sales database records where the State field contains the value "CA". The data is copied until the array rows or the appropriate records run out.

```
USE Sales
REPLACE FROM ARRAY Sold FIELDS ;
   CustNum, SlsRep, TotSale FOR State = "CA"
```

See Also APPEND FROM ARRAY, COPY TO ARRAY, DECLARE

REPORT FORM

Printing a Formatted Report

• SYNTAX

REPORT FORM *file name*/**?** (**PLAIN**) (**HEADING** *expression*) (**NOEJECT**) (**SUMMARY**) (*scope*) (**FOR** *condition*) (**WHILE** *condition*) (**TO PRINTER/TO FILE** *text file name*)

• USAGE REPORT FORM prints a report for the currently open database or view, using a format previously created in the reports design screen (see **CREATE/MODIFY REPORT**). You can direct the report to the screen, the printer, or to a text file.

The PLAIN option suppresses the display of the date and page number on all printed pages and suppresses the page header and footer on all but the first printed page.

The HEADING option specifies an additional title to be displayed at the top of each page. If the heading is literal text, you should enclose it in quotes.

The NOEJECT option combined with the TO PRINTER option suppresses the initial form feed that is usually sent to the printer before report printing begins.

The TO PRINTER option sends output to the printer. The TO FILE option sends output to a file with the file name you specify. If you do not specify an extension for the output file name, dBASE automatically adds the .TXT extension.

The SUMMARY option suppresses the display of detail lines (individual records), displaying only the subtotals and totals specified in the report format.

If the report displays groups or subtotals, the database must be sorted or indexed on the grouping fields for the report to be accurate.

The code generated by the reports design screen always contains the PRINTJOB...ENDPRINTJOB commands, so any changes that you make to the system memory variables before issuing the REPORT FORM command will affect the printed report.

• EXAMPLE The commands

```
USE Customer ORDER LastName
REPORT FORM CustList TO PRINT
```

print data from the Customer.DBF database using the report format named CustList. If LastName is a predefined index of last names, the report is printed in alphabetical order by last name.

See Also CREATE/MODIFY REPORT, LABEL FORM

RESET

Canceling an On-Going Transaction

• SYNTAX

RESET *(***IN** *alias)*

• USAGE Any database involved in a transaction is marked with an integrity tag, which indicates that the database is in a state of change. This tag remains active until an END TRANSACTION or ROLLBACK command terminates the transaction.

The RESET command removes the integrity tag placed in a database file header by the BEGIN TRANSACTION command. You can use it as a safety valve in case a ROLLBACK is not successful. If you remove the integrity tag from a file, you can access the file for another transaction. RESET, with no alias, resets the integrity tag in the current work area only. You can specify the database file name by using the IN option with an alias (a letter "A" through "J," a number 1 through 40, or an open database file name).

Never use the RESET command in a program. Only use it from the dot prompt to regain access to a file in an unusual situation, such as a power failure during a transaction.

See Also BEGIN/END TRANSACTION, ISMARKED(), ROLLBACK, ROLLBACK()

RESTORE

Loading Memory Variables into Memory

• SYNTAX

RESTORE FROM *file name* (**ADDITIVE**)

• USAGE You can use the RESTORE command to load into memory any memory variables that you stored on disk with a SAVE command. Unless you specify the ADDITIVE option, all memory variables currently in memory are erased before the new variables are retrieved. If you use ADDITIVE, retrieved variables are combined with existing variables. If a retrieved and an existing variable both have the same name, the retrieved variable overwrites the existing variable.

Restored variables are always private to the level at which they were restored. To treat restored variables as public to an entire system, you can either restore them at the highest level program in an application or declare them public before you restore them.

RESTORE searches the currently logged disk drive and directory for the specified file unless you have specified a drive or directory in the file name. RESTORE will also search the path specified in a dBASE

SET PATH command. RESTORE assumes that the memory variables are stored in a file with the extension .MEM.

• EXAMPLE This command reads in memory variables from the file named SetUp.MEM without first deleting existing memory variables:

```
RESTORE FROM SetUp ADDITIVE
```

See Also RELEASE, PRIVATE, PUBLIC, SAVE, STORE

RESTORE MACROS

Loading a Macro File

• SYNTAX

RESTORE MACROS FROM *macro file name*

• USAGE The RESTORE MACROS command loads into memory the keystroke macros from a macro file. The default extension .KEY is assumed unless you provide a different extension.

Any keystroke macros in memory with the same names as the restored macros are overwritten. You can only play back keystroke macros that are currently in memory.

• EXAMPLE The following command copies into memory recorded keystroke macros from the CustMac.KEY macro file:

```
RESTORE MACROS FROM CustMac
```

See Also CLEAR, PLAY MACRO, RELEASE, SAVE MACROS, SAVE SCREEN

RESTORE SCREEN

Replacing the Screen Image

• SYNTAX

RESTORE SCREEN FROM *screen file name*

• USAGE The RESTORE SCREEN command replaces the image currently on the screen with one stored in a memory variable. You must use the same name under which the screen was saved.

The saved screen remains in memory until it is removed with the RELEASE command.

• EXAMPLE The following example copies the image stored in SaveScr to the current screen.

```
RESTORE SCREEN FROM SaveScr
```

See Also SAVE SCREEN

RESTORE WINDOW

Loading Saved Window Definitions into Memory

• SYNTAX

RESTORE WINDOW *window name list*/**ALL FROM** *file name*

• USAGE The RESTORE WINDOW command reads windows saved with a SAVE WINDOW command from disk back into memory. The file is assumed to have the default extension .WIN.

Regardless of the number of windows (maximum of 20) in a .WIN file, you can selectively load window definitions by naming the windows in this command and separating them with commas. The ALL option loads all windows in the .WIN file into memory.

• EXAMPLE The next command copies the windows HelpWin and MsgWin from the file named AppWinds.WIN into memory, so they can be displayed by an ACTIVATE WINDOW command:

```
RESTORE WINDOW HelpWin,MsgWin ;
  FROM AppWinds
```

See Also CLEAR, DEFINE WINDOW, RELEASE, SAVE WINDOW

RESUME

Resuming a Suspended Command File

• SYNTAX

```
RESUME
```

• USAGE Use the RESUME command to resume execution of a suspended command file or to return to the debugger after pressing **X** to exit to the dot prompt.

• EXAMPLE After suspending a command file or debugging session, enter this command to resume your work:

```
RESUME
```

See Also BEGIN/END TRANSACTION, CANCEL, CLEAR, DEBUG, RETURN, ROLLBACK, SUSPEND

RETRY

Retrying a Command that Caused an Error

• SYNTAX

RETRY

• USAGE The RETURN command passes control from a called subroutine back to the next line in a calling program. In contrast, RETRY returns control to the line that initiated the branch and retries that same command. Any IF and DO WHILE commands are not evaluated. RETRY is generally used in conjunction with the ON ERROR command to attempt to reexecute the command that caused the error.

You can use RETRY in command files and procedure files. When used in a command file, it closes the called program when it returns control to the calling program. RETRY also resets the ERROR() value to 0.

• EXAMPLE Suppose that an ON ERROR DO ErrTrap command is in effect to pass control to a procedure named ErrTrap as soon as an error occurs during program execution. The ErrTrap procedure might contain the following routine to try to regain access to a locked file on a network:

```
DO CASE
*----- File in use by another.
  CASE ERROR() = 108
    ACTIVATE WINDOW ErrMsg
    ? CHR(7)
    YesNo = .F.
    @ 1,2 SAY "File not accessible. Try again?"
      GET YesNo PICTURE "Y"
    READ
*----- Either pause and retry, or give up.
    IF YesNo
      CLEAR TYPEAHEAD
      WaitASec = INKEY(5)
```

```
    RETRY
  ELSE
    RETURN
  ENDIF
ENDCASE
```

See Also ERROR(), NETWORK(), ON ERROR, RETURN

RETURN

Returning Control to the Calling Program

• SYNTAX

RETURN *(expression/***TO MASTER/TO** *procedure name)*

• USAGE RETURN closes a command file, procedure, or user-defined function and passes control back to the calling program at the command line immediately below the command that called this one. RETURN also erases all private (local) memory variables, but has no effect on public variables or open files.

The TO MASTER option returns control to the highest-level (first) calling command file. Specifying a procedure name in place of MASTER returns control to an active procedure.

You must include an expression with RETURN to terminate a user-defined function. The expression can be a variable name whose contents are returned to the calling command.

• EXAMPLE The PropDate user-defined function that follows is stored in a procedure file named MyProcs.PRG. Note that the RETURN NewDate command passes back the value stored in the NewDate memory variable.

```
********* MyProcs.PRG
FUNCTION PropDate

PARAMETERS AnyDate
```

```
SET TALK OFF

NewDate = CDOW(AnyDate)+" "+ ;
  CMONTH(AnyDate)+" "+ ;
  LTRIM(STR(DAY(AnyDate),2))+", "+ ;
  STR(YEAR(AnyDate),4)

RETURN NewDate
```

When you open the MyProcs procedure file with a SET PROCEDURE command, you can use PropDate() as you would any built-in dBASE IV function. For example, the command

```
? PropDate({12/1/94})
```

displays *Thursday, December 1, 1994.*

See Also COMPILE, DO, ERROR(), FUNCTION, PARAMETERS, PRIVATE, PUBLIC, RESUME, RETRY, SUSPEND

ROLLBACK

Undoing Changes to a Database

• SYNTAX

ROLLBACK *(database file name)*

• USAGE Use ROLLBACK between a BEGIN TRANSACTION and END TRANSACTION command to undo current changes to the database and restores it to its original condition. After the END TRANSACTION command has been executed, you can only use the ROLLBACK command if you specify a database file name. However, after the END TRANSACTION command, ROLLBACK nullifies the database's "in use" flag so that you can manually restore the contents of the database.

ROLLBACK closes all files that were created during a transaction except the text file created by SET ALTERNATE.

• EXAMPLE See the sample routine in the **BEGIN/END TRANSACTION** section.

See Also BEGIN/END TRANSACTION, COMPLETED(), IS-MARKED(), RESET, ROLLBACK()

RUN AND !

Running an External Program

• SYNTAX

RUN! *command*

• USAGE RUN and the equivalent ! command execute a DOS command or an external program that is executable by DOS, and then return control to dBASE.

RUN requires that enough memory be available to load Command.COM and the called program. If there is not enough memory available to run the external program, RUN returns the error message *Insufficient memory* and redisplays the dot prompt.

The DOS Command.COM file must be in the current drive and directory, or in the drive and directory specified by the DOS COMSPEC environmental variable. The DOS SET command displays the current setting of this variable.

To exit dBASE to the DOS prompt temporarily, enter the RUN or ! command with the drive, directory, and Command.COM file name. For example, if Command.COM is stored in the root directory of drive C, enter the dBASE command **RUN C:\Command**.

When the DOS prompt appears, you can enter a series of DOS commands. However, avoid running programs that stay in memory, such as ASSIGN, PRINT, or any TSR (terminate-stay-resident) programs, as these may prevent returning to dBASE and lead to data loss. As an additional safety measure, issue a **CLOSE ALL** command before issuing a **RUN Command.COM** command.

To return to dBASE from the DOS prompt, enter **EXIT** at the DOS prompt.

• EXAMPLE The following commands allow the user to reset the DOS system date and time from within dBASE:

```
RUN Date
RUN Time
```

See Also GETENV(), RUN()

SAVE

Saving Active Memory Variables

• SYNTAX

SAVE TO *file name* (**ALL LIKE/EXCEPT** *skeleton*)

• USAGE The SAVE command places in a disk file a copy of active memory variables and arrays. The file will have the name you supply, followed by the extension .MEM.

If you do not use the ALL LIKE or ALL EXCEPT options, all currently active memory variables and arrays are stored in the file. The ALL LIKE and ALL EXCEPT options allow you to specify skeletal file names with the ? and * wildcard characters (? represents a single character and * represents any group of characters).

• EXAMPLE The next command stores all memory variables and arrays, except those starting with the letters TEMP, in a file named SetUp.MEM:

```
SAVE TO SetUp ALL EXCEPT Temp*
```

See Also CLEAR, RELEASE, RESTORE, STORE

SAVE MACROS

Saving Keystroke Macros to Disk

• SYNTAX

SAVE MACROS TO *macro file name*

• USAGE The SAVE MACROS command saves all keystroke macros currently in memory to a disk file with the default extension .KEY. A single macro file (or *library*) can contain up to 35 keystroke macros named Alt-F1 through Alt-F9, or Alt-F10 followed by any single letter (A through Z).

• EXAMPLE The next command saves all recorded keystroke macros that are currently in memory to a file named UserMacs.KEY:

```
SAVE MACROS TO UserMacs
```

See Also PLAY MACRO, RESTORE MACROS/SCREEN

SAVE SCREEN

Storing the Screen Image

• SYNTAX

SAVE SCREEN TO *screen name*

• USAGE The SAVE SCREEN command copies the image currently on the screen to a memory variable. To restore the image to the screen, use the RESTORE SCREEN FROM command.

Use the RELEASE command to remove the screen images from memory.

• EXAMPLE The following example copies the screen to the variable SaveScr.

```
SAVE SCREEN TO SaveScr
```

See Also CLEAR, RELEASE, RESTORE SCREEN

SAVE WINDOW

Saving Window Definitions to a File

• SYNTAX

SAVE WINDOW *window name list*/**ALL TO** *file name*

• USAGE The SAVE WINDOW command saves the specified window definitions in memory to a disk file. The default extension for the file name is .WIN. If you use another extension, you must specify that extension when you use the RESTORE WINDOW command.

• EXAMPLE The commands that follow save all windows currently defined in memory to a file named AppWinds.WIN. The windows are then cleared from the screen and memory:

```
SAVE WINDOW ALL TO AppWinds
*----- Ok to clear windows.
CLEAR WINDOWS
```

See Also DEFINE WINDOW, RELEASE, RESTORE WINDOW

SCAN AND ENDSCAN

Processing Multiple Database Records

• SYNTAX

SCAN *(scope)* *(* **FOR** *condition)* *(* **WHILE** *condition)*
(commands)
(**LOOP** *)*
(**EXIT** *)*
ENDSCAN

• USAGE The SCAN and ENDSCAN command combination steps through a database file and executes the specified commands on each record that meets the scope, FOR, and WHILE conditions.

The default scope is every record beginning with the first record in the database file. If you specify a FOR condition, dBASE IV tests each record in the scope and executes the commands if the condition is true (.T.). Furthermore, if you specify a WHILE condition, the processing continues until the WHILE condition evaluates to false (.F.).

To prematurely exit the SCAN...ENDSCAN loop, use the EXIT option. When dBASE IV encounters an EXIT inside a SCAN...-ENDSCAN, program execution continues with the command line immediately following the ENDSCAN. LOOP returns control to the beginning of the SCAN segment.

Unlike the DO WHILE .NOT. EOF() command used in earlier versions of dBASE to loop through database records, SCAN...-ENDSCAN automatically advances the record pointer, so a SKIP command is not required. If you include one, SCAN will skip twice, processing every other record.

If an index controls the sort order, SCAN...ENDSCAN advances the record pointer through the database in index rather than record number order. Don't use an index to control the sort order if a REPLACE command within the SCAN...ENDSCAN loop will alter any fields included in the index's key expression. If you do, dBASE will quickly resort the index after each REPLACE, thereby moving the record pointer and perhaps producing incomplete results.

• **EXAMPLE** The following commands call a procedure named InvPost to operate on each record in a database file named Orders.DBF that has .F. in a field named InvPosted. They simultaneously change the setting of InvPosted to .T. and display a list of all records that have been posted.

```
SET TALK OFF
USE Orders
SCAN FOR .NOT. InvPosted
  DO InvPost
  REPLACE InvPosted WITH .T.
  ? OrderNum, CustNo, PartNo, OrdDate
ENDSCAN
```

See Also CONTINUE, DO WHILE, EXIT, LOOP

SEEK

Finding Data in an Indexed File

• **SYNTAX**

SEEK *expression*

• **USAGE** SEEK searches for data stored in the controlling index. Unlike the FIND command, which searches for literal data, SEEK can be used with a memory variable name as the *expression*.

The SEEK command uses the SET NEAR, SET EXACT, SET FILTER, and SET DELETED settings exactly as does the FIND command.

If the index file contains several keys, then the field widths and formats of both the data being searched for and the key expression of the index file must match exactly. SEEK cannot locate characters embedded within the index expression.

If SEEK succeeds, FOUND() returns .T. and RECNO() returns the record number. If SEEK fails to find a record matching the key, the error message *Find not successful* is displayed and FOUND() returns .F..

● **EXAMPLE** Suppose you have a database named Orders that contains the following fields:

NAME	FIELD TYPE	WIDTH	DEC
LastName	Character	15	
FirstName	Character	20	
Amount	Numeric	9	2
OrdDate	Date	8	

To create an index that orders records by name, amount, and date, use the following command:

```
INDEX ON UPPER(LastName+FirstName)+ ;
  STR(Amount,9,2)+DTOS(OrdDate) TAG BigInd
```

The next routine asks the user for values to search for and creates the appropriate search string to match the index expression. Notice that the lengths specified in the SPACE() functions exactly match the lengths specified in the database structure, as required for the SEEK to be successful. Also, the SEEK exactly matches the original INDEX ON key expression, which is necessary for SEEK to work correctly.

```
MLast = SPACE(15)   && As defined in database structure
MFirst = SPACE(20)  && As defined in database structure
MAmount = 0
MOrdDate = {  /  /  }
@ 2,1 SAY "Last Name: " GET MLast
@ 3,1 SAY "First Name: " GET MFirst
@ 4,1 SAY "Amount: " GET MAmount PICTURE "99,999.99"
@ 5,1 SAY "Order date: " GET MOrdDate
READ
USE Orders ORDER BigInd
SEEK UPPER(MLast+MFirst)+STR(MAmount,9,2)+ ;
  DTOS(MOrdDate)
```

Because you *cannot* search for data embedded within the index but *can* search for any leftmost characters within an index, any of the following SEEK commands is valid for the sample BigInd index:

```
SEEK UPPER(MLast)
SEEK UPPER(MLast+MFirst)
SEEK UPPER(MLast)+UPPER(TRIM(MFirst))
SEEK UPPER(MLast+MFirst)+STR(MAmount,9,2)
SEEK UPPER(MLast+MFirst)+STR(MAmount,9,2) + ;
  DTOS(MOrdDate)
```

The following sample routine checks the current setting of the SET NEAR option and the FOUND() function, displaying the results of the SEEK command accordingly:

```
SEEK Anything
*----- Give feedback based on findings.
DO CASE
  CASE FOUND()
    ? "Exact match found"
  CASE .NOT. FOUND()
*----- Return result based on NEAR setting.
    IF SET("NEAR") = "OFF"
      ? "No record available"
    ELSE
      ? "Closest match found"
    ENDIF
ENDCASE
```

Tip: Using the SEEK() function is faster than the SEEK command since it combines two commands, SEEK and IF FOUND(), into one command.

See Also FOUND(), FIND, INDEX, KEY(), LOCATE, SEEK() SET EXACT, SET NEAR, SET ORDER, USE

SELECT

Assigning Databases to Work Areas

• SYNTAX

SELECT *work area/alias*

• USAGE Use the SELECT command both to assign databases to work areas and to move from one work area to another. By assigning databases to separate work areas with the SELECT command, you can open up to 40 database files simultaneously. You can define the first ten work areas as either 1 through 10 or A through J, and the remainder by numbers 11 through 40 or an alias.

Once you have defined work areas with the SELECT and USE commands, you can select a new work area without affecting the record pointers unless the database files are related.

Generally, any command that changes the contents of a field (APPEND, EDIT, BROWSE, READ, and so forth) works only for the currently active database (the one specified by the most recent SELECT command). However, you can display fields from any database by using an alias.

You can use aliases with all dBASE commands that use field names, including MODIFY REPORT, MODIFY LABEL, DISPLAY, ?, @, CALCULATE, and SET FIELDS.

• EXAMPLE In this example, the Orders database is opened in work area A and the Master database is opened in work area B:

```
SELECT A
USE Orders ORDER PartNo
SELECT B
USE Master ORDER PartNo
```

At this point, the Master database is currently selected. To make the Orders database the currently selected database, enter the command

```
SELECT A
```

or

```
SELECT Orders
```

or

```
SELECT 1
```

Instead of using SELECT, you can use the IN option with the USE command to assign databases to work areas while opening them, as follows:

```
USE Orders ORDER PartNo IN 1
USE Master ORDER PartNo IN 2
SELECT Orders
```

See Also ALIAS(), CLOSE, SET CATALOG, USE

SHOW MENU/POPUP

Displaying an Inactive Bar or Pop-Up Menu

• SYNTAX

SHOW MENU *menu name* (**PAD** *pad name*)

or

SHOW POPUP *popup name*

• USAGE SHOW MENU/POPUP displays a horizontal bar or a pop-up menu without activating it. If you use the PAD option with SHOW MENU, the specified option is highlighted. If no option is specified, the left-most option is highlighted.

Use this command during application development to check the appearance of a menu without activating it, or to display an inactive image of a menu while other windows or menus are in effect.

Any message associated with the menu is not displayed with SHOW.

• EXAMPLE The following commands create a horizontal bar menu and show it with the *Exit* option highlighted. The menu is shown, but not active.

```
DEFINE MENU MainMenu
DEFINE PAD Option1 OF MainMenu ;
  PROMPT "Accounts"
DEFINE PAD Option2 OF MainMenu ;
  PROMPT "Inventory"
DEFINE PAD Option3 OF MainMenu ;
  PROMPT "Exit"
SHOW MENU MainMenu PAD Option3
```

These commands define and show a files list without activating it:

```
DEFINE POPUP ShowPrgs FROM 5,32 TO 20,48 ;
  PROMPT FILES LIKE *.PRG
SHOW POPUP ShowPrgs
```

See Also ACTIVATE MENU/POPUP, CLEAR, DEFINE BAR/MENU/PAD/POPUP, DEFINE PAD

SKIP

Moving the Record Pointer

• SYNTAX

SKIP *(number)* **(IN** *alias)*

• USAGE SKIP, without additional parameters, moves the record pointer down one record in the current database file. If an index is controlling the sort order, the record pointer moves to the next record in index order. If the database is not indexed, SKIP moves the record pointer based on record numbers.

The number of records to skip can be any positive or negative number, or the result of a numeric calculation.

The IN option allows you to move the record pointer in another work area without leaving the current work area.

SKIP ignores any records that are hidden by a SET FILTER or SET DELETED ON command.

● **EXAMPLE** Use this command to move the record pointer back one record

```
SKIP -1
```

The next command calculates the number of records to skip using a complex expression and memory variables named Cols and Rows. The record pointer in work area B is moved.

```
SKIP (((Cols-1)*Rows)-1)-1 IN B
```

See Also BOF(), DO WHILE, EOF(), GO/GOTO, RECNO()

SORT

Copying Records in Sequence

● **SYNTAX**

SORT TO *file name* **ON** *field1 (***/A***) (***/C***) (***/D***) (,field2 (***/A***) (***/C***) (***/D***)...) (***ASCENDING/DESCENDING***) (scope) (***FOR** *condition) (***WHILE** *condition)*

● **USAGE** SORT makes a sorted copy of the current database. It does not affect the current database at all. Options used with individual field names are

/A Ascending order

/C Ignores upper- and lowercase

/D Descending order

By default, SORT sorts records into ascending order unless you use /D. You can combine /A or /D with /C, as in /AC.

The ASCENDING and DESCENDING options apply to all fields that do not have an attached /A or /D option.

You may specify a maximum of ten fields in the SORT command, each separated by a comma. However, you cannot sort on logical or memo fields.

If SET SAFETY is on and you attempt to sort to an existing database file, dBASE will ask for permission to overwrite the existing file. If SET SAFETY is off, dBASE will automatically overwrite any existing files.

• **EXAMPLE** The following commands create a database file named DateOrd.DBF that contains records with the year 1994 in the HireDate field.

```
USE Mail
SORT ON HireDate/D, LName/AC, FName/AC ;
 TO DateOrd FOR YEAR(HireDate) = 1994
```

The records in DateOrd are stored in descending order by date (from December 1994 to January 1994), with names listed in ascending alphabetical order within each date. Upper- and lowercase distinctions are ignored.

See Also COPY, INDEX

STORE

Placing a Value in a Memory Variable

• SYNTAX

STORE *value/expression* **TO** *variable name(s)/array element(s)*

• **USAGE** You can use STORE to create a new memory variable and place a value in it or to place a new value in an existing memory variable or array element. The memory variable name can be up to ten characters long, must begin with a letter, cannot contain blank spaces, and may contain numbers and underscores after the first letter.

Avoid using single-letter memory variable names in the range of "A" to "J," or the single letter "M," as these may conflict with aliases. In addition, avoid using dBASE command and function names, including their abbreviations, as variable names. Do not assign the same name to both an array and a single memory variable.

You can also use the STORE command to store values in array elements, provided that you have already defined the array with a DECLARE or PUBLIC ARRAY command.

A faster alternative to the STORE command is the assignment operator (=), with the following syntax:

variable name = expression/value

By default, dBASE allows you to store a maximum of 500 memory variables in memory. However, you can modify this setting using the MVBLKSIZE and MVMAXBLKS options in the Config.DB file.

The STORE command and the assignment operator always place their values in a memory variable, even if the open database includes a field with the same name. On the other hand, commands that display or use memory variables give a field precedence over a memory variable when the field and memory variable have the same name.

When a field and memory variable have the same name, you can use the M-> alias to specify the memory variable. For example, the command

? LastName

displays the value from the LastName field in the currently open database (if any), while the command

? M->LastName

displays the contents of the LastName memory variable.

In fact, you can speed up processing by always using the M-> alias. The M-> prefix indicates that this is a memory variable and dBASE goes directly to the memvar list without searching the field name list first.

The data type of the memory variable being stored is determined by the data being stored in the variable. Be sure to use appropriate delimiters when storing values ("" for character, {} for dates, .T. or .F. for logical, and none for numeric and float). If you attempt to store a memo field in a memory variable, dBASE will store the first 254 characters of the field, with formatting codes. Preferably, use the MLINE() function to store a specific line, stripped of formatting codes, to the variable.

• EXAMPLE This command stores the value 123.45 in a memory variable named Amount as the numeric data type:

```
STORE 123.45 TO Amount
```

The next commands create an array named Day that contains five elements, storing a blank space in each one:

```
DECLARE Day(5)
STORE " " TO Day(1),Day(2),Day(3),Day(4),Day(5)
```

Note that issuing the command

```
STORE " " TO Day
```

would erase the entire Day array, leaving only a single variable named Day.

The following command stores the date that is 90 days from 12/31/94 in a variable named OverdueOn:

```
OverdueOn = {12/31/94}+90
```

See Also &, CLEAR, DECLARE, DISPLAY MEMORY, PARAMETERS, PRIVATE, PUBLIC, RELEASE, RESTORE, SAVE

SUM

Calculating the Sum

• SYNTAX

SUM *(field names/expressions)* **(TO** *memory variables*/**TO ARRAY** *array name) (scope)* **(FOR** *condition)* **(WHILE** *condition)*

• USAGE SUM calculates the sum of numeric fields in the database. If you list no field names or expressions next to the SUM command, all numeric fields are summed.

If SET TALK is on, calculation results are displayed on the screen. If you use the TO option with variable names, results are stored in the named variables. To store the results in an array, you must first declare a one-dimensional array, and then use the TO ARRAY option with the name of the array.

Records hidden by MODIFY QUERY, SET FILTER, or SET DELETED ON are not included in the calculation.

• EXAMPLE Given that Qty and UnitPrice are numeric fields, the command that follows stores the sum of the Qty, UnitPrice, and Qty*UnitPrice values in memory variables named TotQty, TotPrice, TotTotal:

```
SUM Qty,UnitPrice,Qty*UnitPrice TO TotQty,;
  TotPrice,TotTotal
```

See Also AVERAGE, CALCULATE, DECLARE, FIXED(), FLOAT(), STORE, TOTAL

SUSPEND

Suspending Command File Execution

• SYNTAX

SUSPEND

• USAGE The SUSPEND command forces suspension of a program at a specific place (presumably where you've isolated an error). When dBASE encounters a SUSPEND command in a command file, it displays the message *Do suspended* and the dot prompt reappears. All commands, including DISPLAY MEMORY, DISPLAY STRUCTURE, DISPLAY STATUS, DISPLAY HISTORY, and ?, then display information about the program environment at that exact point in the program. This is handy when you are debugging.

To edit a suspended command file, first close the file with the CANCEL command. If you suspend a procedure file, close it with the CLOSE PROCEDURE command before editing. To resume processing without editing, enter **RESUME** at the dot prompt.

If you create any memory variables at the dot prompt while a command file is suspended, those memory variables will be private to the suspended command file.

• EXAMPLE After isolating a program bug near a particular routine, you can check parameters by placing a SUSPEND command near that routine, as follows:

```
SEEK Search
SUSPEND
LIST WHILE .NOT. EOF()
```

When the program runs, it is suspended immediately after the SEEK command is executed. You can then enter commands such as DISPLAY STATUS, DISPLAY MEMORY, and ? at the dot prompt to check the status of variables and files.

See Also CANCEL, COMPILE, DEBUG, DO, RESUME, SET ECHO, SET PROCEDURE, SET STEP, SET TALK, SET TRAP

TEXT AND ENDTEXT

Marking Text for Display

• SYNTAX

```
TEXT
  text to be displayed
ENDTEXT
```

• USAGE To display a large body of text without using a series of @ or ? commands, you should enclose the text within the TEXT and ENDTEXT commands.

Note that dBASE makes no attempt to process any commands, functions, expressions, or macros between the TEXT and ENDTEXT commands. All text is displayed exactly as written in the program. If SET PRINT is on, all text between the TEXT and ENDTEXT commands is channeled to the printer. If a SET ALTERNATE file is active, all text is channeled to the text file.

TEXT and ENDTEXT are used only in command files.

• EXAMPLE The information between the TEXT and ENDTEXT commands is displayed on the screen, verbatim, when the command file containing the code is executed.

```
TEXT
  This text is simply displayed on the screen. dBASE
  makes no attempt to execute a command, such as
  USE CustList
  Nor does it attempt to expand &macros.
ENDTEXT
```

See Also ?/??, @...SAY, DISPLAY, LIST, SET PRINTER

TOTAL

Creating a Summary Database

• SYNTAX

TOTAL ON *key expression* **TO** *file name* (**FIELDS** *field list*) (*scope*) (**FOR** *condition*) (**WHILE** *condition*)

• USAGE TOTAL creates a new database with totals of numeric fields summarized by a key field or expression. The new file contains one record for each distinct value of the key expression. Each of these records contains a subtotal of the specified field for the group of records from the original database file with that key value.

The original database must be sorted or indexed on the key expression. Using TOTAL with an improperly indexed or sorted database will not generate an error message; instead, it will produce an incomplete summary database. All records will be totaled if there is no scope, FOR, or WHILE condition.

The structure of the generated summary database file is identical to that of the original database, except that memo fields are not copied.

Records hidden by MODIFY QUERY, SET FILTER, or SET DELETED ON are not included in the totals. The SET SAFETY setting determines whether dBASE asks for permission before overwriting a file during a TOTAL operation.

• EXAMPLE The sample database named Charges contains the data shown below (it may also contain other fields):

RECORD#	CUSTNO	AMOUNT
1	1001	799.07
2	1002	958.39
3	1001	883.26
4	1001	407.67

5	1003	827.02
6	1002	798.62

To create a summary database with total charges for each customer, first use or create an index of the CustNo field, then issue a TOTAL command as follows:

```
USE Charges
INDEX ON CustNo TAG CustNo
SET ORDER TO CustNo
TOTAL ON CustNo TO TotChrge FIELDS Amount
```

The next two commands display the contents of the new TotChrge.DBF database:

```
USE TotChrge
LIST
```

The TotChrge database contains these records:

RECORD#	CUSTNO	AMOUNT
1	1001	2090.00
2	1002	1757.01
3	1003	827.02

See Also AVERAGE, CALCULATE, CREATE/MODIFY REPORT, MODIFY STRUCTURE, SUM

TYPE

Displaying Text File Contents

• SYNTAX

TYPE *file name* **(TO PRINTER/TO FILE** *file name***)** **(NUMBER)**

• USAGE TYPE displays the contents of any ASCII text file, including dBASE command files and text files created by the TO FILE option available with many dBASE commands. TYPE will also display output from an ALTERNATE file. ASCII files generated by dBASE generally include the .TXT extension.

TYPE cannot display open files. The current drive and directory are assumed unless otherwise specified. You must include the file name extension in the command.

The NUMBER option displays a line number to the left of each printed line in both displayed and printed output.

• EXAMPLE The following command prints the contents of the command file named MyProg.PRG, including line numbers:

```
TYPE MyProg.PRG TO PRINTER NUMBER
```

See Also SET HEADINGS, SET PRINTER

UNLOCK

Releasing a File Lock

• SYNTAX

UNLOCK *[***ALL/IN** *alias]*

• USAGE UNLOCK releases any currently active file or record lock on a shared file so that other users can access that file or record.

When one user locks a file or record to update it with a READ or REPLACE command, other users in the network cannot access that file or record. To return access to other users, the user must issue an UNLOCK command.

The UNLOCK command without any options unlocks the currently selected database file only. UNLOCK ALL releases all locks (both file and record locks) in all work areas. UNLOCK IN *alias* unlocks the file or record in the specified work area only.

• **EXAMPLE** The following commands attempt to replace data in a single record by first locking the record. If the REPLACE command is successful, the UNLOCK command immediately unlocks the record for use by others:

```
IF RLOCK()
  REPLACE UnitPrice WITH UnitPrice * 1.10
  UNLOCK
ELSE
  ? "Can't access record right now..."
ENDIF
```

See Also FLOCK(), NETWORK(), RLOCK(), USER()

UPDATE

Updating One Database from Another

• **SYNTAX**

UPDATE ON *key field* **FROM** *alias* **REPLACE** *field name 1* **WITH** *expression 1 (,field name 2* **WITH** *expression 2 ...)* *(***RANDOM***)* *(***REINDEX***)*

• **USAGE** UPDATE changes the contents of one database file on the basis of the contents of another database file. Both databases must be opened and must have a common field with the same name, data type, length, and width. Records in the two database files are matched on the basis of the values in the key field.

The UPDATE operation will be much faster if the common field is indexed in ascending order in both databases. If only the updated file is indexed, you must use the RANDOM option.

The REINDEX option waits to update the active, noncontrolling indexes until all the changes have been made, rather than updating with each change.

You must precede any field names from the nonselected database file with an alias.

• EXAMPLE In this example, the database named MastFile is indexed on the PartNo field and contains the following records:

PartNo	PartName	InStock	LastSale	YtdSold
A-111	Apples	10	06/01/94	100
B-222	Bananas	10	06/01/94	50

A file named TranFile, which is also indexed on the PartNo field, contains the three sales transactions shown here:

PartNo	QtySold	DateSold	Posted
A-111	1	06/01/94	F
A-111	5	06/02/95	F
B-222	5	07/01/94	F

Enter these commands to subtract the quantities sold from the quantities in stock, replace the LastSale field with the date of the last sale, and increment the YtdSold field by the quantity sold for each part number:

```
USE MastFile ORDER PartNo IN 1
USE TranFile ORDER PartNo IN 2
 *----- && File being updated must be selected.
SELECT MastFile
UPDATE ON PartNo FROM Tranfile ;
  REPLACE InStock WITH InStock – B->QtySold, ;
  LastSale WITH B->DateSold, ;
```

```
YtdSold WITH YtdSold + B->QtySold ;
FOR .NOT. Posted
```

When command execution is finished, the MastFile database will contain the data shown here:

PartNo	PartName	InStock	LastSale	YtdSold
A-111	Apples	4	06/02/94	106
B-222	Bananas	5	07/01/94	55

To prevent the transactions in the TranFile database from inadvertently updating the MastFile database a second time, you could enter the commands

```
SELECT TranFile
REPLACE ALL Posted WITH .T.
```

to convert all of the values in the Posted field to .T. To ensure that these records are not used in a future UPDATE operation, include the FOR .NOT. Posted condition in the UPDATE command. dBASE has no built-in capability to determine which records have and have not already been included in an UPDATE operation. It is the programmer's responsibility to devise a method for excluding posted records from an update.

See Also APPEND FROM, CREATE/MODIFY QUERY, INDEX, JOIN, REPLACE, SELECT, SORT, TOTAL

USE

Opening an Existing File

• SYNTAX

USE *(<database file name>/***?***)* **(IN** *work area number)* **(INDEX** *.ndx or .mdx filename list)*

[**ORDER** *.ndx filename/* [**TAG**] *.mdx tag* [**OF** *.mdx filename*]]
[**ALIAS** *alias name*] [**EXCLUSIVE**] [**NOUPDATE**] [**NOLOG**] [**NOSAVE**] [**AGAIN**]

• USAGE The USE command opens an existing database file. The .DBF extension (which dBASE adds automatically when you create a database) is assumed, unless you specify a different extension. If a catalog is open, entering **?** in lieu of a file name displays a pop-up menu naming files available in the current catalog. If no catalog is open, the ? option displays a pop-up menu of all database files on the current directory. USE with no file name closes the file in the current work area.

The IN option allows you to assign the database file to a specific work area. USE IN with no file name closes the file in the specified work area.

If a production index file with the same name as the database (and the .MDX extension) is available, the index file is opened automatically and all indexes within the production index file are updated to reflect changes to the database.

If the database file contains a memo field, the associated .DBT file will also be opened.

To open indexes other than the production index file, use the INDEX option followed by a list of index file names. Note that you can use the INDEX option to open dBASE III PLUS single index (.NDX) files as well as a tag in a multiple index (.MDX) file. However, if both types of files exist with the same name (for example, Names.MDX and Names.NDX), the INDEX option opens the .MDX file unless you specify the .NDX extension with the index file name.

The ORDER option lets you choose the controlling index. The controlling index determines both the order in which records are displayed and the field that can be searched with the SEEK and FIND commands and the SEEK() function. The controlling index also determines the field that can be used in a SET RELATION TO command.

If several multiple index files are open for a single database, and you wish to use an index outside the production index file as the controlling index, you must use the OF option with the ORDER option. For example, entering the command **USE CustList INDEX Extra ORDER TAG Names OF Extra** makes the Names index of the Extra.MDX index file the controlling index.

You may open up to 40 database files simultaneously, each in a different work area. Create work areas with the SELECT command, or by using the IN option in the USE command.

The ALIAS option allows you to assign a different name to the database. If an ALIAS is not specified, either the work area name or the database file name can be used as the alias.

The EXCLUSIVE option gives the current network user exclusive use of the database. Other users can neither change nor view data in the file until the current user closes the file with the CLOSE ALL, CLOSE DATABASES, USE, or QUIT command. On single-user computers, EXCLUSIVE is ignored.

The NOUPDATE option opens the file for read-only access. The user can view data, but cannot add, change, or delete data.

The NOLOG option prevents changes to the database file from being recorded in the transaction log.

The NOSAVE option defines the database as a temporary file. It will be erased from memory when it is closed.

The AGAIN option allows you to open a second, fully-functioning copy of the same database file in another work area. This is handy when you want to view the contents of the open file but do not want to move the record pointer in the middle of processing. Be sure to keep track of which work area contains the current version.

Tip: To see which databases, index files, and aliases are in use at any given moment, use the DISPLAY STATUS command. To close all open databases, use the CLOSE DATABASES command. To close all active index files, use the CLOSE INDEX command.

You will speed up processing if you keep frequently-used files open instead of reloading them into memory each time they are needed.

• **EXAMPLE** The following commands open two database files named PartList.DBF and Orders.DBF. Orders is opened in work area

1 (or A), and PartList is opened in work area 2 (or B). Each is opened with an indexed field named PartNo as the master (controlling) index. The PartList database is assigned the alias Lookup.

```
USE Orders IN 1 ORDER PartNo
USE PartList IN 2 ORDER PartNo ALIAS Lookup
```

By default, the file name in the USE command is assumed to be literal. To use a variable as the file name, use indirect referencing. For example, the following commands open a database file named MyData.DBF (rather than XFile.DBF):

```
XFile = "MyData"
USE (XFile)
```

See Also CLOSE, COPY INDEXES, COPY TAG, DBF(), DELETE TAG, INDEX, MDX(), NDX(), SELECT, SET CATALOG, SET INDEX, SET RELATION, SET ORDER, TAG()

WAIT

Pausing for a Keystroke

• SYNTAX

WAIT *(prompt)* **TO** *(memory variable)*

• USAGE The WAIT command suspends processing of a program and waits for the user to press any key. It accepts only a single keystroke and does not require that ↵ be pressed. When you use the WAIT command without a prompt, it presents the prompt *Press any key to continue.* To display WAIT with no prompt, use the syntax

```
WAIT " "
```

If you specify a variable name to which to store the keystroke, the keystroke is stored in that memory variable as a character string (whether the user typed a letter or a number).

Note that the INKEY() function provides a similar capability, but can limit the duration of the pause and store nonprinting keystrokes such as ↑, ↓, and ↵.

• **EXAMPLE** This routine asks the user whether to continue with some task. If the answer is **N**, the IF clause returns control to the calling program.

```
WAIT "Do you wish to continue? (Y/N) " TO YesNo

IF UPPER(YesNo) = "N"
  RETURN
ENDIF
```

See Also @, ACCEPT, INKEY(), INPUT, ON KEY

ZAP

Permanently Deleting All Database Records

• **SYNTAX**

```
ZAP
```

• **USAGE** ZAP permanently removes all records from an active database file but leaves the database structure intact. All open index files are also emptied. It has the same effect as entering the commands

```
DELETE ALL
PACK
```

If SET SAFETY is on, dBASE asks for permission before removing all records from the database. If SET SAFETY is off, all records are deleted immediately. You cannot recall records deleted with ZAP.

• **EXAMPLE** In the following example, all records from the Charges.DBF database are appended to the database file named History. ZAP then removes all records from the Charges database.

```
SET SAFETY OFF
USE History
APPEND FROM Charges
USE Charges
ZAP
```

See Also DELETE, PACK, SET SAFETY

Part 3

dBASE IV SET Commands

The SET commands allow you to define general parameters that affect your current dBASE IV session. The settings remain in effect until you either quit dBASE or change them with another SET command.

dBASE lets you set these parameters in three ways:

1. From the Control Center, by making selections from the Tools ➤ Settings menu.
2. By modifying the Config.DB file using MODIFY COMMAND or running the dBSETUP program with RUN DBSETUP. Many of the SET parameters can be specified in the Config.DB file, so that they become the default settings that are automatically activated when you start dBASE. Some of the settings, such as the command to be executed as soon as dBASE is loaded or the command to specify an external word processor, can be set only in the Config.DB file. See Appendix A for more information.
3. By using SET commands that can be issued at the dot prompt or in a program. Part 3 describes these commands and shows examples for their use.

In the following descriptions, the default settings for SET commands are displayed in uppercase. For example, the reference

SET TALK ON/off

indicates that the default setting for the TALK parameter is on, but you can change the setting to off with a SET command.

SET

Setting any dBASE Parameter

• SYNTAX

SET

• USAGE SET provides a full-screen, menu-driven technique for viewing and changing current parameter settings. Use the arrow keys to scroll through options, and press ↵ to select an option or change its status. You can also select an option by moving the mouse pointer to the desired option and double-clicking the left mouse button. Additional instructions appear at the bottom of the screen as you work.

• EXAMPLE Enter the following command at the dot prompt to change the status of SET commands interactively:

SET

See Also LIST/DISPLAY STATUS

SET ALTERNATE

Capturing Output in a File

• SYNTAX

SET ALTERNATE TO *(file name)* (**ADDITIVE**)

or

SET ALTERNATE on/OFF

• USAGE SET ALTERNATE TO opens an ASCII text file to which dBASE can direct output. The text file name will have a .TXT extension unless you specify a different extension in *file name*.

If you use the ADDITIVE option and the named file already exists, the captured text is added to the bottom of the existing file. If you do not use ADDITIVE, SET ALTERNATE TO overwrites existing text. The SET SAFETY command determines whether a warning message will appear when SET ALTERNATE TO is about to overwrite an existing file.

The SET ALTERNATE ON command tells dBASE to record all output, except the output of @...SAY...GET commands, in the currently open alternate file. (To capture @...SAY...GET output in a file, use the SET DEVICE command.) SET ALTERNATE OFF deactivates the alternate file so that ensuing output is not recorded. Reactivate the file to accept more text with another SET ALTERNATE ON command.

Remember that SET ALTERNATE TO *file name* must precede the SET ALTERNATE ON command. After recording output, use the CLOSE ALTERNATE command to close the file.

You can view the contents of a closed alternate file with the TYPE command, or modify those contents with the MODIFY COMMAND/FILE command.

• EXAMPLE The following commands capture output from several LIST commands in a file named MyData.TXT, and then display the contents of the file using TYPE:

```
SET ALTERNATE TO MyData
SET ALTERNATE ON

USE Customer
LIST

LIST STATUS
```

```
LIST MEMORY

SET ALTERNATE OFF
CLOSE ALTERNATE

TYPE MyData.TXT
```

See Also SET DEVICE, CLOSE

SET AUTOSAVE

Setting the Save Frequency

• SYNTAX

```
SET AUTOSAVE on/OFF
```

• USAGE As you add or change database records, dBASE IV temporarily saves each record to a buffer. When the buffer is full, the records are saved to disk in a batch. dBASE writes all remaining data to disk when you close the database file.

To reduce the probability of data loss while new or modified data is stored in the buffer, you can issue the SET AUTOSAVE ON command. With AUTOSAVE on, each new or modified database record is stored to disk immediately. This slows processing but safeguards your data.

In a multiuser environment, SET AUTOSAVE ON ensures that all records are immediately saved to disk and are available to all users without the delay of a buffer.

• EXAMPLE The next command turns the auto-save feature on:

```
SET AUTOSAVE ON
```

SET BELL

Controlling the Bell

• SYNTAX

SET BELL TO *frequency,duration*

or

SET BELL ON/off

• USAGE dBASE IV alerts you with the computer's "bell" (speaker) when a field is completely filled during data entry or editing, or when an error occurs. SET BELL OFF prevents the bell from sounding under these conditions.

To change the frequency (pitch) and duration of the bell, follow the SET BELL TO command by a frequency in the range of 19 to 10,000 Hz (cycles per second), and a duration in the range of 1 to 19 ticks (each tick is approximately 0.0549 seconds). The default frequency is 512 and the default duration is 2.

To resume the default frequency, execute SET BELL TO with no specified frequency or duration.

• EXAMPLE The following commands set the bell to a low pitch and a duration of about one second, and then sound the bell:

```
SET BELL TO 50,19
SET BELL ON
? CHR(7)
```

SET BLOCKSIZE

Controlling Memo and Index File Storage

• SYNTAX

SET BLOCKSIZE TO *number*

• USAGE SET BLOCKSIZE determines the size of memo field and multiple index storage blocks in 512-byte increments. You can set the block size to any value from 1 to 63. The default setting of 1 (512 bytes) is the only setting compatible with dBASE III PLUS.

Larger block sizes provide faster memo field string manipulation, but tend to slow down data entry and editing operations and to increase the size of the memo field (.DBT) and index (.MDX) files.

You can use SET MBLOCK and SET IBLOCK to change the default sizes of memo and index blocks independently to different sizes for optimal performance.

• EXAMPLE The following commands increase the block size of memo field storage to eight blocks (4096 bytes), and copy existing data to a new file named NewCust:

```
SET BLOCKSIZE TO 8
USE Referenc
COPY TO NewCust
```

See Also SET IBLOCK, SET MBLOCK, SET MEMOWIDTH, SET WINDOW OF MEMO

SET BORDER TO

Specifying Border Characters

• SYNTAX

SET BORDER TO (SINGLE/double/panel/none/*border definition string***)**

• USAGE SET BORDER TO defines the border for menus, windows, and the box or line drawn with the @...TO commands. Options are

SINGLE	Borders contain a single line
DOUBLE	Borders contain a double line
PANEL	Borders contain no lines
NONE	Borders are invisible

You can also define a border definition string that lists ASCII character values separated by commas. Each value in the string represents a side or corner of the box in the following order: top line, bottom line, left side, right side, upper-left corner, upper-right corner, lower-left corner, lower-right corner. To use the default single line as a character in a border definition string, include a comma but no number. If you specify a single ASCII character value, the entire border will be composed of that character.

To restore the border definition to the default single-line setting, use SET BORDER TO with no option.

To change the border of a previously defined window, you must use SET BORDER TO, then redefine the window.

• EXAMPLE The commands that follow define a border with single lines at the top and bottom and double lines at the sides and corners:

```
SET BORDER TO ,,186,186,201,187,200,188
```

The command

SET BORDER TO 33

displays a border made up entirely of exclamation points.

See Also @...TO..., DEFINE WINDOW

SET CARRY

Copying Data from One New Record to the Next

• SYNTAX

SET CARRY TO *(field list (***ADDITIVE***))*

or

SET CARRY on/OFF

• USAGE The SET CARRY TO command determines which fields in a database are carried over from one new record to the next during APPEND, BROWSE, or INSERT operations. SET CARRY TO, with no field list, carries over all database fields to new records. The ADDITIVE option adds specified fields to a list of fields already defined with a previous SET CARRY command.

SET CARRY TO does not take effect until you execute SET CARRY ON.

• EXAMPLE The following commands carry the data entered into the State, Zip, and Date fields from one new record to the next as you add new records to the CustList database:

```
USE CustList
SET CARRY TO State,Zip,Date
SET CARRY ON
```

```
SET FORMAT TO MyScreen
APPEND
```

See Also APPEND, BROWSE, EDIT, INSERT, SET FIELDS

SET CATALOG

Storing File Names in a Catalog

• SYNTAX

SET CATALOG TO *(file name/***?***)*

or

SET CATALOG on/OFF

• USAGE SET CATALOG TO creates and activates a new catalog, activates an existing catalog, or closes an open catalog. If you use ? instead of a file name, dBASE lists the names of all catalogs on the current directory, which are stored in a file named Catalog.CAT. If you don't specify a file name, the current catalog is closed.

SET CATALOG ON activates the current catalog and records the names of files created or opened with the CREATE, INDEX, MODIFY, COPY, IMPORT, JOIN, SORT, TOTAL, USE, SET FILTER TO FILE, SET FORMAT, and SET VIEW commands. When SET CATALOG is set to off, new file names are not recorded in the current catalog, but the catalog remains open.

If SET TITLE is on while a catalog is active, dBASE prompts you for a description of each newly created file.

Catalog files have a predefined file structure with the same features, such as field name, size, and type, as database (.DBF) files. You can open them with a USE command if you specify the .CAT extension with the file name. Once they are opened, you can LIST or BROWSE catalog files as you would any database file.

• EXAMPLE These commands create (or activate) a catalog named ARFiles.CAT:

```
SET CATALOG TO ARFiles
SET CATALOG ON
```

See Also SET TITLE

SET CENTURY

Displaying Centuries in Dates

• SYNTAX

```
SET CENTURY on/OFF
```

• USAGE By default, dBASE displays dates without the century (12/31/95 instead of 12/31/1995). However, when SET CENTURY is on, dBASE displays the century in all dates and requires the user to include the century in all new dates entered. When SET CENTURY is off and you enter new dates in mm/dd/yy format, the 20th century is assumed.

• EXAMPLE The following commands prompt the user for a date in the mm/dd/ccyy format:

```
SET CENTURY ON
NewDate = { / / }
@ 5,5 SAY "Enter date " GET NewDate
READ
```

See Also CTOD(), DATE(), DTOC(), DTOS(), SET DATE, YEAR()

SET CLOCK

Controlling the Clock Display

• SYNTAX

SET CLOCK on/OFF

or

SET CLOCK TO *(row,column)*

• USAGE SET CLOCK TO controls the screen position of the system clock. The default position for the clock is row 0, column 68 (0,68). SET CLOCK TO, without row and column coordinates, repositions the clock to the default position.

SET CLOCK OFF erases the clock from the screen. The default setting, SET CLOCK ON, displays the clock on the screen. If you want to change its display position, you should define its coordinates with the SET CLOCK TO command before turning the clock on.

The clock is always displayed in the upper-right corner during full-screen operations such as BROWSE and MODIFY, regardless of the SET CLOCK setting.

• EXAMPLE The following commands set the clock's position to the lower-left corner of the screen beneath the status bar, and display the clock:

```
SET STATUS ON
SET CLOCK TO 23,0
SET CLOCK ON
```

SET COLOR

Controlling Screen Colors

• SYNTAX

SET COLOR ON/OFF

or

SET COLOR TO *(standard) (,(enhanced) (,(perimeter) (,(background))))*

or

SET COLOR OF NORMAL/MESSAGES/TITLES/BOX/ HIGHLIGHT/INFORMATION/FIELDS TO *(color attribute)*

• USAGE

The SET COLOR ON/OFF command switches between color and monochrome monitors on systems that have both. The default setting is determined by the monitor active when dBASE is first started.

The SET COLOR TO command defines the basic screen color scheme. The *standard* option affects text displayed by commands such as ?, LIST, REPORT, and SAY. The *enhanced* option affects reverse-video displays, such as highlighted menu options, window borders, and prompts displayed by the @...GET command. The *perimeter* options affect the screen border, if the monitor has such a border. The *background* option applies only to color monitors that can't set the individual background colors for standard and enhanced display.

The color codes used with the SET COLOR command are listed in Table 3.1.

On monitors that allow you to set both foreground and background colors, you can specify these colors for the standard and enhanced displays, separating the codes with a slash. For example, the command

Table 3.1: SET COLOR Color Codes

Color	Code
Black	N
Blank	X
Blinking	*
Blue	B
Brown	GR or RG
Cyan	BG or GB
Gray	N+
Green	G
High intensity	+
Inverse	I (Monochrome only)
Magenta	RB or BR
Red	R
Underline	U (Monochrome only)
White	W or RGB
Yellow	GR+ or RG+

SET COLOR TO GR+/B,W/R

displays standard text as yellow letters on a blue background and displays enhanced text as white letters on a red background.

The * symbol for blinking and + character for high intensity apply only to the foreground display. Place them to the right of the color code. For example,

SET COLOR TO GR+*/B,W+/R

displays blinking yellow letters on a blue background for standard text, and bright white letters on a red background for enhanced text.

To make text invisible, as when a user is typing in a password, use the X color code.

The SET COLOR TO command, without additional parameters, resets the screen to the default black and white colors. Omitting a color code but including a comma retains the current color setting. For example,

```
SET COLOR TO ,,R
```

retains the current standard and enhanced text colors, but changes the perimeter color to red.

The SET COLOR OF command defines the color attributes of individual display areas. The color codes are the same as for the SET COLOR command. The areas of the screen that each SET COLOR OF command controls are summarized in Table 3.2.

To change the dBASE default color settings, you need to modify the Config.DB file (see Appendix A).

• EXAMPLE The first command that follows sets up a general color scheme of yellow letters on a blue background for standard text, bright white letters on a red background for enhanced (reverse-video) text, and a cyan border. The remaining commands set up additional color schemes for specific areas of the screen:

```
SET COLOR TO GR+/B,W+/R,BG
SET COLOR OF MESSAGES TO N/RB
SET COLOR OF TITLES TO W/B
SET COLOR OF BOX TO GR+/BG
SET COLOR OF FIELDS TO W+/G
```

See Also @, ISCOLOR(), SET DISPLAY, SET INTENSITY

Table 3.2: Screen Areas Controlled by SET COLOR OF Options

Option	Areas Controlled
NORMAL	Dot prompt screen
	@ SAY and @...TO output
	Box borders
	Design screen surfaces
MESSAGES	Message/navigation line text
	Unhighlighted menu options (bright)
	Shaded menu options (dim)
	Box interiors Control Center panels
TITLES	Help box headings
	Control Center titles
	Browse screen field names and grid
BOX	Menu borders
	Error message borders
	Labels design screen box borders
	File window border
	Prompt box borders
HIGHLIGHT	Highlighted menu and list selections
	Highlighted prompt box buttons
	Selected text on design screens
INFORMATION	Clock Status line
	Help box border
	Text, field, or box under cursor in design screens
FIELDS	Editable @...GET fields Selected field in BROWSE
	Prompt box data entry fields

SET CONFIRM

Determining Confirmation Requirements

• SYNTAX

SET CONFIRM on/OFF

• USAGE Normally, when you fill a field during data entry, dBASE automatically moves the cursor to the next field. However, if SET CONFIRM is on, you must press ↵ to complete the entry in one field and move to the next.

• EXAMPLE The following routine lets the user enter a **Y** or **N** character, but requires that the user also press ↵ after entering the character.

```
YesNo = .F.

SET CONFIRM ON

@ 23,1 SAY "Return to menu now? ";
  GET YesNo PICTURE "Y"
READ

SET CONFIRM OFF
```

SET CONSOLE

Enabling or Disabling Screen Display

• SYNTAX

SET CONSOLE ON/off

• USAGE SET CONSOLE turns the screen display off or on for commands other than @...SAY. You typically use it to display a message on the screen while another command, such as REPORT FORM, is sending output to the printer.

• EXAMPLE The following commands display the message *Press End to terminate report* and print a formatted report. The report is not displayed on the screen.

```
SET CONSOLE OFF
@ 2,2 SAY "Press End to terminate report"
REPORT FORM AnyRep WHILE INKEY() # 6 TO PRINTER
SET CONSOLE ON
```

SET CURRENCY TO

Formatting Currency Values

• SYNTAX

SET CURRENCY TO *(character)*

or

SET CURRENCY LEFT/right

• USAGE SET CURRENCY defines the character symbol displayed with the $ picture function. The default symbol is $. You can define up to nine characters as the currency symbol. To prevent multiple leading currency symbols, precede the symbol with a blank space.

For currency symbols that do not have an associated key on the keyboard, first type **SET CURRENCY TO "** and then press **Alt** while typing the three-digit ASCII code for the symbol you want. You must use the numeric keypad (not the numbers above the keyboard letters) when typing the numbers. Then release **Alt** and type the closing quotation mark. The ASCII codes for some common currency symbols are listed here:

Cent	155
Pound	156
Yen	157
Peseta	158
Franc	159

The SET CURRENCY LEFT/right command lets you determine whether the currency symbol appears to the left or right of the number.

• EXAMPLE The next commands display values in the Amount field in the format 12,345.67 ¥:

```
SET CURRENCY TO "(press Alt-157)"
SET CURRENCY RIGHT
LIST TRANSFORM (Amount,"@$ 999,999.99")
```

See Also @, SET POINT, SET SEPARATOR, TRANSFORM()

SET CURSOR

Displaying or Hiding Cursor

• SYNTAX

```
SET CURSOR ON / off
```

• USAGE The SET CURSOR command is used to hide, or by default, display the cursor.

• EXAMPLE The following example hides the cursor.

```
SET CURSOR OFF
```

SET DATE

Determining Date Format

• SYNTAX

SET DATE (TO) AMERICAN/ansi/british/french/german/ italian/japan/usa/mdy/dmy/ymd

• USAGE Regardless of the format used to enter a date, the SET DATE command will display all dates in the specified format. The available date formats are shown in Table 3.3. The century prefix is displayed if SET CENTURY is on.

Table 3.3: Available SET DATE Formats

Setting	Format
AMERICAN	mm/dd/yy
ANSI	yy.mm.dd
BRITISH	dd/mm/yy
FRENCH	dd/mm/yy
GERMAN	dd.mm.yy
ITALIAN	dd-mm-yy
JAPAN	yy/mm/dd
USA	mm-dd-yy
MDY	mm/dd/yy
DMY	dd/mm/yy
YMD	yy/mm/dd

• EXAMPLE To enter and display dates in Japanese format, enter this command:

```
SET DATE TO JAPAN
```

See Also DATE(), DMY(), MDY(), SET CENTURY

SET DBTRAP

Protecting against Program Errors

• SYNTAX

SET DBTRAP ON/off

• USAGE SET DBTRAP protects against program errors when one routine is interrupted to execute another, such as a user-defined function or an interrupt routine (a procedure called by an ON command).

When this setting is on, dBASE monitors the interrupt routine and prevents the execution of commands that might alter the environment or the files. You cannot use any command in a user-defined function or interrupt routine that alters the existing environment or causes any recursive full-screen operations.

With DBTRAP set off, there is very little restriction on commands you can include in a user-defined function or ON routine. You must be sure to restore the environment to its original status before returning to the calling program.

• EXAMPLE The command

```
SET DBTRAP OFF
ON ERROR DO ErrTrap
```

will remove most of the restrictions on the commands contained in the procedure ErrTrap called by the ON ERROR command.

See Also FUNCTION, ON ERROR, ON ESCAPE, ON KEY

SET DEBUG

Echoing Command File Execution on the Printer

• SYNTAX

```
SET DEBUG on/OFF
```

• USAGE When SET DEBUG and SET ECHO are on, the output of the SET ECHO command is directed to the printer rather than the screen. SET DEBUG is helpful for locating errors in programs.

• EXAMPLE To print the progress of program execution on the printer while debugging a command file named MyProg.PRG, enter these commands:

```
SET ECHO ON

SET DEBUG ON
DO MyProg
```

See Also DEBUG, SET ECHO, SET PRINTER, SET TALK, SET TRAP

SET DECIMALS

Determining the Number of Decimal Places to Display

• SYNTAX

SET DECIMALS TO *number*

• USAGE SET DECIMALS determines the number of decimal places to be displayed in calculation results and in the output of all mathematical, financial, and trigonometric functions. SET DECIMALS has no effect on the accuracy of the results. The maximum number of decimal places is 18, the minimum is 0, and the default is 2.

• EXAMPLE The next commands demonstrate the output of the command

```
? PI()
```

with the default number of decimal places and with DECIMALS set to 18:

```
? PI()
        3.14
SET DECIMALS TO 18
? PI()
        3.141592653589793116
```

See Also ROUND(), SET PRECISION

SET DEFAULT

Specifying the Default Disk Drive

• SYNTAX

SET DEFAULT TO *(drive (:))*

• USAGE Use the SET DEFAULT command to change the drive used for reading and writing files. SET DEFAULT does not affect subdirectories. Once the new default disk drive has been specified, all operations will take place there, and all saved files will be stored there unless otherwise directed.

With no drive specified, SET DEFAULT TO restores the default to the startup default drive.

• **EXAMPLE** The following command opens a file named MyFile.DBF on drive B:

```
SET DEFAULT TO B
USE MyFile
```

See Also SET DIRECTORY, SET PATH

SET DELETED

Hiding or Displaying Deleted Records

• **SYNTAX**

```
SET DELETED on/OFF
```

• **USAGE** When SET DELETED is off, records marked for deletion are displayed by all commands. When SET DELETED is on, records marked for deletion are hidden, both from view and from operations like CALCULATE, COPY, and REPLACE.

The GOTO command and commands that use the RECORD scope will position the record pointer to a marked record even if SET DELETED is on.

The commands INDEX and REINDEX include records that are marked for deletion even when SET DELETED is on.

Note that RECALL ALL, RECALL FOR, and RECALL WHILE will not unmark any records if SET DELETED is on, because the marked records are not accessible.

• **EXAMPLE** The following commands exclude records marked for deletion from the COPY command:

```
SET DELETED ON
COPY TO NewBak
```

See Also DELETE, DELETED(), PACK, RECALL, SET FILTER

SET DELIMITERS

Changing, Hiding, or Displaying Delimiters

• SYNTAX

SET DELIMITERS TO *(characters/***DEFAULT***)*

or

SET DELIMITERS on/OFF

• USAGE SET DELIMITERS TO defines the characters that mark the data entry and editing fields. You can specify either one or two characters in the SET DELIMITERS command. If you specify only one character, that character is used on both ends of the field display. If you enter two characters, the first represents the delimiter on the left end and the second represents the delimiter on the right end. The default delimiter is the colon (:).

SET DELIMITERS on/OFF determines whether delimiters are displayed with full-screen operations such as APPEND, EDIT, and READ. The default value, OFF, prevents delimiters from being displayed.

• EXAMPLE The following commands enclose all data-entry fields in square brackets when you issue an APPEND or EDIT command:

```
SET DELIMITERS TO "()"
SET DELIMITERS ON
```

See Also @, SET INTENSITY

SET DESIGN

Controlling Access to Design Screens

• SYNTAX

SET DESIGN ON/off

• USAGE SET DESIGN allows you to determine whether users can access the database, queries, forms, reports, labels, and applications design screens. When SET DESIGN is off, the design screens are inaccessible; the Control Center's Design key (Shift-F2) and all CREATE/MODIFY menu commands are inactivated.

If you modify the Config.DB file so that SET DESIGN is off, you can use the Control Center as the primary user interface for an application and prevent the user from accessing the design mode.

• EXAMPLE The MODIFY REPORT command below returns the message *File cannot be modified because DESIGN mode is set to OFF*:

```
SET DESIGN OFF
MODIFY REPORT YearEnd
```

See Also SET DEVELOPMENT

SET DEVELOPMENT

Preventing Use of Outdated Programs

• SYNTAX

SET DEVELOPMENT ON/off

• USAGE SET DEVELOPMENT determines whether or not dBASE needs to compile new or modified source code before executing it. When SET DEVELOPMENT is on and you execute a DO, SET FORMAT, or SET PROCEDURE command, dBASE compares the creation dates, if any, for the source (.PRG) and compiled (.DBO) file. If the compiled file is older than the source-code file, dBASE recompiles the source before executing it.

If SET DEVELOPMENT is off, dBASE IV does not compare creation dates and times, and executes the existing object file regardless of changes made to the source. To create new object files in this situation, you need to use the COMPILE command.

See Also COMPILE, DO, MODIFY COMMAND, SET PROCEDURE

SET DEVICE

Channeling @...SAY Output

• SYNTAX

SET DEVICE TO SCREEN/Printer/file *file name*

• USAGE When SET DEVICE is set to its default setting, SCREEN, output from @...SAY...GET commands is displayed on the screen only.

SET DEVICE TO PRINTER channels all @...SAY output to the printer. GETs are ignored in printed output. If an @ command specifies a row above the current row, dBASE ejects the page and prints the text on the appropriate row of the next page. On some printers, you may need to issue an EJECT command after channeling output to see the last page of the printed text.

SET DEVICE TO FILE, followed by a file name, channels @...SAY output to the named file. If you don't specify an extension, the file receives the .TXT extension. As with the PRINTER option, GETs are ignored, and attempting to print on a row above the current row places a form feed (Ctrl-L) in the file and displays text on the appropriate row beneath the form feed.

The text file created by SET DEVICE TO FILE is closed when you use SET DEVICE TO SCREEN or SET DEVICE TO PRINTER. You can access the text file with the TYPE or MODIFY COMMAND/FILE command.

• EXAMPLE To store a text image of the custom screen named CustForm to a file named Fig1-1.TXT, enter these commands:

USE CustList
SET DEVICE TO FILE Fig1-1
SET FORMAT TO CustForm
READ
(press Esc)
SET DEVICE TO SCREEN

You will have only the text portions of the custom screen in the file; boxes and lines are not stored.

See Also @, EJECT, SET FORMAT, SET PRINTER

SET DIRECTORY

Set Directory Path

• SYNTAX

SET DIRECTORY TO *((drive:) (path))*

• USAGE The SET DIRECTORY command is used to specify the operating system's current drive and directory. If no path is defined, the default startup path is used.

• EXAMPLE The following example sets the directory to the Sales directory on drive D:

SET DIRECTORY TO d:\sales

See Also SET PATH, SET DEFAULT, DIR

SET DISPLAY

Selecting a Monitor

• SYNTAX

SET DISPLAY TO MONO/COLOR/EGA25/EGA43/ MONO43/VGA25/VGA43/VGA50

• USAGE The SET DISPLAY command changes the display settings for the type of monitor in use. The command selects between monochrome and color monitors, and specifes the number of lines to display on the screen: 25, 43, or 50 lines. Its default setting is determined during installation and stored in the Config.DB file. Options are

MONO	Monochrome
COLOR	Color (CGA)
EGA25	EGA, 25 lines
EGA43	EGA, 43 lines
MONO43	Monochrome, 43 lines
VGA25	VGA, 25 lines
VGA43	VGA, 43 lines
VGA50	VGA, 50 lines

If you SET DISPLAY to a monitor not in your system, dBASE will display an error message.

• EXAMPLE The next command sets the monitor display to 43 lines with a VGA display:

```
SET DISPLAY TO VGA43
```

See Also Config.DB, SET COLOR OF, SET COLOR TO

SET DOHISTORY

Providing dBASE III PLUS Compatibility

• SYNTAX

```
SET DOHISTORY on/OFF
```

• USAGE dBASE IV includes SET DOHISTORY for compatibility with dBASE III PLUS. The command does nothing in dBASE IV.

See Also DEBUG

SET ECHO

Displaying Command File Execution

• SYNTAX

```
SET ECHO on/OFF
```

• USAGE When SET ECHO is on, command lines from the currently running program are displayed on the screen as they execute. If SET DEBUG is on, the output is sent to the printer. You can use this command while debugging.

• EXAMPLE The commands that follow print program command lines as the MyProg.PRG command file is executed:

```
SET ECHO ON
SET DEBUG ON
DO MyProg
SET DEBUG OFF
SET ECHO OFF
```

See Also DEBUG, SET DEBUG, SET PRINTER, SET STEP, SET TALK, SET TRAP

SET ENCRYPTION

Enabling or Disabling File Encryption

• SYNTAX

SET ENCRYPTION ON/off

• USAGE SET ENCRYPTION determines whether or not the files of a newly created or copied database are encrypted. It also applies to copied database files created with COPY, JOIN, or TOTAL. After you have used PROTECT to set up a security scheme, SET ENCRYPTION defaults to ON, and all new files in the database are automatically encrypted so that users who do not have appropriate access levels cannot view the data. Users who log in with an appropriate access level (via the log-in name, group name, and password) will have access to the file in decrypted form. Without PROTECT, SET ENCRYPTION has no effect.

To create a decrypted copy of a file for a single-user system or for storage on a floppy disk as a backup file, use the SET ENCRYPTION OFF command before copying the file. Only users who have complete access to all database records and fields (as defined in the user profile through the PROTECT program) will be able to make exact copies of files in decrypted form. A user who has no access to certain fields cannot produce a decrypted file containing those fields.

• EXAMPLE The following routine makes a decrypted backup copy of a database file, assuming that the user has an access level of 1 or 2. The backup copy is stored on the disk in drive A.

```
IF ACCESS() <= 2
  USE Master
  SET ENCRYPTION OFF
```

```
  COPY TO A:Master
  SET ENCRYPTION ON
ENDIF
```

See Also PROTECT

SET ESCAPE

Enabling or Disabling the Escape Key

• SYNTAX

```
SET ESCAPE ON/off
```

• USAGE SET ESCAPE determines whether the Escape key interrupts processing and whether Ctrl-S stops scrolling of data on the screen. If you press **Esc** while a program is running and SET ESCAPE is on, program execution is aborted.

If SET ESCAPE is off, pressing **Esc** does not interrupt program execution. Be sure to use this option only in programs that are fully debugged. Otherwise, the only way to abort a faulty program is to reboot by pressing **Ctrl-Alt-Del**, which can lead to data loss.

When SET ESCAPE is off, you can not stop scrolling by pressing Ctrl-S, and INKEY() can not record the ESC or Ctrl-S keys.

• EXAMPLE The command

```
SET ESCAPE OFF
```

near the top of an application program prevents the user from interrupting processing by pressing **Esc**.

See Also ON ERROR, ON ESCAPE, INKEY(), READKEY()

SET EXACT

Specifying Character String Matching

• SYNTAX

SET EXACT on/OFF

• USAGE SET EXACT determines how a comparison between two character expressions is evaluated. When SET EXACT is on, the two strings must be the same length and match exactly, character-for-character. When SET EXACT is off, only the first characters of a string must match a shorter string.

SET EXACT affects all character string processing, including the SEEK, FIND, SET RELATION, and SET FILTER commands.

• EXAMPLE When SET EXACT is off, the command

```
LIST FOR FirstName = "Mary"
```

will display Mary, MaryAnn, MaryAnne, Mary Anne, and any other names that begin with the letters "Mary."

When you set SET EXACT on, only character-for-character matches are displayed. Therefore, the command

```
LIST FOR FirstName = "Mary"
```

displays only Mary.

The following commands list all part numbers that begin with the letters "CD":

```
USE Master ORDER PartNo
SET EXACT OFF
SEEK "CD"
LIST WHILE PartNo = "CD"
```

See Also LEFT(), SUBSTR(), TRIM()

SET EXCLUSIVE

Opening a Database File for Exclusive Use

• SYNTAX

SET EXCLUSIVE ON/off

• USAGE SET EXCLUSIVE establishes the file-open attribute for all ensuing USE commands. When SET EXCLUSIVE is on, all opened files can be viewed and changed only by the user who opened the files. When SET EXCLUSIVE is off, the database file is opened in shared mode, and other users in the network will have access to the same database file.

• EXAMPLE The following commands open the Master database for shared use by any user on the network:

```
SET EXCLUSIVE OFF
USE Master ORDER PartNo
```

See Also PROTECT, SET ENCRYPTION, USE

SET FIELDS

Isolating Database Fields

• SYNTAX

SET FIELDS on/OFF

or

SET FIELDS TO *(field name (/**R**)/calculated field)*
*(,field name (/**R**)/calculated field...)*

or

SET FIELDS TO ALL (LIKE/EXCEPT *skeleton)*

• **USAGE** The SET FIELDS TO command specifies the names of fields to access in the current database. Each field name must be separated by a comma. You can place the /R option after a field name to make the field read-only. Be sure to include the slash mark, or the option will not work correctly.

To include a calculated field in a field list, enter a unique name followed by an expression that calculates a result. Calculated fields are always read-only.

You can also specify a group of field names using the ALL or EXCEPT option with a skeletal field name, where ? stands for any single character and * stands for any group of characters.

Consecutive SET FIELDS TO commands are additive. That is, if first the command SET FIELDS TO PartNo is executed, followed by the command SET FIELDS TO PartName, the available fields are PartNo and PartName. SET FIELDS TO ALL provides access to all fields in the database.

If multiple related database files are open and you wish to display a field from the nonselected database, you must include an alias with the field name.

The field list specified in the SET FIELDS TO command is active only while the SET FIELDS command is on. With SET FIELDS OFF, all fields in the current database are accessible again.

While a SET FIELDS TO list is in effect, the following commands hide all fields that are not included in the list: APPEND, AVERAGE, BLANK, BROWSE, CALCULATE, CHANGE, COPY STRUCTURE, COPY TO, CREATE VIEW FROM ENVIRONMENT, DISPLAY, EDIT, EXPORT, JOIN, LIST, SUM, and TOTAL. The DISPLAY/LIST STRUCTURE command lists active fields with a > symbol to the left of the field name.

• **EXAMPLE** This command hides fields whose names begin with the letters "Priv":

SET FIELDS TO ALL EXCEPT Priv*

The next commands open the Orders and Master databases, set up a relationship based on the common PartNo field, and display the PartNo and Qty fields from the Orders database and related PartName and SelPrice fields from the Master database. PartName is included as read-only. An extended price is also displayed using the Qty field from the Orders database and the SelPrice field from the Master database. The fields are then displayed on a Browse screen:

```
USE Orders IN 1
USE Master ORDER PartNo IN 2
SELECT 1
SET RELATION TO PartNo INTO Master

SET FIELDS TO PartNo, Master->PartName /R, ;
              Qty, Master->SelPrice, ;
              ExtPrince = Qty * Master->SelPrice

SET FIELDS ON
BROWSE
```

See Also CLEAR, CREATE/MODIFY VIEW, FLDLIST(), SET RELATION, SET SKIP, SET VIEW

SET FILTER

Specifying Records to Hide

• SYNTAX

SET FILTER TO *(condition)*/(**FILE** *file name*/**?**)

• USAGE SET FILTER hides records that do not match a specified condition. If a condition is given, the SET FILTER command will mask the database, showing only records that meet the condition. SET FILTER applies only to the database file open in the work area where you issue the command. If several database files are open simultaneously, you can set a separate filter for each work area.

Whenever you issue a SET FILTER TO command, you must enter a GO TOP, GO BOTTOM, or SKIP command to move the record pointer and activate the filter.

SET FILTER TO FILE *file name* reads the filter condition from a dBASE III PLUS query (.QRY) file. However, you cannot modify a dBASE III PLUS .QRY file in dBASE IV. To perform a similar operation using a dBASE IV query (.QBE or .QBO) file created in the queries design screen, use the SET VIEW command rather than SET FILTER TO FILE.

Specifying SET FILTER TO without a condition turns off the filter on the active database (including a filter imposed by a SET VIEW command) and makes all records accessible.

• **EXAMPLE** The following command limits future operations on the Sales.DBF database to records that have 10,000 or greater in the Commission field, and a June date in the DateSold field:

```
USE Sales
SET FILTER TO Commission >= 10000 .AND. ;
        Month(DateSold) = 6

GO TOP   && Move the record pointer.
```

Tip: When you are working with a one-to-many relationship between parent and child files, using SET KEY TO to link the files is more efficient than SET FILTER. With SET FILTER, the entire child index is searched, while with SET KEY, dBASE limits the search in the child table to the records whose key field matches the range specifications.

See Also CREATE/MODIFY QUERY, SET DELETED, SET KEY, SET VIEW

SET FIXED

Providing dBASE III PLUS Compatibility

• SYNTAX

SET FIXED on/OFF

• USAGE SET FIXED provides compatibility with dBASE III PLUS. The dBASE IV command SET DECIMALS automatically sets FIXED on, so SET FIXED serves no purpose in dBASE IV.

See Also SET DECIMALS

SET FORMAT

Selecting a Custom Form

• SYNTAX

SET FORMAT TO (file name/**?**)

• USAGE SET FORMAT opens an existing format file containing a custom form. Once a format file is opened, all APPEND, EDIT, READ, CHANGE, and INSERT commands use the form specified in the format file, rather than the simpler default screens these commands usually generate. If you use SET FORMAT with a BROWSE command, all the custom features, such as templates, pictures, and edit options, are used except for the row and column coordinates. BROWSE still displays data in a spreadsheet arrangement.

Once opened, a format file stays in effect until you issue either a CLOSE FORMAT or a SET FORMAT command with a different file name or no file name.

If the format file consists of several pages (screens), pressing the PgUp and PgDn keys will scroll through the pages before they display the next (or previous) record in the database. Note that each page in a format file must be separated by a READ command to store the entered data and clear the GET fields. Furthermore, multiple-page forms work only in format files opened with the SET FORMAT command.

You can open one format file in each work area. A CLOSE FORMAT command closes the format file in the current work area only.

Use CREATE/MODIFY SCREEN to create or edit a format file.

• EXAMPLE Assuming that you've already created a format file named MailScrn.FMT (using the MODIFY SCREEN command or a text editor), the following commands open the Mail database and the MailScrn format files and use the custom form to add new records to the Mail database:

```
USE Mail
SET FORMAT TO MailScrn
APPEND

CLOSE FORMAT
```

See Also @, APPEND, CLOSE, CREATE/MODIFY SCREEN, EDIT, READ, SET DEVICE

SET FULLPATH

Providing dBASE III PLUS Compatibility

• SYNTAX

SET FULLPATH on/OFF

• USAGE The SET FULLPATH command provides compatibility between dBASE III PLUS and dBASE IV programs by suppressing directory names when you use functions such as

CATALOG(), MDX(), NDX(), and DBF(). When SET FULLPATH is on, the full DOS path is returned along with the file name.

• **EXAMPLE** Include the next command at the top of the highest level program written in dBASE III PLUS before running it with dBASE IV:

```
SET FULLPATH ON
```

SET FUNCTION

Programming the Function Keys

• **SYNTAX**

SET FUNCTION *number/key label name* **TO** *string*

• **USAGE** SET FUNCTION allows you to reprogram function keys to type a character expression of up to 254 characters. The character expression represents one or more dBASE commands.

The first expression identifies the function key, and can be a number from 2 to 29 (for example, 2, representing F2) or a key label name (see the **ON KEY** command for a list of key label names).

The *string* expression is the exact sequence of characters to be typed when the user presses the function key. You can place a semicolon anywhere in the string where you want the function key to press ↵. The string must be enclosed in quotation marks.

The programmable function keys are F2 through F10 (numbered 2 through 9), Shift-F1 through Shift-F9 (11 through 19), and Ctrl-F1 through Ctrl-F10 (20 through 29). The F1, Shift-F10, F11, F12, and Alt-key combinations are not programmable.

If both an ON KEY and a SET FUNCTION command assign an action to the same key, ON KEY takes precedence.

The DISPLAY/LIST STATUS command displays the current function key definitions.

• EXAMPLE The next command programs the Shift-F1 function key to enter the commands CLOSE PROCEDURE and CLEAR ALL at the dot prompt:

```
SET FUNCTION Shift-F1 TO "CLOSE
   PROCEDURE;CLEAR ALL;"
```

Notice the semicolons in this example represent pressing ↵ to indicate the end of the command.

You would accomplish the same thing using the number **11** in place of the key label **Shift-F1**.

See Also FKLABEL(), FKMAX(), ON KEY

SET HEADINGS

Displaying Field Names

• SYNTAX

```
SET HEADINGS ON/off
```

• USAGE Normally, the commands DISPLAY, LIST, SUM, AVERAGE, and CALCULATE display a column title for each displayed field, memory variable, or expression. When SET HEADINGS is off, the column titles are not displayed.

• EXAMPLE In the following example, the LIST command displays data but no field names:

```
SET HEADINGS OFF
LIST
```

SET HELP

Activating or Deactivating Immediate Help

• SYNTAX

SET HELP ON/off

• USAGE Usually, when you enter an invalid command at the dot prompt, the error box displays the options *Cancel*, *Edit*, and *Help*. Select **Help**, and the help window displays the syntax and a brief description of the command.

After a SET HELP OFF command, only the *Cancel* and *Edit* options are available in the error box.

See Also HELP, SET INSTRUCT

SET HISTORY

Managing the Dot Prompt History Buffer

• SYNTAX

SET HISTORY ON/off

or

SET HISTORY TO *number*

• USAGE When SET HISTORY is on, you can recall commands that have been entered at the dot prompt by pressing ↑ and ↓. You can use ←, ↓, **Ins**, and **Del** to edit the command currently at the dot prompt, and then press ↵ to execute it.

By default, dBASE stores only the last 20 commands entered in its history file. You can use the SET HISTORY TO command to select any value from 0 to 16,000.

• **EXAMPLE** The following commands set the length of the history buffer to 40 lines and activate it:

```
SET HISTORY TO 40
SET HISTORY ON
```

See Also LIST HISTORY

SET HOURS

Controlling the Time Display

• **SYNTAX**

```
SET HOURS TO (12/24)
```

• **USAGE** By default, dBASE displays the system clock using a 12-hour clock (for instance, 7:30:00 PM). You can change this to a 24-hour clock (7:30:00 PM would be displayed as 19:30:00).

• **EXAMPLE** To set the time display to a 24-hour clock, enter the command:

```
SET HOURS TO 24
```

See Also SET CLOCK, TIME()

SET IBLOCK

Controlling Index Block Size

• SYNTAX

SET IBLOCK *number*

• USAGE SET IBLOCK lets you change the default block size for new index (.MDX) files. The default is 2 units of 512 bytes each, or 1024 bytes. You can set the block size to between 1 unit (512 bytes) and 63 units (32,356 bytes). The index block must be at least 1024 bytes, so if you specify 1, dBASE will default to 2.

If the block size is smaller, less disk space is used but more blocks are needed to store the whole index file. A larger block size reduces the number of physical disk accesses needed to read the whole index file.

SET BLOCKSIZE allows you to specify the same block size for memo and index files. Use SET IBLOCK and SET MBLOCK to specify different block sizes.

• EXAMPLE SET IBLOCK is used to specify the size of new index blocks, but you can change existing index files by copying the database file to a temporary file and creating a new production index file for it. Then copy the file back to the original file. The commands below illustrate this technique:

```
USE Orders
SET IBLOCK TO 8
*----- Copy Orders to TempOrd and create a new .MDX
*----- file
COPY TO TempOrd WITH PRODUCTION
USE TempOrd
SET SAFETY OFF
*----- Copy back to Orders with new block size.
COPY TO Orders WITH PRODUCTION
SET SAFETY ON
*----- Close open work area and delete temporary files.
```

```
USE
ERASE TempOrd.DBF
ERASE TempOrd.MDX
```

See Also SET MBLOCK, SET(), SET BLOCKSIZE

SET INDEX

Activating or Deactivating Index Files

• SYNTAX

SET INDEX TO *(?/file names) (***ORDER** *.ndx file name)*

or

SET INDEX TO *(file names) (***ORDER** *.mdx tag (***OF** *.mdx file name))*

• USAGE SET INDEX activates the list of index (.NDX and .MDX) files for the currently open database file and specifies the controlling order.

The index file listed first in a USE or a SET INDEX TO command is the master index, which determines the sort order of the records in the database. The master index is the only index file that you can search with a SEEK or FIND command. All active index files are updated automatically when data items are changed in the database file.

The ORDER option is used to change the controlling .NDX index file or .MDX index tag. If the desired tag is in a multiple index file other than the production index, use the OF option with the .MDX file name.

SET INDEX TO by itself, like the CLOSE INDEX command, closes all index files for the given database except the production index..

To copy a dBASE III PLUS .NDX index file to a dBASE IV multiple (.MDX) index file, use COPY INDEXES.

● **EXAMPLE** The following commands open the mail database file and its production index file. They then open NameOrd.NDX and ZipOrd.NDX index files that are to be updated automatically whenever information is added to, changed in, or deleted from the Mail database. The production index tag, LastName, determines the sort order and is the only index file that you can search with SEEK or FIND.

```
USE Mail
SET INDEX TO NameOrd,ZipOrd ORDER LastName
```

See Also CLOSE, COPY INDEXES, DELETE TAG, INDEX, KEY(), MDX(), NDX(), ORDER(), REINDEX, SET ORDER, TAG(), USE

SET INSTRUCT

Managing Control Center Prompt Boxes

● **SYNTAX**

```
SET INSTRUCT ON/off
```

● **USAGE** When SET INSTRUCT is on, a prompt box containing action options appears on the screen whenever you select a file name from the Control Center. When SET INSTRUCT is off, prompt boxes are not displayed. If SET TALK is on and SET INSTRUCT is off, dBASE code generated by the labels, reports, or forms designer is displayed.

● **EXAMPLE** If you develop an application that the user can execute from the Control Center, include the following command near the end of the main program to restore the instruct mode before returning to the Control Center:

```
SET INSTRUCT ON
```

SET INTENSITY

Activating or Deactivating Inverse Video

• SYNTAX

SET INTENSITY ON/off

• USAGE When SET INTENSITY is on, dBASE displays @...SAY text in the standard screen colors and @...GET prompts in inverse video. If SET INTENSITY is off, both @...SAY and @...GET display in standard screen colors.

You can use the SET DELIMITERS command to make @...GET fields more visible when SET INTENSITY is off.

• EXAMPLE The following commands allow the user to enter records through a custom screen named CustScre. Entry fields are not displayed in inverse video, but instead are displayed with bracket delimiters.

```
USE AnyFile INDEX AnyIndex
SET FORMAT TO CustScre
SET DELIMITERS TO "( )"
SET DELIMITERS ON
SET INTENSITY OFF
APPEND
```

See Also SET COLOR, SET DELIMITERS, SET DISPLAY

SET KEY

Displaying Selected Records

• SYNTAX

SET KEY TO *(string)(***IN** *alias)*

or

SET KEY TO RANGE *low value, high value/low value (,)/,high value (***IN** *alias)*

• USAGE SET KEY TO is used to filter records to be displayed. dBASE displays only those records whose controlling index key matches the specified range of values or conditions. The specified values must be of the same data type as the controlling index key.

You can select records that are:

- Exact matches
- In the range between low and high values
- Equal to or above a minimum value
- Equal to or below a maximum value

To find exact matches in the index, use SET KEY TO with an expression. To select records in a range, use the RANGE option with low and high values of the key expression. Separate the values with a comma.

To find records equal to or above a certain key value, use SET KEY TO RANGE, followed by the minimum value. To select records equal to or below a certain key value, use SET KEY TO RANGE, followed by a comma and the maximum value. In order for dBASE to distinguish between low and high single values, if the value is intended to be the high value, it must be preceded by a comma.

The IN option lets you select records from another work area.

SET KEY TO with no values turns off the currently active filter range.

Using SET KEY TO when working with one-to-many related files can speed up processing. dBASE limits the search of the child ("many") table to the block of records that satisfy the specified condition, instead of searching the whole index.

• EXAMPLE To display orders in the Orders database file that were placed on June 1, 1994:

```
USE Orders ORDER OrdDate
SET KEY TO {06/01/94}
DISPLAY ALL
```

To display orders placed on or after June 1, 1994:

```
SET KEY TO RANGE {06/01/94}
```

To display orders placed on or before June 1, 1994:

```
SET KEY TO RANGE ,{06/01/94}
```

To display orders placed during the year 1994:

```
SET KEY TO RANGE {01/01/94},{12/31/94}
```

See Also INDEX, KEY(), MDX(), NDX(), SET FILTER, TAG()

SET LDCHECK

Detecting Language Driver Conflicts

• SYNTAX

```
SET LDCHECK ON/off
```

• USAGE Language drivers contain information about the character set and sorting rules that dBASE uses. If you are working with files created with a different dBASE configuration or with different international versions, there may be some conflicts between language drivers.

If you SET LDCHECK on, dBASE checks for conflicts and warns you if any are encountered.

With SET LDCHECK off, language checking is disabled.

• EXAMPLE You can use SET LDCHECK to warn the user that the database file just opened was created using a different language driver. The user may then take corrective action, such as reindexing the file, or continue.

The commands:

```
SET LDCHECK ON
USE IntlCust
SET LDCHECK OFF
```

turn on the language driver checking feature before opening the file name IntlCust. After the user responds to any warning, SET LDCHECK is turned off.

See Also SET()

SET LIBRARY

Accessing Procedures and Functions

• SYNTAX

SET LIBRARY TO *(file name)*

• USAGE Collections of procedures and user-defined functions created for an application can be stored together in a library, much the same as in a procedure file. To open the library for access to the procedures and functions, use SET LIBRARY TO with the library name.

If an active procedure file contains a procedure or user-defined function with the same name as one in the active library, the one in the procedure file takes precedence. dBASE looks for the procedure in the procedure file first and then, if it is not there, looks in the library.

To close the library again, use SET LIBRARY TO with no file name.

• EXAMPLE You have created several procedures and user-defined functions for a sales application and have saved them in a library called SalesLib.PRG. The command:

```
SET LIBRARY TO SalesLib
```

opens the library and

```
SET LIBRARY TO
```

closes it again.

See Also SET PROCEDURE

SET LOCK

Controlling Automatic File Locking

• SYNTAX

```
SET LOCK ON/off
```

• USAGE SET LOCK controls automatic file locking in multi-user operations. When SET LOCK is on, dBASE automatically locks files and records as necessary to prevent several users from editing the same data simultaneously. When one user has locked a file or record, other users can view it but cannot make changes to it. As soon as a user is finished making changes, the file or record is unlocked and other users have full read/write access.

SET LOCK OFF disables automatic file locking for the AVERAGE, CALCULATE, COUNT, LABEL FORM, SUM, and REPORT FORM commands. It also disables locking during the read phase of the COPY INDEX, COPY STRUCTURE, COPY TAG, INDEX, JOIN, SORT, and TOTAL commands, but locks the file as data is being written to it. When you disable automatic record locking, the accuracy of printed data or the results of calculations cannot be guaranteed.

• **EXAMPLE** The following commands perform calculations on the Orders database without locking the file:

```
USE Orders
SET LOCK OFF

CALCULATE SUM(Qty),SUM(Qty*UnitPrice) ;
  TO TotQty,TotSale
```

See Also FLOCK(), NETWORK(), RLOCK(), SET EXCLUSIVE

SET MARGIN

Setting the Printer Left Margin

• **SYNTAX**

SET MARGIN TO *number*

• **USAGE** SET MARGIN adjusts the left margin for all printed output. The default value for the printer margin offset is 0. The SET MARGIN command lets you reset this margin to any number of spaces. SET MARGIN has no effect on video display.

The width you specify in the SET MARGIN command is stored in the _ploffset system memory variable. If you change the value of _ploffset after issuing a SET MARGIN command or print a report that modifies _ploffset, the margin specified in _ploffset will cancel the SET MARGIN setting.

• EXAMPLE If your printer prints ten characters per inch, and you want a 1″ margin at the left of printed output, enter this command:

```
SET MARGIN TO 10
```

See Also PRINTJOB...ENDPRINTJOB, SET PRINTER

SET MARK

Changing the Date Delimiter

• SYNTAX

SET MARK TO *(character)*

• USAGE SET MARK TO defines the delimiter used to separate the month, day, and year in date displays. The default delimiter is determined by the SET DATE command and the country specified when you installed dBASE IV.

If there is no character setting, SET MARK TO restores the default delimiter.

• EXAMPLE The following commands display American dates in the format mm.dd.yy:

```
SET MARK TO "."
```

See Also DATE(), DMY(), MDY(), SET CENTURY, SET DATE

SET MBLOCK

Changing Memo File Block Size

• SYNTAX

SET MBLOCK TO *number*

• USAGE SET MBLOCK lets you change the block size for new memo (.DBT) files. The default is 8 units of 64 bytes each or 512 bytes. You can set the block size to between 1 unit (64 bytes) and 511 units (32,704 bytes). One character takes one byte of disk space.

dBASE reads, writes, and stores memo fields in whole blocks, no matter what size the actual memo is. You can save disk space by setting the memo block to the expected size of the actual memo text plus a little extra space to allow for editing. If a memo exceeds the block size, dBASE uses more than one block for that memo.

SET MBLOCK is similar to SET BLOCKSIZE except that it applies only to memo files, while SET BLOCKSIZE applies to both memo and index files alike. SET MBLOCK also lets you specify smaller block increments (64 bytes each) than SET BLOCKSIZE (512 bytes each).

• EXAMPLE The Notes memo field in the new CustList database file is expected to contain approximately three lines of text, about 180 characters. The optimal memo block size would be approximately 250 characters, leaving room for 70 more characters. The command:

SET MBLOCK TO 4

establishes the memo block size of 256 characters (4 units of 64 bytes each).

Although SET MBLOCK TO is intended for new memo files, you can change the block size of an existing memo file by copying the file to a temporary file, thus creating a new memo file, then copying it back to the original. The commands below reduce the memo block size of CustList.DBT file to 64 characters:

```
USE CustList
SET MBLOCK TO 1
*----- Copy to a temporary file and ceate a new
*----- .MDX file
*----- The .DBT file is copied automatically
COPY TO CustTemp WITH PRODUCTION
USE CustTemp
SET SAFETY OFF
*----- Copy back to the original file
COPY TO CustList WITH PRODUCTION
SET SAFETY ON
*----- Close work area and erase temporary files
USE
ERASE CustTemp.DBF
ERASE CustTemp.MDX
ERASE CustTemp.DBT
```

See Also SET(), SET BLOCKSIZE, SET IBLOCK

SET MEMOWIDTH

Setting Memo Field Widths

• SYNTAX

SET MEMOWIDTH TO *number*

• USAGE The default width for memo field displays is 50 characters. You can use the SET MEMOWIDTH command to alter this width to any value between 8 and 255. Memo fields will be word wrapped within the specified width. SET MEMOWIDTH affects only LIST and DISPLAY commands and does not affect column or template widths defined in the reports design screen.

If a ? command uses the V (vertical stretch) picture function with a defined width, the width specified in the picture function overrides the SET MEMOWIDTH setting. If the V function is equal to 0 or not specified, ? uses the MEMOWIDTH setting.

• EXAMPLE Assuming that Abstract is a memo field in the Referenc database, the following commands print the Abstract field word wrapped in a 40-character wide column:

```
USE Referenc
SET MEMOWIDTH TO 40
LIST Title,Abstract TO PRINTER
```

The next command displays the Abstract memo field word-wrapped within 66 columns, regardless of the current setting of SET MEMOWIDTH:

```
? Abstract FUNCTION "V66"
```

See Also MEMLINES(), MLINE(), MODIFY REPORT

SET MENU

Providing dBASE III PLUS Compatibility

• SYNTAX

```
SET MENU ON/off
```

• USAGE In dBASE III PLUS, SET MENU determined whether or not a menu of editing keys appeared with full-screen operations. SET MENU serves no function in dBASE IV. Instead, commands such as EDIT and BROWSE include a NOMENU option (equivalent to SET MENU OFF) to disable the menus.

SET MESSAGE

Displaying a Custom Message

• SYNTAX

SET MESSAGE TO *(character (***AT** *row, column))*

• USAGE SET MESSAGE defines a message of up to 79 characters that is centered at the bottom of the screen during full-screen editing mode when SET STATUS is on. The message must be enclosed in quotation marks or brackets unless it is stored in a memory variable.

Messages from @ commands, menus, and pop-ups will overwrite the message. The command SET MESSAGE TO with no message erases the message currently at the bottom of the screen.

The AT option is used to display the message at a position other than the center of the screen's bottom line.

The row number can be between 0 and the bottom row on the screen. If no row is specified, the message appears at the bottom line on the screen. If no column is specified, the message is centered in the row. If you specify a column but no row, the column number must be preceded by a comma.

• EXAMPLE The commands that follow display the message *Try again!* centered beneath the status bar:

```
SET MESSAGE TO "Try again!"
SET STATUS ON
```

See Also @, DEFINE MENU, DEFINE POPUP, SET SCOREBOARD, SET STATUS

SET MOUSE

Enabling and Disabling the Mouse

• SYNTAX

```
SET MOUSE ON/off
```

• USAGE If you have a mouse installed in your system, SET MOUSE enables or disables the mouse pointer. Using SET MOUSE ON when a mouse is not installed results in an error message.

Use the ISMOUSE() function to determine if the mouse driver is present and the mouse active.

• EXAMPLE The commands below check for a mouse driver and, if one is present, enables the mouse pointer:

```
IF ISMOUSE()
  SET MOUSE ON
ELSE
  ? "Mouse not installed"
ENDIF
```

See Also ISMOUSE(), MCOL(), MROW(), ON MOUSE, SET()

SET NEAR

Determines Search Behavior of SEEK and FIND

• SYNTAX

```
SET NEAR on/OFF
```

• USAGE SET NEAR specifies the position of the record pointer after an unsuccessful SEEK, SEEK(), or FIND. If SET NEAR is off, the record pointer is positioned after the last record in the database file, FOUND() returns False (.F.), and EOF() returns True (.T.).

If SET NEAR is on and a SEEK or FIND search is unsuccessful, the record pointer is positioned at the record immediately following the potential position of the sought-after value. FOUND() and EOF() both return false (.F.).

The SEEK() function returns false when an exact match cannot be found, regardless of the SET NEAR or SET EXACT settings.

When you relate multiple files using SET RELATION, the child files ignore the SET NEAR setting.

Records hidden by the SET DELETED ON command or a SET FILTER command are also hidden during the search. If SET NEAR is on and a SEEK or FIND search is unsuccessful, the record pointer will be positioned to the closest record that is not hidden.

• EXAMPLE Suppose a database contains an indexed date field named OrdDate. The following commands position the record pointer to and then display the earliest June date in the OrdDate field:

```
SET NEAR ON
SEEK {06/01/94}
DISPLAY
```

See Also EOF(), FIND, FOUND(), LOCATE, SEEK, SEEK(), SET RELATION

SET ODOMETER

Specifying the Odometer Update Frequency

• SYNTAX

SET ODOMETER TO *number*

• USAGE If the SET TALK parameter is on, commands such as COPY, PACK, RECALL, and APPEND FROM display their progress on an "odometer" on the screen. Usually, this odometer counts individual records as the command processes them. You can have it display progress in other increments such as groups of 10 or 100 records by assigning the appropriate value with the SET ODOMETER command. The maximum group interval is 200 records.

If SET TALK is off, the record counter is not displayed at all.

• EXAMPLE The following routine displays progress during a COPY operation, updating the odometer after each batch of 50 records is copied:

```
USE Biggie
? "Copying"+LTRIM(STR(RECCOUNT())+ "records..."

SET TALK ON

SET ODOMETER TO 50
COPY TO BigCopy

SET TALK OFF
```

SET ORDER

Selecting an Index Order

• SYNTAX

SET ORDER TO *(number)*

or

SET ORDER TO (**TAG**) *file name/tag name* (**OF** *.mdx file name*) (**NOSAVE**)

• USAGE The master (or controlling) index determines the sort order in which records are displayed and the fields that can be searched with SEEK and FIND. With the SET ORDER command, you can specify the master index without opening or closing any files and without moving the record pointer.

If you are using dBASE III PLUS .NDX index files, use the SET ORDER TO command followed by a number indicating the position of the index name in the list when opened by a USE or SET INDEX command.

To select an index from a dBASE IV .MDX file, use the SET ORDER TO TAG command followed by the name of the index. If you created indexes at the database design screen by marking the Index column with a Y, the index name is the same as the field name. If the index is included in an .MDX multiple index other than the production index file, use the OF option to specify the name of the multiple index file.

The NOSAVE option creates a temporary tag in a nonproduction .MDX file. The tag is deleted when the database file is closed. This allows you to temporarily order records based on a different field without creating a new index that needs to be kept up-to-date.

The command SET ORDER TO with no additional options disables the controlling index. Records are displayed in natural (record number) order, and no fields can be searched with SEEK or FIND.

• **EXAMPLE** Suppose the Orders database contains three indexed fields named CustNo, PartNo, and OrdDate, and the production index is named Orders.MDX. The next command will make the PartNo index the controlling index for the sort order and for FIND and SEEK searches:

```
USE Orders
SET ORDER TO TAG PartNo
```

See Also FIND, INDEX, KEY(), MDX(), NDX(), ORDER(), SEEK, TAG(), USE

SET PATH

Specifying a Path for File Searches

• **SYNTAX**

SET PATH TO *(path list)*

• **USAGE** SET PATH defines the directory path that dBASE will follow to locate a file not found in the current directory. The path list is expressed as it is in DOS: a drive name, followed by a backslash (\), followed by subdirectory names separated by backslashes. Multiple paths are separated by semicolons, with a maximum of 254 characters.

If dBASE can't find a file in the current directory, it searches paths listed in the SET PATH command one by one until the file is located.

Only dBASE IV's RUN command honors the DOS PATH setting.

The SET PATH command affects only file searches; newly created files are still stored on the current drive and directory unless you specify a different drive or directory in the file name.

Even when SET PATH is active, DIR displays only files on the current drive and directory unless you specify a different drive and directory in the command.

All operations initiated from the Control Center ignore the dBASE SET PATH setting.

• **EXAMPLE** The following commands set the file search path to the \DBASE and \WP subdirectories on drive C:

```
SET PATH TO C:\DBASE; C:\WP
```

The next commands set the dBASE IV search path to be identical to the DOS search path:

```
SPath = GETENV("PATH")
SET PATH TO &SPath
```

See Also DIR, GETENV(), SET DEFAULT, SET DIRECTORY

SET PAUSE

Managing Output from SQL SELECT

• **SYNTAX**

```
SET PAUSE on/OFF
```

• **USAGE** Normally, data output from the SQL SELECT command is displayed without pausing (like output from the dBASE IV LIST command). When SET PAUSE is on, the screen pauses for a keypress after each screenful of output (like the dBASE IV DISPLAY command).

• **EXAMPLE** The commands that follow display all records from the Inventry.DBF database using SQL syntax:

```
SET SQL ON
SET PAUSE ON
SELECT PartNo, Descript FROM Inventry;
```

SET POINT

Defining the Numeric Decimal Point

• SYNTAX

SET POINT TO *(character)*

• USAGE SET POINT defines the character used for displaying the decimal point in numbers. The default is a period. The separator cannot be a blank space, a letter, or a number.

• EXAMPLE The next commands show the effects of the SET POINT and SET SEPARATOR commands on the output of a number:

```
SET SEPARATOR TO "."
SET POINT TO ","
Amount = 123456.78
? Amount PICTURE "99,999.99"
    123.456,78
```

See Also SET CURRENCY, SET SEPARATOR

SET PRECISION

Determining Numeric Precision

• SYNTAX

SET PRECISION TO *number*

• USAGE SET PRECISION specifies the number of significant digits used in calculations with the numeric data type. It has no effect on the float data type. The default value is 16, but you can specify any integer from 10 to 20.

While SET DECIMALS controls the number of decimal places to display without affecting the precision of the results, SET PRECISION actually affects the numeric results by rounding off the numbers to the specified number of significant digits.

Reducing the precision to fewer significant digits increases calculation speed but decreases the accuracy of the results.

• EXAMPLE Note the difference between the results of dividing two numeric memory variables with different SET PRECISION commands in the dot prompt commands:

```
N1 = 123.45678
N2 = 987654321.1
SET DECIMALS TO 15
SET PRECISION TO 10
? N2/N1
   8000000.074000000000000
SET PRECISION TO 20
? N2/N1
   8000000.073710000670800
```

See Also FIXED(), SET DECIMALS

SET PRINTER

Channeling Output to a Printer

• SYNTAX

SET PRINTER on/OFF

or

SET PRINTER TO *(DOS device)*

or

SET PRINTER TO FILE *file name*

or

SET PRINTER TO *computer name**printer name* **=** *destination*

or

SET PRINTER TO \\SPOOLER

or

SET PRINTER TO \\CAPTURE

● **USAGE** SET PRINTER ON channels to the printer all output except output displayed with @...SAY commands. To channel @...SAY displays to the printer, use the SET DEVICE command. Use the NULL device option to simulate an output device for testing purposes.

SET PRINTER TO *DOS device* specifies a local printer. The default value is PRN, but you can specify any valid DOS device such as LPT1, LPT2, LPT3, COM1, or COM2. You still need to issue a SET PRINTER ON command to activate the printer after changing the device. Once you switch to a device other than PRN, you cannot switch back to PRN during the current session.

To channel output to a file, you can use the SET PRINTER TO FILE command followed by the name of the file receiving the output. The file will contain appropriate control codes for the printer in use, as defined by the _pdriver system memory variable. Unless you specify an extension, the output file will have the extension .PRT.

To produce an ASCII text file without printer codes, use the ASCII.PR2 printer driver. In this case, the output file will have the file name extension .TXT.

SET PRINTER TO without a file name closes the file and redirects the printed output to the local DOS device.

On the IBM PC, IBM Token Ring, Ungermann-Bass, and 3Com networks, you can use SET PRINTER to specify a particular printer on the network. Use the syntax

SET PRINTER TO *computer name**printer name* = *destination*

where *computer name* is the network-assigned name for the file server, *printer name* is the network-assigned printer name, and *destination* identifies the shared printer as LPT1, LPT2, or LPT3.

Use \\SPOOLER or \\CAPTURE with the SET PRINTER command to send printed output to a printer in a Novell network. To use these options, you must use the Novell SPOOL or CAPTURE command before starting dBASE.

• EXAMPLE This command sets the printer on to print all future output:

```
SET PRINTER ON
```

The next commands store printed output from the AnyRept report format in an ASCII text file named GrabIt.TXT, and then closes the file:

```
USE AnyFile

_pdriver = "C:\DBASE\ASCII.PR2"
SET PRINTER TO FILE GrabIt.TXT

REPORT FORM AnyRept TO PRINT

SET PRINTER TO
```

The following commands channel output to a shared LaserJet printer off the file server (named Server) designated as LPT1 on that server:

```
SET PRINTER TO \\SERVER\LaserJet=LPT1
```

See Also ?/??/???, EJECT, PRINTJOB...ENDPRINTJOB, REPORT FORM, SET DEVICE

SET PROCEDURE

Loading a Procedure File

• SYNTAX

SET PROCEDURE TO *(file name)*

• USAGE The SET PROCEDURE command opens a procedure file and makes accessible all procedures and user-defined functions within it. Only one procedure file can be open at a time. If you issue the SET PROCEDURE command and another procedure file is already open, that procedure file is closed before the new one is opened.

A procedure file can contain up to 963 procedures, although available RAM may not support that limit.

Unlike a command file, a procedure file can contain only procedures; it cannot have a "main program." As such, it cannot be executed, although its individual procedures can be. Each procedure must begin with the PROCEDURE command and end with the RETURN command.

You can use the MODIFY COMMAND editor to create and modify a procedure file. SET PROCEDURE automatically compiles the source code if it has never been compiled or has been modified since the last compilation. Before modifying a procedure file, release the copy in memory by issuing the CLOSE PROCEDURE command or by issuing the SET PROCEDURE TO command without a file name.

SET PROCEDURE TO is similar to SET LIBRARY TO, but you may also store user-defined functions in a library. Procedures in the procedure file take precedence over those with the same names in the library file.

• EXAMPLE To load a procedure file named MyProcs.PRG into memory and gain access to its procedures, enter this command:

```
SET PROCEDURE TO MyProcs
```

See Also DO, COMPILE, FUNCTION, PARAMETERS, PROCEDURE, RETURN, SET LIBRARY

SET REFRESH

Determining Network Update Frequency

• SYNTAX

SET REFRESH TO *number*

• USAGE SET REFRESH defines in seconds the screen update interval in a multiuser environment for database files that have been converted with the CONVERT command. The default value, 0, can be changed to any integer from 1 to 3600 (one hour).

If SET REFRESH is 0, the system does not refresh.

• EXAMPLE Enter these commands to see every five seconds what changes others have made in a file you are browsing:

```
SET REFRESH TO 5
BROWSE
```

See Also CONVERT

SET RELATION

Defining Relationships among Databases

• SYNTAX

SET RELATION TO *(expression* **INTO** *alias (,expression* **INTO** *alias...))*

• USAGE The SET RELATION command links the currently selected database file to another file in a different work area. The currently selected file, which controls the relationship, is referred to as the *parent* file. The related files in other work areas are referred to as *child* files.

The field used to define the relation must have the same name, data type, width, and decimal places in both files. This common field must be indexed in the child files.

Once you set a relationship, any movement through the parent database moves the record pointer to the related record in the child file. If no value in the child file matches the value in the parent file, the record pointer in the linked file is set to EOF() in the child file. The child files in a relationship do not honor the current setting of the SET NEAR command.

If you use RECNO() as the SET RELATION expression, the open files will be linked on the basis of matching record numbers. In this case, a common field is not required.

• EXAMPLE You have an application that uses three database files: Orders, Customer, and Master. The Orders.DBF database contains the customer number (CustNo) and part number (PartNo) for outstanding orders, but does not store customer names or part names. Customer names are stored in the Customer.DBF database, and part names are stored in the Master.DBF database.

Both the Orders and Customer databases contain a field named CustNo which is identical in type and size in both databases and is indexed in the Customer database. Both Orders and Master have a field named PartNo that is also identical in type and size in both databases and is indexed in the Master database.

The following commands set up a relationship that allows you to list order information with customer names and part names. Note the use of the Customer-> and Master-> aliases in the LIST command to display values from these related files:

```
USE Orders IN 1
USE Customer ORDER CustNo IN 2
```

```
USE Master ORDER PartNo IN 3

*----- Orders is the parent database.
SELECT 1
SET RELATION TO CustNo INTO Customer, ;
            PartNo INTO Master

LIST CustNo, Customer->CustName, ;
        PartNo, Master->PartName
```

See Also FOUND(), INDEX, SELECT, SET FIELDS, SET FILTER, SET SKIP, SET VIEW

SET REPROCESS

Limiting the Network Retry Attempts

• SYNTAX

SET REPROCESS TO *number*

• USAGE You use SET REPROCESS in a network environment to limit the number of times dBASE tries to lock a database file or record before it generates an error. If the file or record is in use by another user, it is already locked and you cannot lock it for your own access.

The default value is 0 and can be changed to any value in the range of –1 to 32,000. A –1 value indicates infinite retries with no mode of escape and should only be used in programs that provide some other means of escape with an ON KEY command.

The default value 0 also tries to access a locked file for an infinite period of time, but displays the message *Please Wait, another user has locked this record or file* while trying to access the file. The user can press **Esc** to stop trying to open the file.

• **EXAMPLE** You could use the following routine in a multi-user environment to open the Orders database file for your exclusive use in a BROWSE screen.

```
USE Orders
SET REPROCESS TO 20
BROWSE
```

dBASE will try 20 times to lock the file for your use before displaying an error message. You can then let dBASE try 20 more times or press **Esc** to give up.

See Also FLOCK(), LOCK(), NETWORK(), ON ERROR, RLOCK(), SET EXCLUSIVE, UNLOCK

SET SAFETY

Managing the File Overwrite Alert Feature

• **SYNTAX**

```
SET SAFETY ON/off
```

• **USAGE** When SET SAFETY is on and a command attempts to overwrite an existing file, the error box displays the message *File already exists* and the options *Overwrite* or *Cancel*. To prevent this message from appearing while your application is running, SET SAFETY should be off.

SET SAFETY also determines whether or not a warning and option to cancel follows a ZAP command.

• **EXAMPLE** In the following example, selected records from the Charges database are copied to a file named ChrgBak.DBF. If a file named ChrgBak already exists, dBASE won't ask for permission before overwriting it:

```
SET SAFETY OFF
USE Charges
COPY TO ChrgBak FOR Posted
```

See Also COPY, ZAP

SET SCOREBOARD

Activating or Deactivating Row 0 Messages

• SYNTAX

```
SET SCOREBOARD ON/off
```

• USAGE When SCOREBOARD is on and STATUS is off, scoreboard messages appear in row 0 on the screen. Scoreboard messages include *Del* (indicating that a record is marked for deletion), and *Ins, Num Lock,* and *Caps Lock* if these keys are on.

When STATUS is on, scoreboard messages appear in the status bar and error line (row 22), regardless of the SET SCOREBOARD status.

• EXAMPLE The commands that follow turn the status bar off and prevent scoreboard messages from overwriting a horizontal bar menu named MainMenu:

```
SET STATUS OFF
SET SCOREBOARD OFF

ACTIVATE MENU MainMenu
```

See Also SET MESSAGE, SET STATUS

SET SEPARATOR

Determining the Thousands Separator in Numbers

• SYNTAX

SET SEPARATOR TO *(character)*

• USAGE SET SEPARATOR defines the character used to separate thousands in numbers. The separator must be a single character, either enclosed in quotes in the SET SEPARATOR command or stored in a character-type memory variable.

The separator character is displayed only in numbers formatted by a picture function or template.

• EXAMPLE See **SET POINT**.

SET SKIP

Controlling Multiple File Relationships

• SYNTAX

SET SKIP TO *(alias1 (,alias2)...)*

• USAGE SET SKIP determines the order in which the record pointer is moved in multiple related files. You generally use it to display records from a database even when there are no matching records in a related file (like the EVERY operator on the queries design screen).

All commands with a FOR or WHILE clause are affected by SET SKIP. The record pointer is advanced in the first database file listed in the SKIP list, then in the second database file listed, and so forth.

You do not need to list the currently selected database in the command.

• EXAMPLE The next commands set up a relationship among the database files Master.DBF, Orders.DBF, and Customer.DBF. The LIST command then displays one record for each customer in the Customer database, with related information from one order:

```
USE Customer IN 1
USE Orders ORDER CustNo IN 2
USE Master ORDER PartNo IN 3

SELECT 2
SET RELATION TO PartNo INTO Master

SELECT 1
SET RELATION TO CustNo INTO Orders

LIST CustNo,Orders->OrdDate, ;
   Orders->PartNo,Master->PartName
```

If you entered the following commands while the previous relationship was still in effect, you would see a line for each order in the Orders database rather than a line for each customer only:

```
SET SKIP TO Orders,Customer,Master

LIST CustNo,Orders->OrdDate, ;
  Orders->PartNo,Master->PartName
```

See Also SET RELATION

SET SPACE

Inserting or Removing Spaces from ? and ??

• SYNTAX

```
SET SPACE ON/off
```

• USAGE If SET SPACE is on, values separated with a comma in a ? or ?? command are printed with a blank space between them. If SET SPACE is off, values separated by a comma are displayed without intervening spaces.

• EXAMPLE These commands, entered at the dot prompt, show the effects of SET SPACE on the ? command:

```
AreaCode = "(213)"
PhoneNum = "555-1234"
? AreaCode, PhoneNum
    (213) 555-1234
SET SPACE OFF
? AreaCode, PhoneNum
    (213)555-1234
```

SET SQL

Using SQL Syntax for Queries

• SYNTAX

SET SQL on/OFF

• USAGE The SET SQL command activates the interactive Structured Query Language (SQL) mode, which allows you to query a database using SQL rather than dBASE syntax. When the SQL mode is active, the dot prompt is replaced by the *SQL.* prompt. The Help (F1) key displays information about using SQL and lists dBASE commands and functions that you can use in SQL mode.

When the *SQL.* prompt is displayed, you can press **Ctrl-Home** to enter long SQL commands, and **Ctrl-End** to transfer the command to the SQL prompt. Remember to end all SQL statements with a semicolon.

You cannot use SET SQL in a command file.

• **EXAMPLE** The following commands display data from the Staff.DBF database using the SQL SELECT command:

SET SQL ON

(press Ctrl-Home)

```
SELECT Location, Count(*)
  FROM Staff
GROUP BY Location;
```

(press Ctrl-End, then Enter)

The resulting table shows the number of salespersons in each city.

SET STATUS

Managing the Status Bar

• **SYNTAX**

SET STATUS ON/off

• **USAGE** When SET STATUS is on, the status bar is displayed in row 22 on the screen. The status bar contains information about the current command, current database in use, current record number, insert/overwrite mode status, and the status of the Caps Lock and Num Lock keys.

When SET STATUS is off, the status bar is removed and you have access to all rows on the screen.

• **EXAMPLE** The following commands remove the status bar and scoreboard messages before displaying a defined menu named MainMenu:

```
SET STATUS OFF
SET SCOREBOARD OFF
ACTIVATE MENU MainMenu
```

See Also SET MESSAGE, SET SCOREBOARD

SET STEP

Single-Stepping through a Command File

- **SYNTAX**

```
SET STEP on/OFF
```

- **USAGE** When SET STEP is on, dBASE stops program execution after each command in a command file is executed, displaying the message *Press SPACE to Step, S to Suspend, or Esc to Cancel....* SET STEP ON is often used in conjunction with SET ECHO ON to help debug command files.

- **EXAMPLE** To watch as dBASE individually executes commands in MyProg.PRG, enter these commands:

```
SET ECHO ON
SET STEP ON
DO MyProg
```

See Also DEBUG, SET DEBUG, SET ECHO, SET TALK, SET TRAP

SET TALK

Hiding or Displaying Progress Messages

- **SYNTAX**

```
SET TALK ON/off
```

• USAGE When SET TALK is on, dBASE displays the progress of commands that do not otherwise display data on the screen. Such commands include APPEND FROM, CALCULATE, COPY, PACK, REINDEX, and STORE. When SET TALK is off, these commands display nothing on the screen.

Compiler warning messages are also suppressed when SET TALK is off.

• EXAMPLE The following commands display progress in a window as a PACK command is executed, turn TALK off, and then remove the window:

```
DEFINE WINDOW PackWind FROM 15,5 TO 20,75
ACTIVATE WINDOW PackWind
SET TALK ON
PACK
SET TALK OFF
DEACTIVATE WINDOW PackWind
```

See Also SET(), SET DEBUG, SET ECHO, SET INSTRUCT, SET ODOMETER, SET SCOREBOARD, SET STEP, SET STATUS

SET TITLE

Managing Catalog File Titles

• SYNTAX

```
SET TITLE ON/off
```

• USAGE When adding a new file to a catalog, you are normally prompted for a catalog file title. When SET TITLE is off, this prompt is not shown.

• EXAMPLE The following commands open and activate a catalog file named ThisApp.CAT, but prevent the catalog title prompts from being displayed.

```
SET CATALOG TO ThisApp
SET CATALOG ON
SET TITLE OFF
```

See Also ASSIST, EDIT, REPLACE, SET CATALOG

SET TRAP

Activating the Debugger Automatically

• SYNTAX

```
SET TRAP on/OFF
```

• USAGE Usually, when dBASE encounters an error while executing a command file, it simply displays an error message with options to cancel, ignore, or suspend. However, if you enter the command SET TRAP ON at the dot prompt before executing the command file, dBASE will activate the debugger as soon as an error is encountered, with the faulty command line highlighted in the editing window.

When SET TRAP is on, you can also call up the debugger by pressing **Esc** to interrupt command file execution.

If the command file you are executing uses the ON ESCAPE, SET ESCAPE OFF, or ON ERROR commands to control interrupts and errors, these take precedence over SET TRAP.

See Also DEBUG, ON ERROR, ON ESCAPE, SET DEVELOPMENT

SET TYPEAHEAD

Determining the Size of the Typeahead Buffer

• SYNTAX

SET TYPEAHEAD TO *number*

• USAGE A typeahead buffer stores keystrokes that are typed too quickly to be processed and then feeds these keystrokes to dBASE when the program is ready to accept them. The SET TYPEAHEAD command determines the number of keystrokes that this typeahead buffer holds. The acceptable range is 0 to 32,000 characters; the default is 20.

During full-screen operations such as Edit or Append, the typeahead buffer is always limited to 20 characters, regardless of the setting.

• EXAMPLE In procedures called by an ON ERROR condition, you can enter

SET TYPEAHEAD TO 0

as the first command to prevent further keystrokes from complicating the error condition. Before returning control to the calling program, issue a SET TYPEAHEAD command again to return to the default value of 20 or to set any other value.

See Also CLEAR TYPEAHEAD, INKEY(), KEYBOARD, ON KEY

SET UNIQUE

Hiding or Displaying Duplicate Key Values

• SYNTAX

SET UNIQUE on/OFF

• USAGE An index created with SET UNIQUE on will contain only unique values within the key fields of the database. Only the first of the duplicate values will be included in the new index file. All future operations act as though only these unique values exist in the database.

Once you create the index file with SET UNIQUE on, the file will keep its unique status even if you SET UNIQUE off and issue a REINDEX command. If you add new records to a database file indexed using the unique status, any duplicate records will be stored in the database file as usual, but will remain hidden from view while the unique index is in use.

To convert a unique index to a regular index, SET UNIQUE to off and use the INDEX ON command without the UNIQUE option to recreate the index.

• EXAMPLE To view a list of unique zip codes in a Mail database, SET UNIQUE to on, index the zip code field, and then use any command to view the zip codes, as shown below:

```
SET UNIQUE ON
INDEX ON Zip TAG UniqZips

*----- View unique zip codes.
LIST Zip
```

See Also FIND, INDEX, REINDEX, SEEK, SEEK(), SET INDEX, SET ORDER, USE

SET VIEW

Opening a View File

• SYNTAX

SET VIEW TO *file name*/**?**

• USAGE When you create a query or a view through the queries design screen, dBASE generates the source code required to execute the query or view and stores the code in a file with the .QBE extension.

To activate that query or view at a later time without going through the queries design screen, use the SET VIEW TO command followed by the name of the query file.

• EXAMPLE The following command activates a query/view stored in BigPict.QBE file:

```
SET VIEW TO BigPict
```

See Also CREATE/MODIFY QUERY, SET FILTER

SET WINDOW OF MEMO

Using a Custom Window to Edit Memo Fields

• SYNTAX

SET WINDOW OF MEMO TO *(window name)*

• USAGE The SET WINDOW OF MEMO command activates a previously defined window for editing memo fields during APPEND, BROWSE, CHANGE, EDIT, and READ operations.

The memo field is still displayed as a marker during these operations. The window is not activated until the user moves the cursor to the memo field marker and presses **Ctrl-Home**.

If you use the WINDOW option with the @...GET command, it overrides the window specified by the SET WINDOW command.

• **EXAMPLE** Assuming that Abstract is the name of a memo field in the Referenc database, the following commands allow the Abstract field to be edited in a window after the cursor is placed in the Abstract field and the user presses **Ctrl-Home**:

```
*----- Define the window.

DFINE WINDOW MemWind FROM 5,5 TO 20,75 DOUBLE

USE Referenc
SET WINDOW OF Memo TO MemWind

@ 5,5 GET Abstract
READ
```

See Also ACTIVATE WINDOW, CLEAR, COPY MEMO, CREATE, DEFINE WINDOW, MOVE WINDOW

Part 4

dBASE IV Functions

dBASE IV provides approximately 170 functions, many of which are used for manipulating character, date, and numeric data, and for performing many mathematical and financial computations. Other functions test the current operating environment, interpret keypresses, or return information about custom menus and pop-ups. This part of the book presents the complete list of dBASE functions with correct syntax, descriptions of usage, and practical examples for each.

& (MACRO SUBSTITUTION)

Substituting Text in a Command

• SYNTAX

&*character memory variable name* **(.)**

• USAGE

The & function substitutes the contents of *character memory variable* into a command line, so that the substituted text actually becomes part of the command. If you use the macro as a prefix to a character string, add a period (.) to indicate the end of the macro.

Since macro substitution usually prevents complete compilation of a command, it is not allowed in user-defined functions or in procedures called by ON commands. Macro substitution also slows down processing in dBASE IV, so you should avoid it as much as possible.

Earlier versions of dBASE required macro substitution in commands that use file names. dBASE IV, in contrast, allows you to use indirect referencing to access file names stored in memory variables, as shown below.

Note that the & macro substitution symbol and the $ substring function are the only dBASE functions that do not require any parentheses.

• EXAMPLE

The following commands tell dBASE to open a database file named MyData.DBF using macro substitution:

```
FileName = "MyData"
USE &FileName
```

The next commands use the faster indirect referencing method to open the MyData database:

```
FileName = "MyData"
USE (FileName)
```

$

Comparing Strings

- **SYNTAX**

string1 **$** *string2*

- **USAGE** The $ substring function is used to compare one character string with another. It is also known as the logical operator *"is contained in."*

$ returns logical true (.T.) if the first string is the same as the second or if it is wholly contained within the second.

- **EXAMPLE** The commands

```
Str1 = "ABC"
Str2 = "ABCDE"
? Str1 $ Str2
```

return .T., while the commands below return .F..

```
Str1 = "ABCDE"
Str2 = "ABC"
? Str1 $ Str2
```

See Also MEMLINES(), MLINE(), SET MEMOWIDTH, SUBSTR()

ABS()

Calculating the Absolute Value

- **SYNTAX**

ABS(*number***)**

• USAGE The ABS() function returns the magnitude of a number. It effectively changes negative numbers to positive and leaves positive numbers unchanged.

• EXAMPLE The following command returns the number of days between two dates, without regard to whether the number is "positive" or "negative":

```
? ABS({9/1/94}-{12/31/94})
```

See Also SIGN(), SQRT()

ACCESS()

Determining the User's Access Level

• SYNTAX

```
ACCESS()
```

• USAGE ACCESS() returns the access level (1–8) of the current user, based on the user profile established in the protection scheme. Use the PROTECT command to assign user profiles.

• EXAMPLE The next routine allows only users with an access privilege of 2 or less to execute the program named PayRoll:

```
IF ACCESS() <= 2
  DO PayRoll
ELSE
  ? "You do not have access to this program!"
ENDIF
```

See Also FLOCK(), NETWORK(), PROTECT, RLOCK(), UNLOCK, USER()

ACOS()

Calculating the Arccosine

• SYNTAX

ACOS(*number***)**

• USAGE The ACOS() (arccosine) function returns the size of an angle expressed in radians, where the cosine is the given number.

• EXAMPLE The command

? ACOS(.0973)

returns the value 1.47.

See Also ASIN(), ATAN(), ATN2(), COS(), DTOR(), PI(), RTOD(), SIN(), TAN()

ALIAS()

Finding the Alias of a Database File

• SYNTAX

ALIAS(*(number)***)**

• USAGE The ALIAS function returns the filename or alias for the database file in a specific work area. If you did not use the ALIAS option with the USE command to select the database file, the name of the database file in the specified work area is returned.

Number specifies the work area containing the database file and can be any whole number from 1 to 40, a character from A to J, or the name of a work area.

• EXAMPLE In the commands that follow, the ? ALIAS(1) command returns *Orders*, the name of the database in work area 1:

```
USE Orders IN 1
USE Master ORDER PartNo IN 2

? ALIAS(1)
```

ASC()

Calculating the ASCII Code for a Character

• SYNTAX

ASC(*character*)

• USAGE ASC() accepts any character string and returns the decimal ASCII code number for that character string. If the argument is longer than one character, ASC returns the ASCII code for the first character only.

• EXAMPLE The Command

```
? ASC("*")
```

returns 42.

See Also CHR()

ASIN()

Calculating the Arcsine

• SYNTAX

ASIN(*number***)**

• USAGE The ASIN() (arcsine) function calculates and returns the size of an angle expressed in radians between $-\pi/2$ and $+\pi/2$. *Number* is the sine of the angle and must be from –1.0 to +1.0, or the *Out of Range* error message is displayed.

• EXAMPLE The Command

? ASIN(.4365)

returns 0.45.

See Also ACOS(), ATAN(), ATN2(), COS(), DTOR(), RTOD(), SET DECIMALS, SET PRECISION, SIN(), TAN()

AT()

Finding One String within Another

• SYNTAX

AT(*string1,string2* (*,number*)**)**

• USAGE The AT() function searches the second character string for the first character string (or the substring expression). If it is found, AT() returns the starting position of the first expression in the second. If no starting point is found, 0 is returned.

The second argument may be a character string, character memory variable or field, or memo field name.

If you included the number argument, AT() returns the starting position of the *n*th occurrence of the first string. AT() is case-sensitive.

• EXAMPLE If Abstract is a memo field, the following command displays the starting position of the word "dBASE" in that field:

```
? AT("dBASE",Abstract)
```

Use the following commands to find that the fourth occurrence of the string "abc" in the longer string begins in the tenth character position.

```
TestStr = "abcabcabcabcabc"
? AT("abc",TestStr,4)
```

See Also LEFT(), RAT(), RIGHT(), STUFF(), SUBSTR()

ATAN()

Calculating the Arctangent

• SYNTAX

ATAN(*number*)

• USAGE The ATAN() (arctangent) function calculates and returns the size of an angle in radians, given the tangent of the angle. The angle passed as the argument must be between $+\pi/2$ and $-\pi/2$ radians, inclusive.

• EXAMPLE The command

```
?ATAN(.2094)
```

returns 0.21.

See Also ACOS(), ASIN(), ATN2(), COS(), DTOR(), RTOD(), SET DECIMALS, SET PRECISION, SIN(), TAN()

ATN2()

Calculating the Four-Quadrant Arctangent

• SYNTAX

ATN2(*number1*,*number2***)**

• USAGE You use the ATN2() function to obtain the size of an angle (in radians) when the sine and cosine of the angle are known. Using ATN2(), you can obtain values in all four quadrants. ATN2() returns a float type number between $-\pi$ and $+\pi$.

• EXAMPLE The commands below convert a 45-degree angle to radians and calculate its sine and cosine. The ATN2() function calculates the arctangent in radians, which is then converted back to 45 degrees.

```
Arg1 = SIN(DTOR(45))
Arg2 = COS(DTOR(45))
? RTOD(ATN2(Arg1,Arg2))
```

See Also ATAN(), COS(), DTOR(), RTOD(), SET DECIMALS, SIN(), TAN()

AVG()

See **CALCULATE** in Part 2.

BAR()

Determining the Pop-Up Menu Selection

• SYNTAX

BAR()

• USAGE The BAR() function returns the number of the bar most recently selected from the currently active pop-up menu.

If you used the DEFINE BAR command to define the bars of a pop-up menu, the number returned is the bar number you specified.

If you used the PROMPT FIELD, STRUCTURE, or FILES option with the DEFINE POPUP command, the returned value is the sequential position of the bar in relation to the first prompt displayed.

If no pop-up is currently active, BAR() returns 0.

• EXAMPLE The BAR function is usually nested in a CASE...ENDCASE statement of a procedure that evaluates the selection from a pop-up menu, as follows:

```
PROCEDURE ExitPop

  DO CASE
    CASE BAR() = 1
      RETURN
    CASE BAR() = 2
      QUIT
```

```
  ENDCASE
RETURN
```

See Also ACTIVATE POPUP, BARCOUNT(), BARPROMPT(), DEFINE BAR/POPUP, ON BAR/POPUP, ON EXIT BAR, ON SELECTION BAR, POPUP(), PROMPT()

BARCOUNT()

Determining the Number of Bars in a Pop-Up Menu

• SYNTAX

BARCOUNT(*(popup name)***)**

• USAGE BARCOUNT() returns the number of bars in the specified pop-up menu. If you do not name a pop-up, the function returns the number of bars in the active pop-up menu. If no pop-up is active, BARCOUNT() returns 0.

Bars defined with the SKIP option are included in the total count.

BARCOUNT() is useful when you need to know how many elements are in a pop-up used to display a fields list (PROMPT FIELDS), a file list (PROMPT FILES), or a structure (PROMPT STRUCTURE).

• EXAMPLE To find out how many database files are in the active catalog:

```
DEFINE POPUP FileList FROM 3,35 TO 20,60 ;
  PROMPT FILES LIKE *.DBF
ACTIVATE POPUP FileList
NumFiles = BARCOUNT()
@ 2,20 SAY "There are "+STR(NumFiles)+" files."
```

See Also BAR(), BARPROMPT(), DEFINE BAR, DEFINE POPUP, ON BAR, ON EXIT BAR, ON SELECTION BAR, POPUP(), PROMPT()

BARPROMPT()

Determining the Text of a Pop-Up Menu Selection

• SYNTAX

BARPROMPT(*bar number (,pop-up name)***)**

• USAGE BARPROMPT() returns the text of the prompt that appears in the specified bar number of a pop-up menu. You can specify the name of the pop-up, if other than the active pop-up.

The pop-up menu and bars must be previously defined. The bars can be explicitly defined with DEFINE BAR commands or implicitly defined with the PROMPT FIELDS (or FILES or STRUCTURE) option of the DEFINE POPUP command.

• EXAMPLE The commands

```
DEFINE POPUP PrnMenu FROM 2,24 TO 8,33
DEFINE BAR 1 OF PrnMenu PROMPT "Roster"
DEFINE BAR 2 OF PrnMenu PROMPT "New Member Letter"
DEFINE BAR 3 OF PrnMenu PROMPT "Renewal Letter"

*----- Define other bars as necessary
*----- Assign actions to bars

ACTIVATE POPUP PrnMenu
?BARPROMPT(3)
```

return "Renewal Letter".

If you have defined a pop-up with the command

```
DEFINE POPUP FormList FROM 2,40 TO 20,60 ;
  PROMPT FILES LIKE *.FRG
```

the function

```
?BARPROMPT(5,FormList)
```

returns the name of the fifth .FRG file in the list.

See Also BAR(), BARCOUNT(), DEFINE BAR, DEFINE POPUP, ON BAR, ON EXIT BAR, POPUP(), PROMPT()

BOF()

Determining the Record Pointer Position

• SYNTAX

BOF(*(alias)*)

• USAGE If the record pointer has been moved to the beginning-of-file marker (which precedes the first record in a database), the function will yield logical true (.T.); otherwise, it will return logical false (.F.). BOF() is useful in applications in which you scan the records in reverse order.

If an alias is not included, the currently selected database is assumed. If the database file contains no records, both BOF() and EOF() return .T..

• EXAMPLE The following loop moves backwards through a database file from the last record to the first:

```
USE AnyFile ORDER AnyIndex
GO BOTTOM

DO WHILE .NOT. BOF()
  DISPLAY
```

```
  SKIP -1
ENDDO
```

See Also EOF(), RECNO(), SKIP

CALL()

Treating Binary Program Modules as Functions

• SYNTAX

CALL(*file name,parameter1 (,parameter2...)***)**

• USAGE The CALL() function executes a previously loaded binary program specified by the file name. The parameters may be memory variables or character strings. The required *parameter1* is the value returned by the called program and is, in turn, the value returned by the CALL() function. Up to six additional parameters may be passed to the binary program as input and are updated in memory but are not returned by the function.

• EXAMPLE Assume that MakeBar is a machine language subroutine that prints bar codes on a laser printer and that it has already been loaded into memory. MakeBar returns logical true (.T.) if printing was successful. The following routine attempts to print the bar code for the part number A-111, and returns an error message if printing failed:

```
PartNo = "A-111"

IF CALL("MakeBar",PartNo)
  ? "Ok"
ELSE
  ? "Cannot convert that to a bar code."
ENDIF
```

See Also BEGIN/END TRANSACTION, DECLARE, CALL, LOAD, RUN, RUN(), STORE

CATALOG()

Identifies the Active Catalog

• SYNTAX

```
CATALOG()
```

• USAGE CATALOG() returns the name of the currently open catalog. If none is open, CATALOG() returns a null string.

• EXAMPLE You have opened a dBASE session and are working with a file named Orders which is included in the Sales catalog. To learn which catalog is currently open, use the command

```
? CATALOG()
```

See Also SET CATALOG, SET FULLPATH, SET TITLE

CDOW()

Finding the Name of a Day

• SYNTAX

CDOW(*date*)

• USAGE The CDOW() function returns the name of the day of the week extracted from the date passed to it. The argument must be of the date data type.

• **EXAMPLE** This command prints "Saturday," the day of the week of December 31, 1994:

```
? CDOW({12/31/94})
```

See Also CMONTH(), CTOD(), DATE(), DAY(), DOW(), DTOC(), YEAR()

CEILING()

Rounding Up to the Next Integer

• **SYNTAX**

CEILING(*number*)

• **USAGE** The CEILING() function returns the smallest integer that is greater than or equal to the argument value. Regardless of the decimal fraction of the number, CEILING() rounds the number up to the next integer. Negative numbers are rounded up to the next higher (less-negative) integer.

• **EXAMPLE** The command

```
? CEILING(5.2)
```

returns 6 and the command

```
? CEILING(–5.2)
```

returns –5.

See Also FLOOR(), INT(), ROUND()

CERROR()

Determining the Number of the Last Compiler Error

• SYNTAX

```
CERROR()
```

• USAGE The CERROR() function returns the number of the last error message produced by the compiler. A zero indicates that no errors occurred. Use this after the COMPILE command to see if any errors were detected.

• EXAMPLE After the program file Test is compiled, it is tested to see if an error occurred. If so, the IF statement is true. This would probably be followed by a command to display a warning to the operator and to abort the current portion of the application.

```
COMPILE Test
IF CERROR() <> 0
...
```

See Also COMPILE, ERROR(), MESSAGE(), ON ERROR

CHANGE()

Determining whether a Record Has Been Changed

• SYNTAX

CHANGE(*(alias)***)**

• USAGE CHANGE() is used in a network environment to find out if a record has been changed since you last used it. The CHANGE() function returns a logical true (.T.) if the current record has been changed. Before the function is valid, you must use the CONVERT command to convert the database file to a multiuser environment file with a _dbaselock field.

Use the alias option to specify a nonactive work area. *Alias* can be a number from 1 to 40, a letter from A to J, or a work area name.

• EXAMPLE The command that follows displays records that have been modified in a converted database:

```
LIST FOR CHANGE()
```

See Also CONVERT, FLOCK(), ISMARKED(), LKSYS(), RLOCK(), SET REFRESH

CHR()

Printing a Character Based on its ASCII Number

• SYNTAX

CHR(*number*)

• USAGE CHR() returns the ASCII character assigned to the number (0–255) in the argument. You can use it to display graphics and other special-effects characters found on most printers and monitors. ASCII characters in the range 0 to 127 are standard on most printers and monitors. The extended ASCII character set (128–255) varies on different screens and printers.

• **EXAMPLE** The following command beeps and prints the message *Please press ↑ ↓ → ← or ↵ to continue.*:

```
? CHR(7)+"Please press",CHR(24),CHR(25), ;
  CHR(26),CHR(27),"or",CHR(17)+CHR(196)+ ;
  CHR(217),"to continue."
```

See Also ???, ASC()

CMONTH()

Printing the Month of a Date

• **SYNTAX**

CMONTH(*expression***)**

• **USAGE** CMONTH() returns the name of the month in a date expression. The value passed to the function must be of the date data type.

• **EXAMPLE** The command

```
? CMONTH({06/01/95})
```

returns June.

See Also CDOW(), DATE(), DAY(), MONTH()

CNT

See **CALCULATE** in Part 2.

COL()

Determining the Cursor's Column Position

• SYNTAX

```
COL()
```

• USAGE COL() returns the current position of the cursor on the screen. It accepts no argument.

• EXAMPLE The next command prints the word *Hello* on the current row, five columns to the right of the current column:

```
@ ROW(),COL()+5 SAY "Hello"
```

See Also @, MCOL(), MROW(), PCOL(), PROW(), ROW()

COMPLETED()

Testing the Success of a Transaction

• SYNTAX

```
COMPLETED()
```

• USAGE COMPLETED() returns a logical true (.T.) after a transaction defined by the BEGIN TRANSACTION...END TRANSACTION commands has been successfully completed.

• **EXAMPLE** The routine that follows displays the status of a database after an END TRANSACTION command has completed a transaction:

```
IF COMPLETED()
? "All changes committed and irreversible"
ENDIF
```

See Also BEGIN/END TRANSACTION, CHANGE(), CONVERT, LKSYS(), ISMARKED(), ROLLBACK, ROLLBACK()

COS()

Calculating the Cosine of an Angle

• **SYNTAX**

COS(*number*)

• **USAGE** The COS() function calculates and returns the cosine of an angle expressed in radians.

• **EXAMPLE** The command below returns 0.71, the cosine of a 45-degree angle:

```
? COS(DTOR(45))
```

See Also ACOS(), ASIN(), ATAN(), ATN2(), DTOR(), RTOD(), SET DECIMALS, SIN(), TAN()

CTOD()

Converting a Character String to a Date

• SYNTAX

CTOD(*character*)

• USAGE CTOD() converts a character variable in date format to the date data type. The character expression passed to the function must be in the date format currently determined by the SET DATE, SET CENTURY, and SET MARK commands.

• EXAMPLE When dBASE is set to its default date format, SET DATE AMERICAN and SET CENTURY OFF, the following command will convert the character string 12/31/94 to the date data type:

```
Date = CTOD("12/31/94")
```

See Also DATE(), DTOC(), DTOS(), SET CENTURY, SET DATE, SET MARK

DATE()

Accessing the System Date

• SYNTAX

DATE()

• USAGE The DATE() function returns the system date using the date data type. The returned date is in the mm/dd/yy format unless it is changed by the SET CENTURY, SET DATE, or SET MARK commands.

• **EXAMPLE** The following command stores the current system date in the OrdDate field of a database, where OrdDate is currently empty:

```
REPLACE OrdDate WITH DATE();
  FOR OrdDate = { / / }
```

See Also SET CENTURY, SET DATE, SET MARK

DAY()

Isolating the Day in a Date

• **SYNTAX**

DAY(*date*)

• **USAGE** DAY() returns the numeric value of the day of the month from a date passed to the function. The date passed to the DAY() function must be of the date data type.

• **EXAMPLE** The following command displays 15, because the date falls on the fifteenth day of the month.

```
? DAY({12/15/94})
```

See Also CDOW(), DATE(), DOW()

DBF()

Identifying the Current Database File

• **SYNTAX**

DBF(*(alias)*)

• USAGE DBF() returns the name of the currently selected database file. The character string returned by DBF() contains the current drive designator with the file name, but not the current directory unless SET FULLPATH is on. Use the alias option to get the name of a database file in another work area.

A null string is returned if no database file is in use in the current or specified work area.

• EXAMPLE If there is no currently open database, the following routine calls a files list popup named ShowDbf and allows the user to select a database from the pop-up list.

```
IF DBF() = ""
   ACTIVATE POPUP ShowDbf
   USE (PROMPT())
ENDIF
```

To learn the name of the database file open in work area 6, use the command:

```
? DBF(6)
```

See Also ALIAS(), FIELD(), MDX(), NDX(), SET FULLPATH, TAG()

DELETED()

Finding Records Marked for Deletion

• SYNTAX

DELETED(*(alias)***)**

• USAGE DELETED() returns logical true (.T.) if the current record has been marked for deletion; otherwise, it returns logical false (.F.). If the optional alias is excluded, the currently selected work area is assumed.

• **EXAMPLE** The following command lists records that have been marked for deletion:

```
LIST FOR DELETED()
```

See Also PACK, RECALL, SET DELETED

DESCENDING

Determining the Sort Order of an Index File

• **SYNTAX**

DESCENDING(*((mdx filename,) number (,alias))***)**

• **USAGE** DESCENDING() returns logical true (.T.) if the tag number of the specified multiple index file is a descending key created with the DESCENDING option. The *mdx filename* must be enclosed in quotation marks. If no tag number is specified, the controlling index is assumed. If you specify a tag number but no .MDX file name, dBASE assumes the production index file.

You can examine the sort order of any .MDX tag in another work area by using the alias option.

• **EXAMPLE** To find out the sort order of tag number 3 in the AltInd.MDX index file of the database file open in work area 32, use the command:

```
? DESCENDING("AltInd.MDX",3,32)
```

See Also FOR(), KEY(), MDX(), ORDER(), SET(), TAG(), TAGCOUNT(), TAGNO(), UNIQUE()

DIFFERENCE()

Comparing Sounds

• SYNTAX

DIFFERENCE(*character1,character2*)

• USAGE The DIFFERENCE() function creates SOUNDEX() codes for the two character expressions, compares them, calculates the difference, and returns a number from 0 to 4. If the two character expressions are closely matched, the returned value is 4. If no letters are the same in the expressions, the returned value is 0.

• EXAMPLE The next command displays records that have names that sound somewhat like "Smith" in the LastName field:

```
LIST FOR DIFFERENCE(LastName,"Smith") ≥ 3
```

See Also SOUNDEX()

DISKSPACE()

Determining Available Disk Space

• SYNTAX

DISKSPACE()

• USAGE DISKSPACE() returns the number of bytes available on the default disk drive. In routines that involve backing up data to floppy disks, this function can ensure that the target disks have sufficient room for the file transfer.

• EXAMPLE The following routine determines whether or not there is enough room on the disk in drive A to copy a file named MyData.DBF, and then performs the copy if possible:

```
USE MyDATA
FileSize = (RECCOUNT() * RECSIZE()) + 2000
SET DEFAULT TO A
IF DISKSPACE() > FileSize
  SET DEFAULT TO C
  COPY TO A:MyData
ELSE
  SET DEFAULT TO C
  ? "Not enough room for copy..."
ENDIF
```

See Also RECCOUNT(), RECSIZE()

DMY()

Converting a Date Format

• SYNTAX

DMY(*date*)

• USAGE The DMY() function converts a valid dBASE IV date to the dd Month yy format. The day of the month is displayed without leading zeros, the month is spelled out, and the year is displayed in two digits.

If SET CENTURY is on, the year is expressed as a four-digit number.

• EXAMPLE The command that follows displays *31 December 94:*

```
? DMY({12/31/94})
```

See Also CDOW(), CMONTH(), DATE(), DOW(), MDY(), MONTH(), SET CENTURY, SET DATE, YEAR()

DOW()

Calculating the Day of the Week as a Number

• SYNTAX

DOW(*date*)

• USAGE DOW() returns a number that indicates the day of the week. The value passed to the DOW() function must be of the date data type. The value returned is a number between 1 and 7; Sunday represents 1, Monday represents 2, and so on.

• EXAMPLE The following command lists all records with dates that fall on a weekend, assuming that the SelDate field is of the date data type.

```
LIST FOR DOW(SelDate) = 1 .OR. DOW(SelDate) = 7
```

See Also CDOW(), DATE(), DAY()

DTOC()

Converting a Date to a Character String

• SYNTAX

DTOC(*date*)

• USAGE The DTOC() function converts date data to character data. A date must be converted to a character string in order to concatenate it with other character strings for use in display or index tags.

• EXAMPLE This command displays *Today is* followed by the current date:

```
@ 5,1 SAY "Today is " + DTOC(DATE())
```

See Also CTOD(), DATE(), DTOS(), SET CENTURY, SET DATE

DTOR()

Converting Degrees to Radians

• SYNTAX

DTOR(*number***)**

• USAGE The DTOR() function converts the size of an angle from degrees to radians.

• EXAMPLE To see 45 degrees converted to radians, enter the command

```
? DTOR(45)
```

which returns 0.79.

See Also ACOS(), ATAN(), ATN2(), COS(), RTOD(), SET DECIMALS, SIN()

DTOS()

Converting Date Fields for Indexing

• SYNTAX

DTOS(*date*)

• USAGE The DTOS() function converts a date data type variable to a character string in the ccyymmdd format for indexing purposes. The function ignores any current SET CENTURY or SET DATE settings.

• EXAMPLE The next commands create an index that displays records sorted by name, and by date within each name:

```
INDEX ON UPPER(LastName+FirstName) + ;
  DTOS(Date) TAG NameDate
```

See Also CTOD(), DATE(), DTOC(), INDEX, SET CENTURY, SET DATE

EOF()

Determining the End of File Position

• SYNTAX

EOF(*[alias]*)

• USAGE EOF() returns logical true (.T.) as soon as the record pointer moves past the last logical record in the database file (either the highest record number or the last record in the index order). If the optional alias is omitted, the currently selected database is assumed.

• **EXAMPLE** The following loop is the equivalent of a loop issued with the command SCAN FOR .NOT. InvPosted. However, it requires an IF clause to isolate records with .F. in the InvPosted field, and a SKIP command to advance the record pointer:

```
USE AnyFile ORDER AnyTag
DO WHILE .NOT. EOF()
  IF .NOT. InvPosted
    DO PostIt
  ENDIF
  SKIP
ENDDO
```

See Also BOF(), ERROR(), FIND, FOUND(), LOCATE, RECCOUNT(), RECNO(), SEEK, SEEK()

ERROR()

Accessing an Error Number

• **SYNTAX**

```
ERROR()
```

• **USAGE** When an ON ERROR condition is triggered, the ERROR() function returns the number that corresponds to the error. RETURN and RETRY clear the ERROR() function, so be sure to access the error number before issuing one of those commands.

• **EXAMPLE** See **ON ERROR** in Part 2.

See Also CERROR(), DEBUG, LINENO(), MESSAGE(), ON ERROR, PROGRAM(), RETRY, RETURN

EXP()

Calculating an Exponential

• SYNTAX

EXP(*number*)

• USAGE

The EXP() function returns the value of the constant **e** (which is approximately equal to 2.7182818285), raised to a power. The number passed to the function is the value of the exponent (*x* in the expression $\mathbf{e}^x$). The value returned is the inverse of the LOG() function.

• EXAMPLE

```
SET DECIMALS TO 6
? EXP(1)
? EXP(2.5)
```

return 2.718282 and 12.182494.

See Also LOG(), SET DECIMALS, SET PRECISION

FCLOSE()

Closing a Low-Level File

• SYNTAX

FCLOSE(*file handle*)

• USAGE

FCLOSE() closes the low-level I/O file specified by its file handle. The handle was assigned to the file by the operating system when it was opened with FOPEN() or FCREATE().

If the file is successfully closed, FCLOSE() returns logical true (.T.). Otherwise, FCLOSE() returns logical false (.F.). If FCLOSE() is not successful, you can use FERROR() to return the operating system error number in an ON ERROR interrupt routine.

Once the file is closed, you can modify the file using MODIFY COMMAND or any other word processor.

CLOSE ALL and CLEAR ALL close all open low-level files.

• EXAMPLE The commands below open and close the low-level file named LowFile.TXT. If an error occurs in either operation, the error procedure FileErr is called.

```
ON ERROR DO FileErr
*----- Open LowFile for read and write operations
FHandle = FOPEN("LowFile","RW")

*----- Low-level file operations

Clsd = FCLOSE(FHandle)
IF Clsd
  @ 2,2 SAY "File closed successfully"
ENDIF
```

See Also CLOSE ALL, DISPLAY STATUS, FCREATE(), FEOF(), FERROR(), FFLUSH(), FGETS(), FOPEN(), FREAD(), FSEEK(), FWRITE(),

FCREATE()

Creating a Low-Level File

• SYNTAX

FCREATE(*file name (,privilege)***)**

• USAGE FCREATE() creates and opens a new low-level file with the specified file name and extension. If FCREATE() is successful, it returns a positive integer that represents the file handle assigned by the operating system. You must refer to that file handle in all subsequent file operations.

The handle is temporary and is released when you close the file. When you open the file again, the operating system assigns a new handle. You can store the handle in a memory variable after opening or creating the file and have it accessible for later operations.

If FCREATE() is not successful, it returns a null string. You can use FERROR() to identify the error with an ON ERROR routine unless dBASE intercepts the error before it reaches the operating system.

You can specify various levels of user privilege with one of the following privilege codes:

Code	Permitted Operations
R	Read only
W	Write anywhere in the file
A	Append only at the end of the file
RW or WR	Read and write (anywhere)
RA or AR	Read and append (end only)

If you do not specify an access privilege, the file is automatically opened for reading and writing. Both the file name and the privilege must be enclosed in quotation marks.

• EXAMPLE To create and open an input/output file named NewFile with read and write privileges:

```
FHandle = FCREATE("LowFile.TXT")
```

See Also FCLOSE(), FEOF(), FERROR(), FFLUSH(), FGETS(), FOPEN(), FPUTS(), FREAD(), FSEEK(), FWRITE()

FDATE()

Determining Date of Last Change

• SYNTAX

FDATE(*file name*)

• USAGE FDATE() returns the date on which the specified file was last modified. The date is displayed in the mm/dd/yy format unless SET DATE, SET CENTURY, or SET MARK has changed it.

The file name must include the DOS path and file extension and be enclosed in quotation marks. No wild card characters are allowed in the file name.

• EXAMPLE To find out the date of the last edit of the CustList database file:

```
? FDATE("C:\DBASE\CustList.DBF")
```

See Also DISKSPACE(), FILE(), FSIZE(), FTIME(), SET CENTURY, SET DATE, SET MARK

FEOF()

Determining the End of File Position in a Low-Level File

• SYNTAX

FEOF(*file handle*)

• USAGE FEOF() returns logical true (.T.) if the file pointer is at the end of the specified low-level file. Otherwise, FEOF() returns logical false (.F.).

• EXAMPLE Use FEOF() in a DO WHILE loop to process all the characters in a low-level file:

```
DO WHILE .NOT. FEOF()
*----- Read characters from the file
ENDDO
```

See Also FCLOSE(), FCREATE(), FERROR(), FFLUSH(), FGETS(), FOPEN(), FPUTS(), FREAD(), FSEEK(), FWRITE(),

FERROR()

Determining the Cause of a Low-Level File Error

• SYNTAX

```
FERROR()
```

• USAGE FERROR() returns the operating system error number when an error occurs during low-level file operations. You can trap and identify the error with an ON ERROR interrupt routine. FERROR() returns zero if no error occurred.

If dBASE detects and traps an error before it is recognized by the operating system, FERROR() returns zero. You must then use the dBASE ERROR() or MESSAGE() function to identify the cause of the error.

• EXAMPLE You can use the following procedure to trap and identify errors that occur during low-level file operations.

```
PROCEDURE FileErr
  Err = FERROR()
  DO CASE
    CASE Err = 2
      @ 2,20 SAY "File does not exist"
```

```
    CASE Err = 3
      @ 2, 20 SAY "Path not found"

*----- Other cases

  ENDCASE
RETURN
```

See Also FCLOSE(), FCREATE(), FEOF(), FFLUSH(), FGETS(), FOPEN(), FPUTS(), FREAD(), FSEEK(), FWRITE(),

FFLUSH()

Saving Contents of I/O Buffer

• SYNTAX

FFLUSH(*file handle*)

• USAGE FFLUSH() writes the contents of the low-level file buffer to a disk file and returns logical true (.T.) if successful. Usually, the data in the buffer is written to disk only when the buffer is full or when you close the file. You can use FFLUSH() to periodically save the new data and safeguard against power failure or other accidents.

• EXAMPLE The commands below open a low-level file for read and write operations. During the processing, the buffer is emptied and a message is displayed, indicating successful completion:

```
FHandle = FOPEN("LowFile","RW")

*----- File operations

IF FFLUSH(FHandle)
  @ 2,20 SAY "Buffer emptied"
ENDIF
```

See Also FCLOSE(), FCREATE(), FEOF(), FERROR(), FGETS(), FOPEN(), FPUTS(), FREAD(), FSEEK(), FWRITE()

FGETS()

Reading from a Low-Level File

• SYNTAX

FGETS(*file handle (,number)(,EOL character)***)**

• USAGE FGETS() reads characters from a low-level input file and returns the character string to dBASE. FGETS() starts at the current file pointer position and reads the specified number of characters, or reads characters until a End-of-Line indicator is reached. The file pointer is then positioned at the next character following the group just read. If unsuccessful, FGETS() returns a null string.

The file handle is the identifier assigned by the operation system when the file was opened with FOPEN() or FCREATE(). The optional number is the number of characters to read. If none is specified, FGETS() defaults to 254. The final option specifies the character to be recognized as the End-of-Line indicator, if other than the default Carriage Return and Line Feed.

FREAD() also reads character strings from a low-level file but does not stop at an EOL indicator. If it encounters one within the specified string length, the indicator is included with the characters read. FGETS() does not include EOL indicates.

• EXAMPLE To open the file Remarks.TXT as a low-level file and read and display groups of 60 or less characters, use the following commands:

```
FHandle = FOPEN("Remarks.TXT","R")
DO WHILE .NOT. FEOF(FHandle)
  FLine = FGETS(FHandle,60)
```

```
  @ 2,2 SAY FLine
  WAIT
ENDDO
```

See Also FCLOSE(), FCREATE(), FEOF(), FERROR(), FFLUSH(), FOPEN(), FPUTS(), FREAD(), FSEEK(), FWRITE()

FIELD()

Accessing a Field Name

• SYNTAX

FIELD(*number, alias***)**

• USAGE FIELD() returns the name of a field corresponding to a numeric position in the file structure of the active database file. The first field in a database file is number 1, or FIELD(1). The largest possible field number is 255. If you pass the function a number that is greater than the number of fields in the database file or greater than 255, the function will return a null string.

If you omit the optional second parameter, *alias*, then the currently selected database is assumed.

• EXAMPLE The following commands determine the number of fields in the structure of the database file open in work area 5, then return the name of the last field.

```
NumFlds = FLDCOUNT(5)
? FIELD(NumFlds,5)
```

See Also DBF(), FLDCOUNT(), FLDLIST(), NDX(), RECCOUNT(), RECSIZE(), VARREAD()

FILE()

Determining whether a File Exists

• SYNTAX

FILE(*file name*)

• USAGE FILE() returns logical true (.T.) if dBASE finds the file name passed to the function. Otherwise, it returns logical false (.F.). If the file name passed to the function is not contained in a memory variable, you must enclose it in single or double quotation marks or brackets. The file name must include the file extension. Also, you must explicitly state the drive or directory if you do not use the default drive or directory.

• EXAMPLE This routine prints a warning if the file named CustList.DBF cannot be found on the current drive and directory. Use the string functions LEFT and LEN to display the file name without the extension.

```
lsFile = "CustList.DBF"
IF .NOT. FILE(lsFile)
  @ 5,10 SAY "Can't find the "+ ;
    LEFT(lsFile,LEN(lsFile)-4)+" database file."
ENDIF
```

See Also DIR, SET DEFAULT, SET DIRECTORY, SET PATH

FIXED()

Converting Float Data to Numeric Data

• SYNTAX

FIXED(*number***)**

• USAGE The FIXED() function converts binary coded decimal numbers (Numeric data type) to IEEE long floating-point numbers (Float data type) in the range of 0.1E–307 to 0.9E308. The conversion affects the way dBASE stores the number but it does not affect the display.

• EXAMPLE The following command stores the value of π as a numeric data type:

```
NPi = FIXED(PI())
```

See Also FLOAT(), TYPE()

FKLABEL()

Accessing a Function Key Label

• SYNTAX

FKLABEL(*number***)**

• USAGE FKLABEL() returns the name assigned to the function key specified by the numeric argument between 1 and 28. Although most keyboards use the standard function key names F1, F2, F3, and so forth, you can assign different names. The FKLABEL() function returns the label that has been assigned to it on the user's keyboard. FKLABEL() can access only programmable function keys. On terminals that use the F1 key as the Help key, the lowest programmable function key is F2. In this case, the function FKLABEL(1) actually refers to the F2 key. See **SET FUNCTION** in Part 3 for the key numbers that correspond to key labels.

• EXAMPLE The following commands initialize function key F2 to enter the QUIT command and then display the prompt *Press F2 to Exit*, assuming that the user's keyboard uses F2 as the label for function key number 1. If the label for function key number 1 is User 1 rather than F2, the prompt displays the message *Press User 1 to Exit*.

```
SET FUNCTION 2 TO "QUIT;"
Prompt = "Press " + FKLABEL(1)+ " to exit"
@ 2,1 SAY Prompt
```

See Also FKMAX(), ON KEY, SET FUNCTION

FKMAX()

Finding the Number of Function Keys

• SYNTAX

```
FKMAX()
```

• USAGE FKMAX() returns the maximum number of programmable function keys on the keyboard in use. On a 101-key keyboard, this is usually 28 (the sum of F2 through F10, Shift-F1 through Shift-F9, and Ctrl-F1 through Ctrl-F10). Function keys F1, Shift-F10, F11, and F12 are not programmable.

• EXAMPLE The next command declares an array named FuncKey that contains as many elements as there are programmable function keys:

```
DECLARE FuncKey(FKMAX)
```

See Also FKLABEL(), SET FUNCTION

FLDCOUNT()

Determining the Number of Fields in a Structure

• SYNTAX

FLDCOUNT(*(alias)***)**

• USAGE FLDCOUNT() returns the number of fields in the structure of the specified database file. If no alias is named, the currently active database file is assumed. If no database file is active, FLDCOUNT() returns zero.

• EXAMPLE To find out how many fields are in the Orders.DBF structure, use the following commands:

```
USE Orders IN 12
? FLDCOUNT(12)
```

See Also FIELD(), FLDLIST(), LIST/DISPLAY STRUCTURE, RECCOUNT(), RECSIZE()

FLDLIST()

Identifying a Field in a Field List

• SYNTAX

FLDLIST(*(number)***)**

• USAGE FLDLIST() returns the name of the specified field or evaluated field expression. The name is returned as it appears in the list created by SET FIELDS TO.

Since the field list is additive and may contain fields from several database files, FLDLIST() returns the entire field name, including the file or alias name. If the field is specified as read-only, FLDLIST() adds **/R** to the field name.

The optional number indicates the position of the field in the list. The number must be a positive integer. If no number is specified, FLDLIST() returns the entire list, up to a maximum of 254 characters. Characters beyond 254 are ignored. Field names are separated by commas.

If the field list has been cleared with SET FIELDS TO (no field list), FLDLIST() returns a null string. FLDLIST() ignores the SET FIELDS OFF setting.

• EXAMPLE The commands below return CustList->State, the third field name in the field list.

```
SET FIELDS TO                &&Empty the list
USE CustList IN 2
SET FIELDS TO LastName, Company, State, Paid, Phone
? FLDLIST(3)
```

See Also DISPLAY STRUCTURE, FIELD(), FLDCOUNT(), RECCOUNT(), RECSIZE(), SET FIELDS

FLOAT()

Converting Numeric Data to Float Data

• SYNTAX

FLOAT(*number***)**

• USAGE The FLOAT() function converts binary coded decimal numbers (the Numeric data type) to IEEE long, floating-point numbers (the Float data type). The conversion affects only the way dBASE stores the number, not the display.

• **EXAMPLE** The following command stores the number 3 in a float memory variable named X1:

```
X1 = FLOAT(3)
```

See Also FIXED(), TYPE()

FLOCK()

Locking a Database File

• **SYNTAX**

FLOCK([*alias*]**)**

• **USAGE** FLOCK() operates more like a command than a function. Without the optional alias, the function attempts to lock the currently selected file. You can also specify an alias to lock a file in an unselected work area. The alias must be the name of the file (as returned by the ALIAS() function), enclosed in quotation marks or square brackets, a number between 1 and 40, or a letter between A and J.

If the file is not already locked, FLOCK() locks the file and returns logical true (.T.) If the file is already locked by another user and cannot be locked, FLOCK() returns logical false (.F.).

While a file is locked by one user, other users can still view the file but cannot change it in any way. Once locked, the file remains locked until the locking workstation issues an UNLOCK command, closes the file, or exits dBASE IV.

If you lock a file that is related to other files by a SET RELATION command, all related files are locked. UNLOCK, in turn, unlocks all related files.

• **EXAMPLE** The routine that follows attempts to lock the AnyFile.DBF database for exclusive use in the Browse screen. If you cannot lock the file, a message is returned instead.

```
USE AnyFile

IF FLOCK()
  BROWSE
ELSE
  ? "File not available."
  ? "Try again later"
ENDIF
```

See Also ACCESS(), LOCK(), RLOCK(), SET LOCK, SET REPROCESS, UNLOCK

FLOOR()

Calculating the Next Smaller Integer

• SYNTAX

FLOOR(*number*)

• USAGE FLOOR() returns the largest integer that is less than or equal to its *number* argument. Regardless of the number's decimal value or sign, FLOOR() rounds it to the next lower integer.

• EXAMPLE

```
? FLOOR(99.999)
? FLOOR(–5.765)
```

display 99 and –6.

See Also CEILING(), INT(), MOD(), ROUND()

FOPEN()

Opening a Low-Level I/O File

• SYNTAX

FOPEN(*file name (,privilege)***)**

• USAGE FOPEN() opens an existing low-level I/O file and returns the numeric file handle assigned by the operating system. If an error occurs and the file cannot be opened, FOPEN() returns zero.

You can open the file with specific privileges, just as with FCREATE():

Code	Permitted Operations
R	Read only
W	Write anywhere in the file
A	Append only to the end of the file
RW or WR	Read and write (anywhere)
RA or AR	Read and append (end only)

If you do not specify an access privilege, R is assumed.

Both the file name and the privilege code must be enclosed in quotation marks.

• EXAMPLE The command:

```
FHandle = FOPEN("LowFile.TXT", "RA")
```

opens the low-level file named LowFile.TXT for reading and appending only. The user may not edit any existing data in the file. FHandle is the numeric file handle assigned by the operating system.

See Also FCLOSE(), FCREATE(), FEOF(), FERROR(), FFLUSH(), FGETS(), FPUTS(), FREAD(), FSEEK(), FWRITE()

FOR()

Determining the Filter Condition of an Index

• SYNTAX

FOR(*((mdx file name,) number (,alias))***)**

• USAGE FOR() returns the FOR filter condition used with the specified .MDX tag number. The controlling index tag is assumed if no tag number is specified. The currently active .MDX file is assumed unless a different one is named. Use the alias to examine the index FOR clause in another work area.

FOR() returns a null string if no FOR clause is included in the index or if you have specified an .NDX file.

• EXAMPLE The following commands index the Orders database file on date of order for only those orders placed more than 90 days ago. FOR() then returns DATE()-OrdDate>90:

```
USE Orders
INDEX ON OrdDate TAG OrdDate FOR DATE()-OrdDate>90
? FOR()
```

See Also DESCENDING(), INDEX, KEY(), SET(), TAG(), TAGCOUNT(), TAGNO(), UNIQUE()

FOUND()

Determining the Results of a Search

• SYNTAX

FOUND(*(alias)***)**

• **USAGE** FOUND() tests whether the previous SEEK, LOCATE, CONTINUE, or FIND command or a SEEK() or LOOKUP() function was successful in the specified work area. It returns logical true (.T.) if the search was successful. Otherwise, it returns logical false (.F.).

• **EXAMPLE** The following commands hide records in the Master.-DBF database that do not have part numbers listed in the Orders.DBF database:

```
USE Master IN 1
USE Orders ORDER PartNo IN 2

SELECT 1
SET RELATION TO PartNo INTO 2
SET FILTER TO FOUND(2)
```

See Also CONTINUE, EOF(), FIND, LOCATE, LOOKUP(), SEEK, SEEK(), SET NEAR, SET RELATION

FPUTS()

Writing to a Low-Level File

• **SYNTAX**

FPUTS(*file handle*,*character string* (,*number*)(,*EOL character*)**)**

• **USAGE** FPUTS() writes a specified character string to the low-level output file beginning at the current file pointer position. You can specify the number of characters to be written at one time by including the *number* option. After FPUTS() writes that number of characters, it appends an End-of-Line (EOL) indicator either as specified or as the default Carriage Return and Line Feed. The file pointer is then positioned at the next character position.

FPUTS() returns the number of characters written. FPUTS() returns zero and FERROR() can be used to trap and identify the type of error if an error occurs.

FWRITE() also writes characters to a file but does not append an EOL indicator.

• EXAMPLE The commands below create and open a low-level output file named Remarks.TXT for reading and writing. Then, if it was created successfully, a character string is written to it with the default EOL indicator. FPUTS() returns 20: 18 characters plus a 2-byte EOL indicator.

```
FHandle = FCREATE("Remarks.TXT","RW")
IF FHandle > 0
  FPUTS(FHandle,"Now is the time...")
ENDIF
```

See Also FCLOSE(), FCREATE(), FEOF(), FERROR(), FFLUSH(), FGETS(), FOPEN(), FREAD(), FSEEK(), FWRITE()

FREAD()

Reading from a Low-Level Input File

• SYNTAX

FREAD(*file handle,number***)**

• USAGE FREAD() reads the specified number of characters from a low-level input file, beginning at the current file pointer position. FREAD() returns the string of characters read, including any EOL indicators. Unlike FGETS(), which stops reading characters when a EOL indicator is encountered, FREAD() treats them as just another character.

At the end of the read, the file pointer is positioned at the character following the last one read.

• EXAMPLE The following commands open a low-level file named Remarks.TXT as read-only and, if successful, read all the characters into an empty Remarks.DBF database file, 60 characters at a time. Each set of 60 characters is placed in a record with a single field, RemLine. Any carriage returns or other EOL indicators are included, and may appear strange on your screen.

```
FHandle = FOPEN("Remarks.TXT","R")
IF FHandle < 0
  DO FileErr                    && Branch to error handler
ELSE
  USE Remarks IN 1
  ZAP
  DO WHILE .NOT. FEOF(FHandle)
    CharStr = FREAD (FHandle,60)
    APPEND BLANK
    REPLACE RemLine WITH CharStr
  ENDDO
ENDIF
```

See Also FCLOSE(), FCREATE(), FEOF(), FERROR(), FFLUSH(), FGETS(), FOPEN(), FPUTS(), FSEEK(), FWRITE()

FSEEK()

Moving the File Pointer in a Low-Level File

• SYNTAX

FSEEK(*file handle,number (,reference number)***)**

• USAGE FSEEK() is used to move the file pointer in a low-level file. You can specify the number of characters, the direction to move, and indicate the starting position from which to count. FSEEK() returns the new file pointer position.

The file handle is the numeric identifier assigned by the operating system with FOPEN() or FCREATE(). The number specifies the number of characters to move the pointer. A negative number moves the pointer toward the beginning of the file.

To start counting from the beginning of the file, use 0 as the reference number; to use the current file pointer position as the starting position, use 1; and for the end of the file, use 2. If you do not specify a reference point, FSEEK() starts at the beginning of the file.

• EXAMPLE Use the commands below to perform the following actions.

To move the file pointer to the beginning of the file:

```
Posit = FSEEK(FHandle,0)
```

To move the pointer 100 characters closer to the end of the file from the current position:

```
Posit = FSEEK(FHandle,100,1)
```

To find out how many characters are in the file, move the pointer to the end. FSEEK() returns the position of the last character:

```
? FSEEK(FHandle, 0, 2)
```

See Also FCLOSE(), FCREATE(), FEOF(), FERROR(), FFLUSH(), FGETS(), FOPEN(), FPUTS(), FREAD(), FWRITE()

FSIZE()

Determining the Size of a File

• SYNTAX

FSIZE(*file name***)**

• USAGE FSIZE() returns the size, in bytes, of the specified file. If the file is not in the current directory, you must include the DOS path with the file name and enclose it in quotes. No wild cards are permitted.

• **EXAMPLE** To find the size of the Orders database file, use the following:

```
? FSIZE("C:\DBASE\ORDERS.DBF")
```

See Also DISKSPACE(), FDATE(), FILE(), FTIME()

FTIME()

Determining the Time of Last Change

• **SYNTAX**

FTIME(*file name***)**

• **USAGE** FTIME() returns the time that the specified file was last changed. The time is displayed in hh:mm:ss format, the same as is returned by the TIME() function.

You must include the DOS path with the file name and extension, both enclosed in quotation marks. Wild cards are not allowed.

• **EXAMPLE** To find out when the GetNew.PRG command file was last modified:

```
? FTIME("C:\DBASE\GetNew.PRG")
```

See Also DISKSPACE(), FDATE(), FILE(), FSIZE(), SET HOURS, TIME()

FV()

Calculating the Future Value

• SYNTAX

FV(*payment,rate,periods*)

• USAGE The FV() function returns the future value of an investment made in equal payments with a defined interest rate and number of payments where:

- *Payment* is the periodic payment
- *Rate* is the fixed interest rate for each period (in decimal form)
- *Periods* is the number of fixed periods of the investment

The interest rate and number of periods must match. For example, your payments are monthly, the interest rate is annual, and the periods are expressed in years. When using FV(), you must convert the annual interest rate to a monthly rate by dividing by 12 and convert the duration (years) to months by multiplying by 12.

• EXAMPLE Suppose you plan to deposit $166 monthly to an IRA account that pays 10.5 percent (.105 in decimal form) interest annually (compounded monthly) for 20 years. The value of the IRA at the end of 20 years can be displayed with the following commands:

```
Payment = 166.00            && Monthly deposit
APR = .105                  && 10.5% annual interest
Years  =  20
? FV(Payment,APR/12,Years*12)
```

See Also CALCULATE, LOG10(), PAYMENT(), PV()

FWRITE()

Writing to a Low-Level Output File

• SYNTAX

FWRITE(*file handle,character string (,number)***)**

• USAGE FWRITE() writes a character string to the specified low-level output file. The file handle is the numeric identifier assigned by the operating system when the file was opened by FOPEN() or FCREATE(). If you use FOPEN(), you must specify the write or append privilege. If you opened a new file with FCREATE(), it is automatically opened for reading and writing (RW).

The writing begins at the current file pointer position and, unlike FPUTS(), no End-of-Line indicator is appended to the end of the string. The file pointer is positioned at the end of the written characters.

FWRITE() returns the number of characters written if the write was successful and zero if it was not. If an error occurs, you can use FERROR() in an error trapping routine to identify the cause of the error.

• EXAMPLE The commands below write the specified character string to the low-level file LowFile.TXT and return 18, the number of characters in the string.

```
ON ERROR DO FileErr
FHandle = FCREATE("LowFile.TXT","RW")
NumChar = FWRITE(FHandle,"Now is the time...")
```

See Also FCLOSE(), FCREATE(), FEOF(), FERROR(), FFLUSH(), FGETS(), FOPEN(), FPUTS(), FREAD(), FSEEK(), ON ERROR

GETENV()

Accessing DOS Environmental Variables

• SYNTAX

GETENV(*character*)

• USAGE GETENV() returns a character string containing the setting or definition of a DOS environmental variable such as PROMPT, PATH, and COMSPEC. If the argument does not match a DOS environmental variable, the function returns a null string.

You can view the current contents of DOS environmental variables by entering the command **RUN SET** at the dot prompt.

• EXAMPLE The following command displays the location of the Command.COM file:

```
? GETENV("COMSPEC")
```

See Also OS()

HOME()

Determining the Startup Path

• SYNTAX

HOME()

• USAGE HOME() returns the path you used to start the current dBASE session.

• EXAMPLE If you are running dBASE from the C drive and dBASE directory,

```
? HOME()
```

returns C:\DBASE\

See Also ID(), NETWORK(), OS()

ID()

Identifying the User on the Network

• SYNTAX

```
ID()
```

• USAGE ID() returns the eight-character log-in name of the current user on a network. If no user is currently logged onto the network, ID() returns a null string.

• EXAMPLE To see the name of the current user, use the command:

```
? ID()
```

See Also LIST USERS, NETWORK(), USER()

IIF()

Executing an Immediate IF Command

• SYNTAX

IIF(*expression*,*value1*,*value2***)**

• USAGE IIF() makes an IF...ELSE decision within a command line, LABEL/REPORT column, or @ command. If the expression evaluates to logical true (.T.), the first value is returned. If it evaluates to logical false (.F.), the second value is returned. Either argument may be an expression that evaluates to a value not necessarily of the same data types.

Note that you cannot use IIF() to execute dBASE commands, only to return values. To execute commands based on a conditional expression, use the IF...ELSE...ENDIF command.

• EXAMPLE The following command, whether used in a program or a MODIFY REPORT or MODIFY LABEL column, displays the extended price with 8.5% tax added if a logical variable or field named Taxable contains .T. Otherwise, it displays the extended price without tax added.

```
IIF(Taxable,(Qty*UnitPrice)*1.085,Qty*UnitPrice)
```

See Also IF...ELSE...ENDIF

INKEY()

Checking for a Keypress

• SYNTAX

INKEY([*n*]**)**

• USAGE The INKEY() function returns the number that represents the most recent key pressed. The value returned is a numeric code, as listed in Table 4.1.

The optional argument specifies the number of seconds to wait for a key to be pressed. Enter an integer to have INKEY() wait that number of seconds and, if no key is pressed during that time, for dBASE to resume processing.

A zero argument causes INKEY() to wait indefinitely for a new keypress.

Table 4.1: Keypresses and Their INKEY() Values

Key Label	Value
→	4
←	19
↑	5
↓	24
↵	13
0 to 9	48 to 57
Backspace	127
Ctrl-→	6
Ctrl-←	1
Ctrl-↵	–402
Ctrl-Backspace	–401
Ctrl-End	23
Ctrl-F1 to Ctrl-F10	–10 to –19
Ctrl-Home	29
Ctrl-PgDn	30
Ctrl-PgUp	31
A to Z	65 to 90
a to z	97 to 122
Del (or Delete)	7
Esc (or Escape)	27
F2 to F10	–1 to –9
Home	26
Ins (or Insert)	22
PgDn	3
PgUp	18
Shift-Tab	–400
Space Bar	32
Tab	9

Table 4.1: Keypresses and Their INKEY() Values (Continued)

Key Label	Value
Shift-F1 to Shift-F9	–20 to –28
Alt-A to Alt-Z	–435 to –410
Alt-0 to Alt-9	–452 to –443

• EXAMPLE The following command prints a report until the user presses the spacebar to stop printing:

```
REPORT FORM AnyRep WHILE INKEY() <> 32
```

The next commands wait indefinitely for a keypress and store the user's keypress in a numeric memory variable named UserPress:

```
CLEAR TYPEAHEAD
UserPress = INKEY(0)
```

These commands pause for five seconds, or until a key is pressed, whichever comes first, then resume processing:

```
CLEAR TYPEAHEAD
X = INKEY(5)
```

See Also CHR(), KEYBOARD, LASTKEY(), ON KEY, READ, READKEY(), SET TYPEAHEAD, WAIT

INT()

Truncating Decimal Values

• SYNTAX

INT(*number*)

• **USAGE** INT() converts any numeric expression to an integer by truncating all digits to the right of the decimal place without rounding.

• **EXAMPLE** The commands

```
? INT(99.9999999)
? INT(16/5)
```

return 99 and 3, respectively.

See Also MOD(), ROUND(), FLOOR(), CEILING()

ISALPHA()

Determining whether a String Begins with a Letter

• **SYNTAX**

ISALPHA(*character*)

• **USAGE** If an argument begins with a letter, ISALPHA() returns logical true (.T.) Otherwise, ISALPHA() returns logical false (.F.).

• **EXAMPLE** The following ? command returns .F. because the Address variable begins with a number.

```
Address = "123 Oak Tree Lane"
? ISALPHA(Address)
.F.
```

See Also ISLOWER(), ISUPPER(), LOWER(), UPPER(), VAL()

ISBLANK()

Determining whether a Field is Blank

• SYNTAX

ISBLANK(*expression*)

• USAGE ISBLANK() returns logical true (.T.) if the specified expression is blank. A record added to a database file with APPEND BLANK contains what are defined as blank values in every field. Blank values differ by data type:

Data Type	Blank Value
Char	All spaces
Date	{ / / }
Float	No data
Logical	No data
Memo	No data
Numeric	No data

In Numeric and Float type fields, although the field may be blank, zero is displayed on the screen. Logical values, when blank, display as .F. but ISBLANK() returns .T. A logical field that contains an authentic .F. returns .F. with ISBLANK(), since it actually contains data.

• EXAMPLE To make sure all member records in the Members database file contain addresses complete with Zip codes, use the following commands:

```
USE Members
SCAN
  AddZip = "          "
  IF ISBLANK(Zip)
    @ 2,2 SAY TRIM(FirstName)+TRIM(LastName)+;
      " is missing the zip code. Please enter:" ;
```

```
      GET AddZip
    READ
    REPLACE Zip WITH AddZip
  ENDIF
ENDSCAN
```

See Also APPEND BLANK, BLANK, ISALPHA(), SPACE()

ISCOLOR()

Determining whether a Color Monitor is Available

• SYNTAX

ISCOLOR()

• EXAMPLE ISCOLOR() returns logical true (.T.) if the computer is currently using a color monitor and logical false (.F.) if the computer is using a monochrome video card.

• EXAMPLE The following routine illustrates the typical method of setting video attributes based on the type of monitor in use:

```
IF ISCOLOR()
  SET COLOR TO GR+/B,W/R
ELSE
  SET COLOR TO W+
ENDIF
```

See Also SET COLOR, SET DISPLAY

ISLOWER()

Determining a Lowercase First Letter

• SYNTAX

ISLOWER(*character*)

• USAGE ISLOWER() returns logical true (.T.) if the character expression passed to the function begins with a lowercase letter. Otherwise, it returns logical false (.F.).

• EXAMPLE This ? command displays .F. because the memory variable named LastName begins with an uppercase letter:

```
LastName = "Smith"
? ISLOWER(M->LastName)
```

See Also ISALPHA(), ISUPPER(), LOWER(), UPPER()

ISMARKED()

Determining whether a Transaction is in Progress

• SYNTAX

ISMARKED(*(alias)*)

• USAGE The ISMARKED() function checks the integrity flag in the database file header and returns a logical true (.T.) if the database file was changed during transaction processing. If the file was opened with the NOLOG keyword, no transaction log was written and ISMARKED() will return logical false (.F.) even if the file was changed.

Unless you specify an optional alias within the parentheses, ISMARKED() checks the file in the current work area.

• EXAMPLE The following routine prevents a user from accessing the Master.DBF database, currently open in a separate work area, if it is currently involved in transaction processing:

```
IF ISMARKED("Master")
   ? "Cannot use Master.DBF right now..."
ELSE
   SELECT Master
ENDIF
```

See Also BEGIN/END TRANSACTION, CHANGE(), COMPLETED(), RESET, ROLLBACK, ROLLBACK(), USE

ISMOUSE()

Determining whether a Mouse is Installed

• SYNTAX

```
ISMOUSE()
```

• USAGE ISMOUSE() returns logical true (.T.) if a mouse driver is installed and logical false (.F.) if one is not.

• EXAMPLE The commands below check to make sure a mouse can be used to make menu selections, then advises the user.

```
IF ISMOUSE()
   @20,1 SAY "You may use your mouse to select."
ELSE
   @20,1 SAY "Sorry, no mouse installed."
```

See Also MCOL(), MROW(), ON MOUSE, SET MOUSE, SET()

ISUPPER()

Determining an Uppercase First Letter

• SYNTAX

ISUPPER()

• USAGE ISUPPER() returns logical true (.T.) if the argument begins with an uppercase letter. Otherwise, it returns logical false (.F.).

• EXAMPLE The next command converts all PartCode values in the current database that begin with a lowercase letter to their uppercase equivalents:

```
REPLACE PartCode WITH UPPER(PartCode) ;
  FOR .NOT. ISUPPER(PartCode)
```

See Also ISALPHA(), ISLOWER(), LOWER(), UPPER()

KEY()

Determining the Key Expression for an Index

• SYNTAX

KEY(*((mdx filename,) number (,alias))***)**

• USAGE The KEY() function returns the key expression for the index file specified by tag number. If the specified index file does not exist, KEY() returns a null string. If no multiple index (.MDX) file exists, dBASE considers all open indexes, including .NDX files. The number then represents the position of the .NDX file in the index list.

KEY() assumes the database and index file in the current work area unless you specify a different work area in an alias. The alias may be a work area number (1–40), the work area letter (A–J), or the database name or alias specified in the USE command.

• **EXAMPLE** Suppose that Master.DBF has a production index file named Master.MDX, which contains indexes named PartNo and PartName. The PartName index was created using the expression UPPER(PartName).

Assuming that the Master database was opened in work area 2 with the following USE command, the ? command displays UPPER(PartName), the name of the second tag in the Master.MDX index file:

```
USE Master IN 2
? KEY(2,"Master")
```

See Also INDEX, MDX(), NDX(), ORDER(), TAG()

KEYMATCH()

Looking for an Index Key Value

• **SYNTAX**

KEYMATCH(*expression [,[mdx file name,]*
*tag number/ndx number [,alias]]***)**

• **USAGE** KEYMATCH() is useful for maintaining the integrity of a database file when entering or appending records. You can check for new records which have the same index key as existing records.

KEYMATCH() returns logical true (.T.) if the specified key expression is found in the specified index. It returns logical false (.F.) if the key is not found.

The index to be searched is specified either by the tag number of an .MDX file or the numeric position of an .NDX file in the list of indexes. You can use DISPLAY STATUS or TAGNO() to find out the position of the .NDX file in the list.

If no tag or .NDX file number is specified, KEYMATCH() searches the controlling index for a key with the same value.

If you use a work area number as an alias, you must also use a tag or .NDX number, separated with a comma, to avoid ambiguity.

KEYMATCH() ignores the status of the SET DELETED, SET FILTER, and SET KEY settings and searches the entire index, even though you are working with only part of the file.

You can use KEYMATCH() to search for the expression in any index key without changing the active index or moving the record pointer.

• EXAMPLE Suppose the Master database file contains the master list of part numbers with associated information, one record per part number. The file is keyed on the unique part number and problems would occur if records were added using an already existing part number. The commands below ensure that new entries will have new part numbers.

```
USE Master Order PartNo
@ 2,2 SAY "Enter new parts:"
NewPart = SPACE(5)
@ 4,2 SAY "Part Number:  " GET NewPart
READ
OldPart = TAGNO("PartNo")
IF KEYMATCH(NewPart,OldPart)
*----- If duplicate, call procedure to get different number
    DO FixDupe WITH NewPart
ELSE
    APPEND BLANK
    REPLACE PartNo WITH NewPart
*----- And enter rest of data.
ENDIF
RETURN
```

See Also FIND, INDEX, LOOKUP(), SEEK, SEEK()

LASTKEY()

Determining the Last Key Pressed

• SYNTAX

LASTKEY()

• USAGE LASTKEY() returns the numeric code of the last key pressed by the user when exiting a full-screen operation such as BROWSE, READ, or EDIT. It returns the last keypress even if INKEY() has already stored that value in a memory variable. See **INKEY()** for a list of the returned numeric codes.

• EXAMPLE You could use the IF condition below within a procedure or user-defined function to determine whether the user changed data during a full-screen operation. The ASCII code 13 represents ↵, and the codes between 32 and 122 are alphabetic and numeric keyboard characters.

```
IF LASTKEY() = 13 .OR. ;
  LASTKEY() >= 32 .AND. LASTKEY() <= 122
```

See Also INKEY(), READKEY()

LEFT()

Accessing the Leftmost Characters

• SYNTAX

LEFT(*character,number***)**

• USAGE LEFT() extracts and returns a specified number of characters from a character string or memo field. The number of characters counts from the leftmost character (1). If the numeric expression is larger than the length of the character expression, the whole character string is returned. If the numeric expression is 0 or a negative number, a null string is returned.

In dBASE IV, unlike earlier versions, LEFT() can extract up to 254 characters from any string or memo field.

• **EXAMPLE** This command lists all records that have the letter "A" as the first character in the character field named PartNo:

```
LIST FOR UPPER(LEFT(PartNo,1)) = "A"
```

See Also AT(), LTRIM(), RIGHT(), STUFF(), SUBSTR(), TRIM()

LEN()

Determining the Length of a Character String

• **SYNTAX**

LEN(*character***)**

• **USAGE** LEN() returns the length of a character string. The character string being measured can be stored in any character memory variable, character field, or memo field. The length of a null (empty) string is 0.

• **EXAMPLE** The following command calculates the widest PartName (with blanks trimmed off) in a character field named LastName, storing that width in a numeric variable named Widest:

```
CALCULATE MAX(LEN(TRIM(PartName))) TO Widest
```

See Also @, LTRIM(), STUFF(), SUBSTR(), TRIM()

LIKE()

Comparing Strings to a Pattern

• SYNTAX

LIKE(*pattern,character*)

• USAGE The LIKE() function compares a pattern with a character string and returns logical true (.T.) if they match. The pattern may consist of any letters and numbers, plus the wildcard ? to match any single character and * to match any group of characters.

LIKE() is case-sensitive.

• EXAMPLE The next command lists last names that begin with the letters "SM," followed by any single character, followed by the letter "T," followed by any other characters, without regard to upper- or lowercase:

```
LIST FOR LIKE("SM?T*",UPPER(LastName))
```

See Also DIFFERENCE(), LOOKUP(), SOUNDEX()

LINENO()

Determining the Number of a Command Line

• SYNTAX

LINENO()

• USAGE The LINENO() function returns the line number of the current command line in a program or procedure being executed. You can use the function as a breakpoint in the debugger or to display the line number in an ON ERROR procedure.

• EXAMPLE The following procedure opens a window named BadLine, displays an error message, and waits for the programmer's response:

```
PROCEDURE ErrProc
   ACTIVATE WINDOW BadLine
   ? "Problem with line",LINENO(),
     "of "+PROGRAM()
   WAIT
   CLOSE ALL
RETURN
```

See Also DEBUG, ERROR(), ON ERROR, PROGRAM(), SET DEVELOPMENT

LKSYS()

Determining the Source of a Lock

• SYNTAX

LKSYS(*number***)**

• USAGE LKSYS() returns information about a locked file, depending on the number argument. This information is useful when a lock request has been denied. If the user did not convert the database file with CONVERT, LKSYS() returns a null string.

The LKSYS() function reads the _dbaselock field of the converted file for the specified information. Arguments 0 through 2 return information about a locked file and arguments 3 through 5 return similar information about an unlocked file. Optional values for the *number* argument return the following information:

0	Returns the time when the lock was placed on the file or record.
1	Returns the date when the lock was placed on the file or record.
2	Returns the log-in name of the user who locked the file or record.
3	Returns the time of the last update or lock.
4	Returns the date of the last update or lock.
5	Returns the log-in of the user who last updated or locked the record.

• **EXAMPLE** The following routine attempts to lock the currently open database file. If it cannot lock the file, it displays the name of the user who has the file locked:

```
IF FLOCK()
  BROWSE
ELSE
  ? "File in use by", LKSYS(2)
ENDIF
```

See Also CHANGE(), CONVERT, FLOCK(), RLOCK(), SET LOCK, UNLOCK

LOCK()

See **RLOCK()**.

LOG()

Calculating the Natural Logarithm

• SYNTAX

LOG(*number*)

• USAGE LOG() returns the natural logarithm of the number passed to it. The natural logarithm has a base of **e** (a mathematical constant approximately equal to 2.7182818285).

• EXAMPLE The following command displays 1.473710, the natural logarithm of 4.3654:

```
SET DECIMALS TO 6
? LOG(4.3654)
```

See Also EXP(), LOG10(), SET DECIMALS, SET PRECISION, SIGN()

LOG10()

Calculating the Common Log to the Base 10

• SYNTAX

LOG10(*number*)

• USAGE LOG10() calculates the common (base 10) log of a specified number. The returned number is the Float data type.

• EXAMPLE The CAGR() user-defined function that follows returns the compound annual growth rate (interest rate) required for an initial deposit to reach some value within a specified number of years. For example, the command

```
? CAGR(5000,10000,7)
```

returns 0.10, indicating that an interest rate of ten percent is required to turn $5000 into $10,000 within seven years:

```
FUNCTION CAGR
PARAMETERS Initial,Goal,Years
  CAGR=(10^((LOG10(Goal/Initial))/Years))-1
RETURN CAGR
```

See Also EXP(), LOG()

LOOKUP()

Searching a Database File for Information

• SYNTAX

LOOKUP(*return exp***,***look-for exp***,***look-in field***)**

• USAGE The LOOKUP() function performs a sequential search of the database for a specified value (the *look-for exp*) in a particular field (the *look-in field*) and returns the contents of another field in the located record (the *return exp*). Unless you specify an alias in *return exp* and *look-in field*, the database in the current work area is searched.

The field being searched need not be indexed, but the search will be faster if it is.

If no match is found, FOUND() returns logical false (.F.) and EOF() returns logical true (.T.).

• EXAMPLE This command looks up A-111 in the PartNo field of the open Master.DBF database and returns the PartName for that part number:

```
? LOOKUP(Master->PartName,"A-111,;
  Master->PartNo)
```

See Also FIND(), FIND, LOOKUP, SEEK(), SEEK

LOWER()

Converting Letters to Lowercase

• SYNTAX

LOWER(*character*)

• USAGE LOWER() converts all letters in a character string to lowercase. It has no effect on other characters.

• EXAMPLE The next command converts all values in a non-memo field named FName to initial capitalization followed by lowercase letters (for instance, JOHN is converted to John):

```
REPLACE ALL FName WITH ;
    UPPER(LEFT(FName,1))+ ;
    LOWER(RIGHT(FName,LEN(FName)-1))
```

See Also ISALPHA(), ISLOWER(), ISUPPER(), MLINE(), UPPER()

LTRIM()

Trimming Leading Blanks

• SYNTAX

LTRIM(*character*)

• USAGE LTRIM() removes leading blanks from a character string. You can use it in conjunction with the STR() function to remove leading blanks from converted numeric and float data.

• EXAMPLE The following commands display the string *You have won $100.00 dollars!*

```
Prize = 100
? "You have won $"+LTRIM(STR(Prize,9,2))+ "dollars!"
```

See Also RIGHT(), RTRIM(), STR(), SUBSTR(), TRIM()

LUPDATE()

Determining the Date of the Last Change

• SYNTAX

LUPDATE(*(alias)***)**

• USAGE LUPDATE() returns the date on which the database file was last updated. The returned value is the date data type. If the optional alias is excluded, the currently selected database is assumed.

• EXAMPLE The next command prints the number of days since the currently selected database file was last changed:

```
? "This file was last changed "+ ;
    LTRIM(STR(DATE()-LUPDATE()))+ ;
    "days ago."
```

See Also DATE(), LIST STRUCTURE

MAX()

Finding the Larger of Two Numbers

• SYNTAX

MAX(*expression1,expression2***)**

• USAGE The MAX() function determines the higher of any two expressions, including numeric, character, or date expressions. Typically, you use it to establish a lower limit on some numeric value or to return the later of two dates.

• EXAMPLE The following command displays an overhead cost using either ten percent or the value stored in the field named Overhead, whichever is higher (that is, ten percent is the minimum overhead):

```
LIST "Total with overhead = ", ;
     Cost*MAX(.10,Overhead)
```

See Also CALCULATE, MIN()

MCOL()

Determining the Mouse Cursor's Column Position

• SYNTAX

MCOL()

• USAGE MCOL() returns the column number of the current position of the mouse cursor on the screen. It returns zero if no mouse is installed.

• EXAMPLE The following commands allow you to reposition a previously defined window with the mouse. The message appears below the status bar if SET STATUS is on. Move the mouse pointer somewhere on the screen outside the window and click the left button. The mouse position is the new upper-left corner of the window.

```
DEFINE WINDOW Wind1 FROM 2,40 TO 10,65
IF ISMOUSE()
   ACTIVATE WINDOW Wind1
   SET MESSAGE TO "Move mouse to new window ;
  location and click left button."
   ON MOUSE MOVE WINDOW Wind1 TO MROW(), MCOL()
ELSE
   @ 2,2 SAY "Sorry, no mouse installed!"
ENDIF
```

See Also COL(), ISMOUSE(), MROW(), ON MOUSE, PCOL(), PROW(), ROW(), SET MOUSE

MDX()

Determining the Name of the .MDX File

• SYNTAX

MDX(*[number [,alias]]***)**

• USAGE MDX() returns the file name of the active .MDX file specified by the index order number. If no index order number is specified, the master index is assumed. If there is no .MDX file associated with *number* or there is no list of active .MDX files, dBASE IV returns a null string.

The optional *alias* argument allows you to specify a database that is open in any other work area.

• **EXAMPLE** This command displays the name of the first-opened index file for the currently open Master.DBF database:

```
? MDX(1,"Master")
```

See Also KEY(), NDX(), ORDER(), TAG()

MDY()

Converting a Date to Month-Day-Year Format

• **SYNTAX**

MDY(*date***)**

• **USAGE** The MDY() function converts a valid dBASE IV date to the Month dd, yy format. If SET CENTURY is on, the year is expressed with the century prefix.

• **EXAMPLE** These commands display *June 01, 1994*:

```
SET CENTURY ON
? MDY({06/01/94})
```

See Also DMY(), SET CENTURY, SET DATE, SET MARK

MEMLINES()

Counting the Printed Lines for a Memo Field

• SYNTAX

MEMLINES(*memo field name***)**

• USAGE The MEMLINES() function counts the number of lines required to print a memo field using the current setting of SET MEMOWIDTH.

• EXAMPLE In the following routine, MEMLINES() prevents memo fields from being split by a page break:

```
USE Referenc
SET MEMOWIDTH TO 65

SCAN ALL
    ? Author
    ? Title
    IF MEMLINES(Abstract) > _plength - _plineno
      EJECT
    ENDIF
    ? Abstract
ENDSCAN
```

See Also MLINE(), SET MEMOWIDTH

MEMORY()

Determining Available Memory

• SYNTAX

MEMORY(*(number)***)**

• USAGE MEMORY() returns the amount of unused RAM available in kilobytes (1024-byte increments). The optional argument returns the amounts of different types of available memory, as shown in Table 4.2.

Table 4.2: Arguments Used with MEMORY()

Argument Value	Returns
0 or none	Amount of available memory (sum of values returned by 3 and 6)
1	Amount of memory in the heap and available to dBASE.
2	Amount of low DOS memory (in 640K region) available for binary files
3 or 4	Amount of extended memory unallocated
5	Amount of memory under control to the Virtual Memory Manager
6	Amount of memory currently allocated to the dBASE buffer manager
7	Size of the swap file, if any

• **EXAMPLE** The following routine runs an external program named QuikCalc only if there is at least 128K of RAM available:

```
IF MEMORY(0) >= 128
   RUN QuikCalc
ELSE
   ? "Not enough memory available"
ENDIF
```

See Also DISKSPACE(), GETENV(), OS()

MENU()

Determining the Name of the Active Menu

• **SYNTAX**

```
MENU()
```

• **USAGE** MENU() returns the name of the most recently activated horizontal bar menu. If no menu is active, a null string is returned. You can use MENU() in a procedure to display a help screen relevant to the current menu.

• **EXAMPLE** This program segment displays the contents of the file named MainHelp.TXT if the currently active menu is named MainMenu:

```
CASE MENU() = "MAINMENU"
     DISPLAY WINDOW HelpMsg
     TYPE MainHelp.TXT
```

See Also ACTIVATE MENU, DEFINE MENU

MESSAGE()

Accessing Error Messages

• SYNTAX

MESSAGE()

• USAGE MESSAGE() returns the error message describing the error that triggered an ON ERROR condition.

• EXAMPLE See **ON ERROR** in Part 2.

See Also CERROR(), ERROR(), ON ERROR

MIN()

Finding the Smaller of Two Expressions

• SYNTAX

MIN(*expression1*,*expression2***)**

• USAGE MIN() returns the lower value of any two expressions, including numeric, character, or date expressions. You can use it to place a ceiling (maximum) on a numeric value or to return the earlier of two dates.

• EXAMPLE The following command calculates tax on a field named Cost, using either seven percent or the value stored in the field named TaxAmt, whichever is smaller (that is, seven percent is the maximum tax amount):

```
LIST "Total with tax = ",Cost*MIN(.07,TaxAmt)
```

The next command displays 12/31/94 or the current date, whichever is smaller:

```
? MIN({12/31/94},DATE())
```

See Also CALCULATE, MAX()

MLINE()

Extracting a Line from a Memo Field

• SYNTAX

MLINE(*memo field name,number***)**

• USAGE MLINE() returns a specified line of text from a memo field. It interacts with the current SET MEMOWIDTH setting to determine the number and content of the line.

• EXAMPLE If Abstract is a memo field that contains the text *Now is the time for all good men to come to the aid…,* and SET MEMOWIDTH is set to 20, the command

```
? MLINE(Abstract,2)
```

displays *all good men to come* (the second line when Abstract is word wrapped within 20 columns).

See Also MEMLINES(), SET MEMOWIDTH

MOD()

Calculating the Modulus

• SYNTAX

MOD(*number1*,*number2*)

• USAGE MOD() returns the remainder, or *modulus*, from the division of the numbers specified in the argument. If *number1* is evenly divisible by *number2*, MOD() returns 0. To find the integer part of the dividend, use INT(). *Number2* cannot be 0.

• EXAMPLE The command below returns the remainder 3:

```
? MOD(33,15)
```

The following command lists every tenth record in a database:

```
LIST FOR MOD(RECNO(),10) = 0
```

See Also CEILING(), FLOOR(), INT()

MONTH()

Isolating the Month in a Date

• SYNTAX

MONTH(*date*)

• USAGE MONTH() returns the number of the month from any date expression. The value returned is a number from 1 to 12, where 1 is January and 12 is December.

• **EXAMPLE** This command lists records that have June 1994 dates in the OrdDate field:

```
LIST FOR MONTH(OrdDate)=6;
   .AND. YEAR(OrdDate) = 1994
```

See Also CMONTH(), DAY(), YEAR()

MROW()

Determining the Mouse Cursor's Row Position

• **SYNTAX**

MROW()

• **USAGE** MROW() returns the row number of the current position of the mouse cursor on the screen. It returns zero if no mouse is installed.

• **EXAMPLE** See **MCOL()**.

See Also COL(), ISMOUSE(), MCOL(), ON MOUSE, PCOL(), PROW(), ROW(), SET MOUSE

NDX()

Determining an Index File Name

• **SYNTAX**

NDX(*[number[,alias]]***)**

• USAGE NDX() returns the name of an index (.NDX) file based on its position in the list specified by a SET INDEX TO or USE...INDEX command. The argument must be a number between one and seven. If you do not specify an alias, the current work area is assumed. If no index number is specified, NDX() returns the name of the controlling .NDX file, if any.

To access names of indexes stored in a multiple (.MDX) index file, use the MDX() function. DISPLAY STATUS shows a list of all indexes associated with the database file.

Only the drive and the file names are returned unless SET FULLPATH is on.

• EXAMPLE The following commands display *C:FNAME.NDX*, the name of the second listed index file:

```
USE OldData INDEX LName,FName
? NDX(2,"OldData")
```

See Also ALIAS(), DBF(), FIELD(), LUPDATE(), MDX(), ORDER(), RECCOUNT(), RECSIZE(), SET FULLPATH, SET INDEX, SET ORDER, USE

NETWORK()

Determining Network Installation

• SYNTAX

```
NETWORK()
```

• USAGE NETWORK() returns logical true (.T.) if dBASE IV is currently running on a network. If you are developing an application to run on either a network or single-user system, use this function to check the current environment and branch to appropriate record-keeping routines.

• EXAMPLE This routine calls a procedure named GetUser only if the program is currently running on a network:

```
IF NETWORK()
   DO GetUser
ENDIF
```

See Also GETENV(), OS()

NPV()

See **CALCULATE** in Part 2.

ORDER()

Determining which Index File or Tag is Active

• SYNTAX

ORDER(*[alias]***)**

• USAGE ORDER() returns the name of the active index file or .MDX tag. Unless you use the *alias* option, the ORDER() function examines the active work area. ORDER() returns a null string if there is no active index.

• EXAMPLE The following command returns the name of the index file or tag controlling the database in the work area named PartList:

```
? ORDER("PartList")
```

See Also KEY(), MDX(), NDX(), SET ORDER, TAG()

OS()

Determining the Current Operating System

• SYNTAX

```
OS()
```

• USAGE OS() returns the name and version number of the operating system currently in use.

• EXAMPLE You can use the general structure of the following IF clause to perform different commands under the DOS and UNIX operating systems:

```
SET EXACT OFF
IF OS() = "DOS"
  commands...
ENDIF

IF OS() = "UNIX"
  commands...
ENDIF
```

See Also GETENV(), RUN, VERSION()

PAD()

Determining the Bar Menu Selection

• SYNTAX

```
PAD()
```

• USAGE The PAD() function returns the name of the most recently selected option (called a pad) from a horizontal bar menu.

The value returned is the name specified in the DEFINE PAD command. PAD() does not receive a value until the user selects the pad by highlighting the option and pressing ↵.

If no menu has been defined or none is active, PAD() returns a null string.

• **EXAMPLE** If the second option on a horizontal bar menu was defined with the command

DEFINE PAD Option2 OF MainMenu PROMPT "Edit"

and the user selects that option when the menu is activated, the PAD() function will return OPTION2.

See Also BARCOUNT(), BARPROMPT(), DEFINE BAR, DEFINE MENU, DEFINE PAD, DEFINE POPUP, MENU(), ON MENU/PAD, ON SELECTION MENU/PAD, PADPROMPT(), POPUP()

PADPROMPT()

Determining the Text of the Bar Menu Selection

• **SYNTAX**

PADPROMPT(*pad name (,menu name)***)**

• **USAGE** PADPROMPT() returns the text of the specified option (pad) from a horizontal bar menu. The text returned is the expression specified as the PROMPT in the DEFINE PAD command. The named menu must be defined but need not be active.

If no menu is specified, the active menu is assumed. If no menu has been defined, PADPROMPT() returns a null string.

• EXAMPLE If you define the third option of the horizontal bar menu MainMenu with:

```
DEFINE PAD Option3 OF MainMenu PROMPT "Print Report"
```

the function

```
PADPROMPT(Option3,MainMenu)
```

returns *Print Report* whether the MainMenu is active or not.

See Also ACTIVATE MENU, DEFINE MENU/PAD, MENU(), ON EXIT MENU/PAD, ON MENU/PAD, ON SELECTION MENU/PAD, PAD(), PROMPT(), POPUP()

PAYMENT()

Calculating Payment on a Loan

• SYNTAX

PAYMENT(*principal,rate,periods***)**

• USAGE PAYMENT() calculates the periodic payment required to amortize a loan with a specified *principal* and interest *rate,* and which is spread over a certain number of payment *periods*. The period of the interest rate must match the period of the payment. The interest rate must be expressed as (or converted to) a decimal.

• EXAMPLE The following commands display $1,230.26, the monthly payment on a loan of $160,000. Note that the annual interest rate (APR) is divided by 1200 to determine the monthly interest rate as a decimal value. The term (years) is multiplied by 12 to determine the number of monthly payments:

```
LoanAmt = 160000
APR = 8.5
Years = 30
? PAYMENT(LoanAmt,APR/1200,Years*12)
```

See Also CALCULATE, FV(), PV()

PCOL()

Determining the Printer Column Position

• SYNTAX

```
PCOL()
```

• USAGE PCOL() returns the current column position of the printer print head.

• EXAMPLE The commands that follow print the contents of the field or variable named Address at the current row position, five columns to the right of the current column position:

```
? Address AT PCOL()+5
```

See Also @, ?, COL(), PRINTJOB...ENDPRINTJOB, PROW(), ROW(), SET MARGIN

PCOUNT()

Determining the Number of Parameters

• SYNTAX

```
PCOUNT()
```

• USAGE PCOUNT() returns the number of parameters that are passed to a procedure or a user-defined function. It can be used to trap and correct errors that can occur when too many or too few parameters are passed. It can also be used to fill in with a default value for a parameter that is optional.

• EXAMPLE The CAGR user-defined function for calculating the compound annual growth rate is described in the LOG10() paragraph. CAGR requires three parameters; however, you can get away with specifying just two of them—the Initial value and the Goal—and leave the Years as a default value. The following commands added to the CAGR function provide the default value of 10 years if only two parameters are passed:

```
FUNCTION CAGR
PARAMETERS Initial, Goal, Years
ParaNum = PCOUNT()
IF ParaNum = 2
    Years = 10
ENDIF
CAGR = (10^((LOG10(Goal/Initial))/Years))-1
RETURN CAGR
```

Then the command

```
? CAGR(5000,10000)
```

returns .07 or seven percent.

See Also DEBUG, DO, FUNCTION, PARAMETERS, PROCEDURE

PI()

Using the Value of PI (π)

• SYNTAX

```
PI()
```

• USAGE The PI() function returns the value of π (3.14159). Use SET PRECISION and SET DECIMALS to control the accuracy and number of displayed decimal places.

• **EXAMPLE** This command calculates and displays the area of a circle with a radius of 12 centimeters:

```
SET DECIMALS TO 10
SET PRECISION TO 10
? PI()*12^2
```

POPUP()

Determining the Name of the Active Pop-Up

• **SYNTAX**

```
POPUP()
```

• **USAGE** The POPUP() function returns the name of the active pop-up menu. If no pop-up menu is active, even if the pop-up menu has just been deactivated in an ON SELECTION POPUP command, POPUP() returns a null string.

You typically use POPUP() in procedures called by an ON KEY command to determine the currently active menu and display an appropriate help screen.

• **EXAMPLE** The following commands display the contents of a text file named HelpAdd.TXT in a window name HelpWind when the current pop-up menu is named AddMenu:

```
CASE POPUP() = "ADDMENU"
     ACTIVATE WINDOW HelpWind
     TYPE HelpAdd.TXT
```

See Also ACTIVATE POPUP, BAR(), BARCOUNT(), BARPROMPT(), DEFINE POPUP, MENU(), ON EXIT POPUP, ON POPUP, ON SELECTION POPUP, PAD(), PADPROMPT(), PROMPT()

PRINTSTATUS()

Checking the Printer Status

- **SYNTAX**

PRINTSTATUS()

- **USAGE** PRINTSTATUS() returns logical true (.T.) if the printer is ready to accept output. Otherwise, it returns logical false (.F.). This may not be accurate when used with a network printer on a server.

- **EXAMPLE** If the printer is not ready, the following routine will beep and ask the user to prepare the printer and press any key to continue:

```
DO WHILE .NOT. PRINTSTATUS()
  ACTIVATE WINDOW ErrMsg
  ? CHR(7)
  ? "Please prepare printer, then: "
  WAIT
  DEACTIVATE WINDOW ErrMsg
ENDDO
```

See Also SET DEVICE, SET PRINTER

PROGRAM()

Determining the Active Command File

- **SYNTAX**

PROGRAM()

• USAGE The PROGRAM() function is a debugging tool that returns the name of the currently running program or the program that was running when an error condition occurred. If the error condition was caused by a procedure in a procedure file, PROGRAM() returns the name of the procedure, not the name of the procedure file.

• EXAMPLE See **LINENO()**.

See Also DEBUG, LINENO(), ON ERROR, RESUME, SET DEVELOPMENT, SUSPEND

PROMPT()

Determining the Option Selected from a Menu

• SYNTAX

PROMPT()

• USAGE PROMPT() returns the text of the most recently selected option from a horizontal bar menu, pop-up menu, or list. If you include in the associated DEFINE POPUP command a PROMPT definition with the FIELDS, FILES, or STRUCTURE option, the PROMPT() function returns the name selected from the list that is displayed on the screen.

If PROMPT is defined in the DEFINE BAR or DEFINE PAD command, PROMPT() returns the text specified in the PROMPT portion of the command.

If there are no pop-ups or menus in memory, or if the user pressed **Esc** instead of selecting an option, PROMPT() returns a null string.

• EXAMPLE The routine that follows displays in a files list the names of files with the .DBF extension. The file name that the user selected is stored in a memory variable named dbFileName:

```
DEFINE POPUP FileList FROM 5,5 ;
    PROMPT FILES LIKE *.DBF
ON SELECTION POPUP FileList DEACTIVATE POPUP

ACTIVATE POPUP FileList
dbFileName = PROMPT()

USE (dbFileName)
```

See Also BAR(), BARCOUNT(), DEFINE BAR/MENU/PAD/POPUP, ON BAR/MENU/PAD/POPUP, ON EXIT BAR/MENU/PAD/POPUP, ON SELECTION BAR/MENU/PAD/POPUP, PADPROMPT(), POPUP()

PROW()

Determining the Printer Row Position

• SYNTAX

```
PROW()
```

• USAGE PROW() returns the current row position of the printer print head. You can use it for relative addressing on the printer, so that the location of the next row to be printed depends on the current row. But since the printer can only scroll forward, if you subtract from the current row position, dBASE ejects the current page and prints on the specified row on the next page.

• EXAMPLE The next command prints the contents of the Address field one row beneath the current row at column 32:

```
SET DEVICE TO PRINT
@ PROW()+1,32 SAY Address
```

See Also COL(), EJECT, PCOL(), ROW(), SET DEVICE, SET PRINTER

PV()

Calculating an Investment's Present Value

• SYNTAX

PV(*payment,rate,periods*)

• USAGE PV() calculates the present value of an investment where *payment* is a numeric expression representing a fixed regular payment, *rate* is a decimal expression representing the interest rate, and *periods* is a whole number representing the number of payment periods. As with PAYMENT(), the payment amount, interest rate, and number of periods must agree in time and frequency. The interest rate must be in decimal form.

• EXAMPLE Suppose you've paid $1,000 per month for 5 years on a 30-year mortgage borrowed at 8 percent annual interest. To determine the present value (principal paid) at the end of the fifth year, you could enter these commands:

```
Payment = 1000
APR = .08
ThisYear = 5
? PV(Payment,APR/12,ThisYear*12)
```

See Also CALCULATE, FV(), PAYMENT()

RAND()

Generating a Random Number

• SYNTAX

RAND(*(number)***)**

• USAGE RAND() returns a random number from 0 to 0.999999, using a default seed number of 100001. You can specify your own seed number by using the optional *number* parameter. If the seed number is negative, the seed is taken from the system clock.

To return the next random number in a series, repeat RAND() with no argument. To reset the random number generator to the default seed, use RAND(1000001).

• EXAMPLE The following routine plays a series of 40 randomly selected tones:

```
SET TALK OFF
Counter = 1
DO WHILE Counter <= 40
  SET BELL TO MAX(RAND()*5000,19),1
  CHR(7)+CHR(14)
  Counter=Counter + 1
ENDDO
```

RAT()

Finding One String within Another

• SYNTAX

RAT(*string1,string2 (,number)***)**

• **USAGE** The RAT() function searches the second character string for the first character string (or substring expression). RAT() is the same as AT() except that it starts the search from the right end of the string. The second argument can be a character string, character memory variable or field, or a memo field name. When searching a long memo field, RAT() searches only the first 64K of data.

If the first string is found, RAT() returns the starting position (as counted from the beginning of the string, not the end) of the first expression in the second. If no starting position is found or the first string is longer than the second string, RAT() returns zero.

If you include the optional number argument, RAT() returns the starting position of the *n*th occurrence of the first string in the second (counted from the beginning).

RAT() is case-sensitive.

• **EXAMPLE** The function

```
RAT("abc","abcabcabc")
```

returns 7, while the function

```
RAT("ABC","abcabcabc")
```

returns 0, and the function

```
RAT("abc","abcabcabc",2)
```

returns 4.

See Also AT(), LEFT(), RIGHT(), STUFF(), SUBSTR()

READKEY()

Determining the Key Used to Exit a Screen

• **SYNTAX**

```
READKEY()
```

• USAGE READKEY() returns an integer corresponding to the key that was pressed to exit from a full-screen operation (APPEND, BROWSE, EDIT, MODIFY, or READ). READKEY() returns one of two possible values for a single keypress, depending on whether any data items on the screen were altered. If no changes were made to the data, READKEY() has a value from 0 to 36. If any field on the screen was changed, the READKEY() value is increased by 256.

Table 4.3 lists values returned by READKEY() for both edited and unchanged data. Pressing Ctrl-key equivalents returns the same result. For example, pressing **Ctrl-Q** returns the same result as **Esc**; pressing **Ctrl-S** returns the same result as ←.

Table 4.3: Values Returned by READKEY()

Key Pressed	READKEY() When Data Not Changed	READKEY() When Data Changed
←	0	256
→	1	257
↑	4	260
↓	5	261
↵ (or screen filled)	15	271
↵ (empty APPEND screen)	16	
Backspace		256
Ctrl-End		270
Ctrl-Home	33	289
Ctrl-←	2	258
Ctrl-M	15	271
Ctrl-PgDn	35	291
Ctrl-PgUp	34	290
Ctrl-→	3	259
End	3	259

Table 4.3: Values Returned by READKEY() (Continued)

Key Pressed	READKEY() When Data Not Changed	READKEY() When Data Changed
Esc	12	
F1	36	292
PgDn	7	263
PgUp	6	262

• **EXAMPLE** The next routine copies array data to a database only if the key pressed to exit the READ command indicates that changes were made:

```
READ
IF READKEY() >= 256
   APPEND FROM ARRAY OnScreen
ENDIF
```

See Also INKEY(), LASTKEY(), ON KEY, READ

RECCOUNT()

Determining the Number of Records

• **SYNTAX**

RECCOUNT(*[alias]***)**

• **USAGE** RECCOUNT() returns the total number of records in a database, regardless of a current filter or the SET DELETED setting. If you do not specify an alias, the number of records in the currently selected database is displayed.

• EXAMPLE You could use the following @...SAY command inside a SCAN...ENDSCAN loop to display the loop's progress:

```
@ 2,2 SAY "Processing record "+ ;
    LTRIM(STR(RECNO()))+" of "+ ;
    LTRIM(STR(RECCOUNT()))
```

See Also DBF(), DISKSPACE(), FIELD(), RECNO(), RECSIZE()

RECNO()

Accessing the Current Record Number

• SYNTAX

RECNO(*[alias]***)**

• USAGE RECNO() returns the number of the current record. If you do not specify an alias, RECNO() displays the record number in the current work area. RECNO() returns 1 if the record pointer is at the first record or if there are no records in the database file. RECNO() returns 0 if no database file is currently in use.

• EXAMPLE This command displays the record number in the currently selected database and in the database open in work area 2:

```
? RECNO(), RECNO(2)
```

See Also RECCOUNT()

RECSIZE()

Calculating the Size of Database Records

• SYNTAX

RECSIZE(*[alias]***)**

• USAGE RECSIZE() returns the number of bytes used by a single record in the specified database file. If you do not specify an alias, the size of each record in the currently selected database is returned. If no file is currently in use, RECSIZE() returns zero.

• EXAMPLE The next command shows the size of a record in the Master database, open in another work area:

```
? RECSIZE("Master")
```

See Also DBF(), DISKSPACE(), RECCOUNT()

REPLICATE()

Repeating a Character String

• SYNTAX

REPLICATE(*character,number***)**

• USAGE REPLICATE() repeats a character string a specified number of times. The maximum length of the resulting character string is 254 characters.

• EXAMPLE Assuming that the field named Weight contains values in the range of 10 to 100, the following command displays the contents of the Weight field along with a small horizontal bar graph:

```
LIST WEIGHT,REPLICATE("*",Weight/10)
```

RIGHT()

Accessing the Rightmost Characters

• SYNTAX

RIGHT(*character,number***)**

• USAGE RIGHT() returns a specified number of characters starting from the right end of a character string or a memo field. If the numeric expression is less than 1, a null string is returned. If the numeric expression is greater than the length of the character expression, the entire character string is returned (up to 254 characters).

• EXAMPLE The command below returns the file name extension (.DBF) from the currently open database file:

```
? RIGHT(DBF(),4)
```

See Also AT(), LEFT(), LTRIM(), STUFF(), SUBSTR(), TRIM()

RLOCK()

Locking a Record

• SYNTAX

RLOCK(*(number list,alias)/(alias)***)**

• USAGE RLOCK() operates more like a command than a function. It attempts to lock one or more records in the current or specified work area. If the records are not already locked, RLOCK() locks them and returns logical true (.T.). If any one of the records in the list is already locked by another user and cannot be locked, RLOCK() returns logical false (.F.) and none of the records are locked. This all-or-none feature prevents processing deadlock in a multiuser environment.

The optional *number list* lists record numbers to be locked, separated by commas. The optional *alias* specifies a work area other than the current work area. The work area can be a number (1–40), letter (A–J), or the database or alias specified in a previous USE command. If you use the alias without a list of record numbers, dBASE attempts to lock the current record in that file.

A record that is locked by one user can be viewed, but not changed, by other users. Closing the file, quitting dBASE, or executing an UNLOCK command releases the record lock.

In dBASE IV, unlike earlier versions of dBASE, RLOCK() is additive; it does not unlock a previously requested lock. That is, each record locked with RLOCK() remains locked until an UNLOCK command is issued.

The maximum number of simultaneous locks is 100.

LOCK() is an alternative syntax for the RLOCK() function.

• EXAMPLE The following command attempts to lock record numbers 2, 5, 10, 13, and 15 in the Master database for an edit, and returns a message if any one of the records cannot be locked:

```
IF RLOCK(2,5,10,13,15,"Master")
    EDIT
ELSE
  ? "Can't lock the records, one already in use."
ENDIF
```

See Also FLOCK(), NETWORK(), SET ENCRYPTION, SET LOCK, UNLOCK

ROLLBACK()

Testing the Success of a Rollback

• SYNTAX

ROLLBACK()

• USAGE ROLLBACK() returns logical true (.T.) if the last ROLLBACK command was successful. Otherwise, it returns logical false (.F.).

• EXAMPLE The following lines display one of two screen messages, depending on the success of the ROLLBACK command.

```
ROLLBACK
IF ROLLBACK()
  ? "Original values restored"
ELSE
  ? "Could not retrieve original data"
ENDIF
```

See Also BEGIN/END TRANSACTION, COMPLETED(), ISMARKED(), ROLLBACK

ROUND()

Rounding off a Number

• SYNTAX

ROUND(*number1,number2***)**

• USAGE The ROUND() function rounds off the first number to the number of decimal places specified by the second number. If the second number is negative, the function begins rounding the integer portion of the number, counting the number of places leftward from the decimal point.

• EXAMPLE The following commands demonstrate the various effects of the ROUND() function on the number 123.4567.

```
? ROUND(123.4567,3)
   123.457

? ROUND(123.4567,0)
   123.000

? ROUND(123.4567,-2)
   100.000
```

See Also CEILING(), FLOOR(), INT(), SET DECIMALS, STR(), VAL()

ROW()

Determining the Row Position of the Cursor

• SYNTAX

```
ROW()
```

• USAGE The ROW() function returns the current row position of the cursor on the screen.

• EXAMPLE The next command displays the contents of the Amount field two rows beneath the current row, at column 5:

```
@ ROW () + 2,5 SAY Amount PICTURE "9,999.99"
```

See Also @, COL(), PCOL(), PROW()

RTOD()

Converting Radians to Degrees

• SYNTAX

RTOD(*number***)**

• USAGE RTOD() converts an angle size from radians to degrees.

• EXAMPLE The command that follows converts $\pi/2$ radians to 90 degrees:

```
? RTOD((PI)/2)
```

See Also ACOS(), ASIN(), ATAN(), ATN2(), COS(), DTOR(), SIN(), TAN()

RTRIM()

See **TRIM()**.

RUN()

Running an External Program

• SYNTAX

RUN(*(expression1,) command (,expression2)***)**

• USAGE The RUN() function instructs an external DOS command or program to execute and, depending on the command, returns a completion code.

Both expressions evaluate to a logical true (.T.) or false (.F.) and indicate how the external program is to be executed. If the first expression evaluates to .T., the command is passed to the operating system for execution. If it evaluates to .F. or not included, the dBASE command interpreter is called.

If the second expression evaluates to .T., dBASE makes more memory available for the external program. If it evaluates to .F. or is not included, dBASE does not swap out of memory and the external program must run in the available memory.

• EXAMPLE To copy all database files to the Temp directory, use

```
command = "COPY *.DBF \TEMP"
RUN(&command)
```

Tip: Do not run any Terminate-and-Stay-Resident (TSR) programs with the RUN() function.

See Also CALL, CALL(), LOAD, RUN/!

SEEK()

Searching an Index

• SYNTAX

SEEK(*expression [,alias]***)**

• USAGE SEEK() searches the controlling index of a database for a specified value. If SEEK() finds an exact match, it returns logical true (.T.) and positions the record pointer at the appropriate record. If unsuccessful, SEEK() returns logical false (.F.) and positions the record pointer at EOF(). SET NEAR does not affect the results of the SEEK() function.

• EXAMPLE The following commands allow a new PartNo to be added to the Orders database only if the part number exists in the PartNo index of the Master.DBF database:

```
USE Orders IN 1
USE Master ORDER PartNo IN 2

SELECT 1
APPEND BLANK
@ 2,2 GET PartNo PICTURE "!!!!!" ;
    VALID SEEK(Orders->PartNo,"Master")

READ
```

See Also FIND, FOUND(), LOOKUP(), SEEK, SET NEAR

SELECT()

Finding an Unused Work Area

• SYNTAX

SELECT(*[alias]***)**

• USAGE SELECT() returns the next unused work area as a number between 1 and 40 or the number of the work area that contains the specified file alias.

• EXAMPLE To open the CustList database in the next available work area, then display that work area number, enter

```
USE CustList IN SELECT()
? SELECT("CustList")
```

See Also ALIAS()

SET()

Determining the Status of a SET Command

• SYNTAX

SET(*character***)**

• USAGE SET() returns the status of a SET command. The argument must be a valid SET option, enclosed in quotation marks. SET() works with SET commands that use ON, OFF, or an integer value setting. It also returns the setting for many other parameters such as ATTRIBUTES, DIRECTORY, FILTER, PATH, PROCEDURE, RELATION, and VIEW. SET() returns up to 254 characters of the more lengthy settings such as PATH.

• EXAMPLE This routine sets the TALK parameter on while reindexing a database. Then it sets TALK to its original setting.

```
CurrStatus = SET("TALK")
SET TALK ON
REINDEX
IF CurrStatus = "OFF"
  SET TALK OFF
ENDIF
```

See Also LIST/DISPLAY STATUS, SET

SIGN()

Determining the Sign of a Number

• SYNTAX

SIGN(*number***)**

• USAGE SIGN() evaluates a number or numeric expression and returns the mathematical sign of the results. SIGN() returns a 1 if the number is positive, –1 if the number is negative, and 0 if the number is 0.

• EXAMPLE A computed field, X1, is not allowed to go negative and, if it does, is set to zero:

```
X1 = <formula>
IF SIGN(X1) < 0
  X1 = 0
ENDIF
```

See Also ABS()

SIN()

Calculating the Sine of an Angle

• SYNTAX

SIN(*number*)

• USAGE SIN() calculates the sine of an angle expressed in radians. The value returned by SIN() is a Float data type number between –1 and +1.

• EXAMPLE The command below displays the sine of a 45-degree angle:

```
? SIN(DTOR(45))
```

See Also ACOS(), ASIN(), ATAN(), ATN2(), COS(), DTOR(), PI(), RTOD(), TAN()

SOUNDEX()

Determining Sound-Alike Codes

• SYNTAX

SOUNDEX(*character*)

• USAGE SOUNDEX() returns a four-character (letter, digit, digit, digit) code representing the phonetic spelling of a character string. The first character matches the first letter of the original string. All vowels plus h and w are dropped unless they are the first letter of the string.

All remaining alphabetic characters are assigned a number according to the following list:

bfpv	1
cgjkqsxz	2
dt	3
l	4
mn	5
r	6

All but the first occurrence of two or more adjacent codes are dropped. Leading blanks are ignored. The first non-alphabetic character stops the creation of the code. If the code is less than four characters long, trailing zeros are added.

If the first nonblank character is non-alphabetic, four zeros (0000) are returned.

SOUNDEX() is used to locate close matches between character strings by using sound instead of having to adhere to the correct spelling.

• EXAMPLE The commands that follow create an index of SOUNDEX codes. The SEEK and LIST commands use the index to display values that sound like Smith (SOUNDEX code S530):

```
INDEX ON SOUNDEX(LastName) TAG Sounds
SET ORDER TO Sounds
SEEK SOUNDEX("Smith")
LIST WHILE SOUNDEX(LastName)= ;
  SOUNDEX("Smith")
```

See Also DIFFERENCE(), LOCATE

SPACE()

Creating Blank Spaces

• SYNTAX

SPACE(*number*)

• USAGE SPACE() creates a character string containing a specified number of blank spaces. SPACE() is frequently used to initialize character memory variables.

• EXAMPLE The following command assigns 20 blank spaces to a variable named LookFor and displays a 20-character field on the screen for the user to fill in:

```
LookFor = SPACE(20)

@ 5,5 SAY "Enter name to look for ";
    GET LookFor
READ
```

SQRT()

Calculating the Square Root

• SYNTAX

SQRT(*number*)

• USAGE SQRT() returns the square root of the number passed to the function. The value returned is a number with either the default number of decimal places or the number of decimal places in the expression, whichever is larger.

Use the ABS() function to change a negative number to positive before taking its square root. Attempting to find the square root of a negative number will cause an error.

• EXAMPLE The following commands display the square root of 3213.56.

```
Numb = 3213.56
? SQRT(Numb)
56.69
```

The next command displays the cube root of 27:

```
? 27^(1/3)
3
```

STD()

See **CALCULATE** in Part 2.

STR()

Converting a Number to a String

• SYNTAX

STR(*number(,length (,decimal))***)**

• Usage STR() converts a number to a character string. The *length* argument sets the total length of the character expression (including any decimal digits, the decimal point itself, and the minus sign), and the *decimal* argument sets the number of decimal places to be included. If you omit either parameter, dBASE uses the default setting of ten characters and no decimal places.

If you specify a length smaller than the number of digits to the left of the decimal point in the numeric expression, dBASE returns asterisks in place of the number. If you specify fewer decimal digits than are in the numeric expression, dBASE rounds the result to the specified number of decimal places.

You can use LTRIM() to remove leading blanks from a converted number in displayed text, but do not use it in an index expression. This would result in key values of differing lengths.

• EXAMPLE The following command creates an index named DateQty that will order records by OrdDate order and by the numeric Qty field within each date:

```
INDEX ON DTOS(OrdDate)+STR(Qty,3) TAG DateQty
```

See Also LTRIM(), TRANSFORM(), VAL()

STUFF()

Inserting or Replacing a String

• SYNTAX

STUFF(*target,start,replace,bullet***)**

• USAGE STUFF() combines two character expressions to produce a third character expression.

STUFF() lets you insert the character string listed as *bullet* into the *target* character string, starting at the numeric *start* position and replacing the number of characters specified in *replace*.

If the *replace* value is 0 or a negative number, no characters in the target string are overwritten, so the *bullet* is inserted into the *target* string. If *bullet* is a null string, STUFF() removes characters from the *target* string, because the overwritten characters are replaced by nothing.

The *target* string must be character type, not memo data type.

• EXAMPLE The following commands illustrate the outcome of various STUFF() operations with two strings named Target and Bullet:

```
Target = "This is a long sentence"
Bullet = "IN WE GO"

? STUFF(Target,5,0,Bullet)
  ThisIN WE GO is a long sentence
? STUFF(Target,5,0," "+Bullet)
  This IN WE GO is a long sentence
? STUFF(Target,6,4,Bullet)
  This IN WE GO long sentence
? STUFF(Target,6,10,"")
  This sentence
```

See Also LEFT(), RIGHT(), SUBSTR()

SUBSTR()

Extracting a Substring

• SYNTAX

SUBSTR(*character,start[,length]***)**

• USAGE SUBSTR() extracts a smaller string from a larger string or a memo field. The *start* argument is a number indicating the starting point of the string to be extracted. The optional *length* argument is a number representing the number of characters to be extracted. If you omit *length,* SUBSTR() will extract all characters to the right of the *start* position.

• EXAMPLE These commands show how you can use SUBSTR() with the AT() function to extract a substring from a larger string when you do not know the numeric position of the starting character:

```
? SUBSTR(DBF(),AT(".",DBF()),4)
```

displays .DBF.

See Also AT(), LEFT(), LTRIM(), RIGHT(), STR(), STUFF()

SUM()

See **CALCULATE** in Part 2.

TAG()

Determining the TAG Name in an .MDX File

• SYNTAX

TAG(*((mdx filename,) number (,alias))***)**

• USAGE TAG() returns the name of the specified tag in an open .MDX file. If you omit the .MDX file name, the production index file is assumed. If you omit the alias, the database in the current work area is assumed. If no index is active, TAG() with no argument returns a null string.

• EXAMPLE

```
USE CustList
? TAG(2)
```

displays Zip, the tag assigned to the second index in the production index file.

See Also DBF(), KEY(), MDX(), NDX(), ORDER()

TAGCOUNT()

Counting Active Tags

• SYNTAX

TAGCOUNT(*(mdx filename (,alias))***)**

• USAGE TAGCOUNT() returns the number of active tags in the specified .MDX file. If no .MDX file name is included, all active indexes are counted, including .NDX files. If no alias is included, the currently active work area is assumed.

• EXAMPLE The Orders database file is indexed with two tags in the production index, on the PartNo, and Date. Then

```
? TAGCOUNT()
```

returns 2.

See Also KEY(), MDX(), TAG(), TAGNO()

TAGNO()

Determining the Index Number

• SYNTAX

TAGNO(*[tag name/ndx filename [, mdx filename [,alias]]]***)**

• USAGE TAGNO() with no arguments returns the index number of the controlling index tag. Include a tag name or an .NDX file name to return its index number. If the tag is in another .MDX file, include the file name.

The alias specifies another work area with a number from 1 to 40, a letter from A to J, or a work area name.

Use DISPLAY STATUS to see all the tags in the multiple index files and all the .NDX files.

• EXAMPLE You have created four index tags for the CustList database file: UPPER(LastName+FirstName), STATE, ZIP, and SOUNDS. The commands below return 3.

```
USE CustList ORDER Zip

? TAGNO()
```

See Also KEY(), MDX(), ORDER(), TAG(), TAGCOUNT()

TAN()

Calculating the Tangent of an Angle

• SYNTAX

TAN(*number*)

• USAGE TAN() returns the trigonometric tangent of an angle measured in radians.

• EXAMPLE

? TAN(DTOR(45))

returns 1.

See Also ACOS(), ASIN(), ATAN(), ATN2(), COS(), DTOR(), RTOD(), SIN()

TIME()

Accessing the System Time

• SYNTAX

TIME(*(expression)*)

• USAGE TIME() returns the system time in the common format HH:MM:SS or in the HH:MM:SS:hh format where hh represents hundredths of a second. Because TIME() is returned as a character string, you cannot perform time arithmetic directly.

The optional argument, which can be any valid dBASE expression, returns the system time with hundredths of a second in the time string. TIME() always returns the time using the 24-hour clock, regardless of the SET HOURS TO setting.

- **EXAMPLE** The commands

```
? TIME()
? TIME("X")
```

return the system time as 18:35:26 and 18:35:26:88, respectively.

See Also DATE(), SET HOURS

TRANSFORM()

Formatting Data

- **SYNTAX**

TRANSFORM(*data,format***)**

- **USAGE** TRANSFORM() extends picture formatting to commands such as DISPLAY, LABEL, LIST, and REPORT. The first argument can be a numeric or character variable. The second argument (enclose in quotation marks) is a template, or the name of a variable containing the template, that defines the format. Table 2.3 (shown earlier) shows valid PICTURE template characters.

- **EXAMPLE** The next commands lists social security numbers (stored in the format 123456789) and amounts (stored in the format 12345.67), in the formats 123-45-6789 and $12,345.67:

```
SET CURRENCY TO " $"

LIST TRANSFORM(SSN,"999-99-9999"), ;
     TRANSFORM(Amount,"$999,999.99")
```

See Also @, MODIFY REPORT

TRIM()

Trimming Trailing Blanks

• SYNTAX

TRIM(*character***)**

• USAGE TRIM() removes trailing blanks from a character expression. The trailing blanks are typically those used to pad the string to a width defined in a database field or to a predefined width created by a SPACE function before a READ command.

RTRIM() is an alternative syntax for the TRIM() function; the two functions are identical.

Never use TRIM() or RTRIM() in an index key expression, as this produces unequal key lengths within the index file and unpredictable results.

• EXAMPLE The following command prints the City, State, and Zip fields with trailing blanks removed and a comma and single spaces inserted, to display the data in the format San Diego, CA 92067:

```
? TRIM(City)+", "+TRIM(State),Zip
```

See Also LEFT(), LTRIM(), RIGHT(), SEEK

TYPE()

Determining the Data Type

• SYNTAX

TYPE(*expression***)**

• **USAGE** The TYPE() function evaluates the expression and returns the data type. If the item does not exist, a U (for undefined) is returned. If the item does exist, one of the following characters is returned:

C	Character
N	Numeric
F	Float
D	Date
L	Logical
M	Memo

• **EXAMPLE** The next command returns C, the data type of a field or memory variable named Zip. The command returns U if Zip does not exist.

```
? TYPE("Zip")
```

See Also FIELD()

UNIQUE()

Determining whether an Index is Unique

• **SYNTAX**

UNIQUE(*([mdx filename,] number [,alias])***)**

• **USAGE** UNIQUE() returns logical true (.T.) if the specified .MDX tag was created using the UNIQUE keyword or with the command SET UNIQUE on. With no arguments, the controlling index is assumed.

Include a tag number to examine a nonactive tag and .MDX file name if the tag is in another multiple index. The .MDX file name must be enclosed in quotation marks.

UNIQUE() applies only to .MDX files and always returns logical false (.F.) if an .NDX file is specified. The UNIQUE keyword is available only when creating .MDX index tags.

- **EXAMPLE** The commands

```
USE Orders
INDEX ON CustNo TAG CustNo UNIQUE

? UNIQUE()
```

return .T..

See Also DESCENDING(), FOR(), INDEX, KEY(), MDX(), NDX(), ORDER(), SET UNIQUE, TAG(), TAGCOUNT(), TAGNO()

UPPER()

Converting Letters to Uppercase

- **SYNTAX**

UPPER(*character***)**

- **USAGE** UPPER() converts all lowercase letters in a character string to uppercase. It has no effect on numeric characters or punctuation. You can use UPPER() in index file expressions to prevent case distinctions from affecting sort orders and searches. This function does not work with the memo data type.

- **EXAMPLE** The commands that follow show how to sort a database into proper LastName and FirstName order, as well as how to seek a last name in the index:

```
INDEX ON UPPER(LastName+FirstName) TAG Names
SET ORDER TO Names
LookFor = "Smith"
SEEK UPPER(LookFor)
```

See Also ISALPHA(), ISLOWER(), ISUPPER(), LOWER(), MLINE(), SEEK

USER()

Displaying User Names in a Protected System

• **SYNTAX**

```
USER()
```

• **USAGE** USER() returns the eight-character log-in name of a user currently logged into a protected application. If no name is included in the dbsystem.DB file or the system does not use PROTECT, USER() returns a null string.

• **EXAMPLE** Only the user named HONCHO can access the PROTECT command in this IF clause:

```
IF USER() = "HONCHO"
  PROTECT
ENDIF
```

See Also LIST/DISPLAY USERS, PROTECT

VAL()

Converting a Character String to a Number

• **SYNTAX**

VAL(*character***)**

• **USAGE** VAL() converts numbers stored as character strings to the numeric data type. Any nonnumeric characters following the numbers are ignored. If the argument consists of leading nonnumeric characters (other than blanks), the function returns 0. The number of decimal digits returned by the function is determined by the SET DECIMALS command.

• **EXAMPLE** The command

```
StreetNo = VAL("123 Rainbow Dr.")
```

stores the number 123 in a numeric memory variable named StreetNo.

If the current database includes a character field named Address that stores addresses in the format "123 Oak Tree Lane," the following commands display the lowest and highest street number for addresses on Rainbow Dr.:

```
CALCULATE MIN(VAL(Address)), ;
     MAX(VAL(Address)), ;
     FOR "RAINBOW DR." $ UPPER(Address)
```

See Also SET DECIMALS, STR(), TIME(), TRANSFORM()

VAR

See **CALCULATE** in Part 2.

VARREAD()

Determining which Variable is Being Edited

• SYNTAX

```
VARREAD()
```

• USAGE VARREAD() returns the name of the field or memory variable currently being edited in a full-screen operation such as APPEND, EDIT, BROWSE, or READ. The name is returned in uppercase letters.

Usually, you use VARREAD() within a DO CASE clause in a procedure called by an ON KEY command to provide context-sensitive help while entering data or editing.

• EXAMPLE In the following example, the user can edit the Company and Phone fields from a database named Customer.DBF. If the user presses **F1**, help text relevant to the field currently being edited is displayed in a window named HelpWndo:

```
*----- Define window for help messages.
DEFINE WINDOW HelpWndo FROM 16,5 TO 20,74

*----- Reroute F1 key to GetHelp procedure.
ON KEY LABEL F1 DO GetHelp

*----- Display editing screen.
USE Customer
CLEAR
@ 10,10 SAY "Enter Company Name: " GET Company
@ 12,10 SAY "Enter Phone Number: " GET Phone

READ
RETURN
*----- End of main program.
```

```
PROCEDURE GetHelp
  CLEAR TYPEAHEAD  && Get rid of extra keystrokes.
  ACTIVATE WINDOW HelpWndo

  DO CASE
    CASE VARREAD() = "COMPANY"
       ? "Enter the full legal name of the company"
    CASE VARREAD() = "PHONE"
       ? "Include the area code with the phone;
         number"
  ENDCASE

  HoldIt = INKEY(0)   && Pause until a keypress.
  DEACTIVATE WINDOW HelpWndo

RETURN
```

See Also @, APPEND, BROWSE, EDIT, FIELD(), READ

VERSION()

Accessing the Version Number of dBASE IV

• SYNTAX

VERSION(*(number)***)**

• USAGE VERSION() returns a character expression containing the version number of the dBASE IV program in use. The optional number argument displays the Borland "build" number for the current version, and the date that the version was created.

• EXAMPLE The following command displays the full version number of dBASE IV currently in use:

```
? dBASE IV  2.0xx54 (03/09/93) VERSION(1)
```

See Also GETENV(), OS()

WINDOW()

Determining the Name of the Currently Active Window

• SYNTAX

WINDOW()

• USAGE The WINDOW() function returns the name of the currently active window as a character string. A null string indicates no window is active.

• EXAMPLE To get the name of the current active window, enter

```
? WINDOW()
```

See Also ACTIVATE WINDOW, DEFINE WINDOW

YEAR()

Isolating the Year in a Date

• SYNTAX

YEAR(*date*)

• USAGE YEAR() returns a four-digit number of the year for a given date.

• EXAMPLE The following example copies only records with order dates in the year 1994 to a file called LastYear.DBF:

```
COPY TO LastYear FOR YEAR(OrdDate) = 1994
```

Appendix A

Installing and Configuring dBASE IV

Before you can use dBASE IV 2.0 on your computer, you must install it. You need only go through the installation process once. This appendix discusses general techniques for installing dBASE IV on a single-user computer. If you wish to install dBASE IV on a network, refer to the network installation instructions that came with your dBASE IV package.

SYSTEM REQUIREMENTS

The minimum system requirements for running dBASE IV are:

- A 286 or higher 100 percent IBM-compatible microcomputer.
- IBM DOS or MS-DOS version 3.3x or higher and, for Windows installation, MicroSoft Windows 3.0 or higher.
- At least 2 megabytes (MB) of RAM, with 1MB of extended memory available when starting dBASE IV.
- A hard disk with about 4.5MB of available disk space to install only dBASE system files; 7.5MB to install all dBASE IV files; and during installation, 2MB more.
- For network operation, Novell Netware 286 v2.2, Netware 386 v3.11, Lantastic 4.0, or Banyan Vines 4.01.

PREVIOUS VERSIONS OF dBASE

If you have an earlier version of dBASE such as dBASE IV version 1.5 or dBASE III PLUS on your computer, you might want to uninstall those or move them to another directory. You may be able to use the install program that came with that earlier version of program to uninstall it. dBASE IV 2.0 also gives you the opportunity during installation to protect the old dBASE IV system files.

If you want to keep an earlier version of dBASE on your hard disk, make sure that you do not install dBASE IV 2.0 on the same directory as that earlier version. Either move the earlier version to another directory, or use a new directory name when installing dBASE IV 2.0.

DISK CACHING

Disk caching (pronounced *cashing*) is a technique version 2.0 of dBASE IV uses to speed processing. New buffer management improves the performance of the dBASE IV 2.0 internal cache. dBASE uses extended memory (XMS) for storing both data and programs in a way that fits the higher level dBASE file structures.

You can instead use an external cache such as SMARTDRV, Hyper-Disk, or Norton Cache, which speed up DOS directory access. However, if you use external cache, you should allocate a small amount of memory to it and save the rest for the dBASE internal buffer manager.

dBASE IV also caches index blocks in memory. You can set the maximum number of 1KB blocks to reserve for the indexes. Use the INDEXBYTES command in the Config.DB file to specify from 2K to 2MB blocks. For example,

```
INDEXBYTES = 1024
```

sets the default number of index blocks to 1024K. You can also change the index block size (see **SET IBLOCK** in Part 3). When you close the database or the index tags, the index buffer memory is released and available for other data.

If you start dBASE from Windows, its memory management system will be active and dBASE caching will not be installed. However, if you have already installed dBASE caching and exit Windows before starting dBASE, the dBASE cache will be activated when you start dBASE from the DOS prompt.

VIRTUAL MEMORY

Virtual memory is a way of making disk space appear to be additional RAM. This allows you to run programs that require more RAM than your system has. For example, you can run a program that requires 4.5MB of memory on a computer with only 1MB by using virtual memory.

The dBASE Virtual Memory Manager (VMM) establishes a swap file on the hard drive where it stores program and data segments. As they are needed, they are loaded into RAM. After they are used they are swapped back to disk, freeing up the limited memory.

If your computer has less than 4.5MB of extended memory, the dBASE IV 2.0 VMM runs automatically when you start up, and gives you access to 5MB of virtual memory. dBASE automatically analyzes the system configuration and sets the sizes of the virtual memory, the swap file, and the maximum extended memory to use. You can change any of these default values to suit your application development. See your dBASE IV 2.0 documentation for more information.

Use the MEMORY() function to see whether dBASE VMM is running and how much memory is under VMM control.

If you run dBASE IV under OS/2 or Windows, the dBASE VMM is disabled, since both OS/2 and Windows have their own VMM.

INSTALLING dBASE IV

The steps listed below apply to the basic single-user installation of dBASE IV. If you are installing dBASE IV from another drive, make the appropriate changes in the steps below.

INSTALLING WITH DOS

To execute a single-user installation with DOS, follow these steps:

1. Start your computer in the usual manner and get to the DOS command prompt.
2. Insert the dBASE IV Install Disk in disk drive A.
3. Type **A:** and press ↵ to switch to drive A.
4. Type **INSTALL** and press ↵.
5. After a few moments, you'll see a dBASE IV screen followed by a Copyright screen. When instructed at the bottom of the screen, press ↵ to proceed with the installation.
6. You are then asked to verify that the source drive you are installing from is A (or B). Press ↵ to accept or enter another drive name to change and press ↵.
7. Choose StandAlone installation from the next dialog box. Press **F2** (DO-IT!) or ↵.

8. Next you will be prompted to enter your name (required), your company (optional), and the dBASE IV 2.0 serial number, which is on Disk 1. Press ↵ to open the text box for each entry and press ↵ again after entering the data.

9. You can also change the code page for this installation if you are using a different language driver. Press ↵ to toggle between 437 and 850.

10. When finished, press **F2** (DO-IT!).

11. The next screen gives you several options. The first is to change the directory in which to install dBASE. To change the directory from the default C:\DBASE, highlight the Directory line and press ↵. Enter the desired directory and press ↵ again. Press **Esc** to return to main installation window.

12. The next line allows you to choose which dBASE files to add to the configuration: the dBASE System Files, Samples, Tutorial, Template Language, and DBSETUP Utilities. All default options are YES. To leave one out of this installation, press ↵ with the Configuration line highlighted. Then highlight the option you want to remove and press ↵ to toggle to NO. When you have finished, press **Esc** to return to the main window. You can run Install again and add the options later if you decide you want them.

13. The third line allows you to specify install options such as to protect or remove existing dBASE IV system files and to shield or replace old SQL system files. Again, the defaults are all YES. Press ↵ to open the pull-down menu, then highlight the option and press ↵ to toggle to NO. When finished, press **Esc** to return to the main window.

14. When all changes have been made, press **F2** (DO-IT!). You may get a message that there is not enough room on your hard disk to accommodate all the options you have selected. If so, return to the screen and remove some of the configuration options.

15. If dBASE IV is already installed on your system, you will get a message that you may either remove the old files by

changing the Protect Old dBASE IV System Files setting to NO, or change the directory to install dBASE elsewhere.

16. After the files on Disk 1 are copied and unzipped, you are prompted to insert the remaining system disks into the source drive so that all the files may be copied.

17. A message is then displayed indicating that installation is complete and reminding you to modify the Config.SYS file so that Files is set to at least 99 and Buffers is set to at least 15. It also reminds you to add DBASE to the PATH statement in the Autoexec.BAT file.

At this point, the basic installation is complete and you should be at the drive and directory where dBASE IV was installed (typically C:\DBASE).

INSTALLING THROUGH WINDOWS

You can install dBASE IV 2.0 through MicroSoft Windows by invoking the Program Manager:

1. Open the Program Manager window.
2. Insert dBASE IV Install disk in drive A (or the desired drive).
3. Select **File➤Run**.
4. Type **A:Install** at the Command Line in the dialog box.

Then proceed as with the DOS installation.

When installation is complete, you should have a dBASE group window with three icons: dBASE program, DBSETUP, and DBINFO. Double-click on these icons to start dBASE, run DBSETUP, or to display information about the current dBASE system configuration.

If Windows is installed in a directory that doesn't have WINDOWS as part of its name (for example, WIN486), or if you install Windows after installing dBASE IV, the icons will not appear. You must then carefully edit the Program Manager initialization file named PROGMAN.INI, which is in the same directory as Windows. To make changes, exit Windows, then edit the file using any text editor or the dBASE MODIFY COMMAND editor.

Add a line to the end of PROGMAN.INI as follows:

Group*n* = *dbase directory***DBASEIV.GRP**

Replace *n* with the next available group number and specify the directory that holds dBASE. DBASEIV.GRP is the file name of the group icon and includes the three individual icons.

After making the changes, save the PROGMAN.INI as an unformatted ASCII file, exit the editor, and restart Windows. This is usually done by entering the command **WIN** at the DOS prompt.

RUNNING dBASE IV

After dBASE IV 2.0 is installed you can run it from DOS, OS/2, or Windows. If you changed the Autoexec.BAT or the Config.SYS files during installation, reboot by removing the floppy disks from their drives and simultaneously pressing **Ctrl**, **Alt**, and **Del**. You can then start dBASE either through the DOS prompt or the Windows Program Manager.

RUNNING IN DOS

To start dBASE IV after installation, change to the directory where you installed dBASE and enter the following command at the DOS prompt:

DBASE **(/C** *.db filename***)** **(***program name***)**
(*parameter1***)** **(,***parameter2...***)**

You can use the /C option with a custom .DB file name to configure the dBASE session with parameters other than those in the Config.DB file.

To execute a program inside dBASE at startup, specify the program name and, if desired, pass one or more parameters to it. To open the session with the Control Center, add COMMAND=ASSIST to the Config.DB file.

If you added DBASE to the PATH statement in the Autoexec.BAT file, you can start dBASE from any directory.

RUNNING dBASE IV WITH MICROSOFT WINDOWS

To start dBASE from Windows, open the dBASE group window by double-clicking the group icon. Then double-click the dBASE program icon. If you want a program to execute at startup, add the following command to the Config.DB file. Make sure you have added the dBASE directory to your path so windows can find it.

COMMAND = MyProg

If you want to start up in the Control Center, specify ASSIST as the command.

When you start dBASE from Windows, it looks for the Config.DB file in the Windows directory. Make sure you have a copy of the same Config.DB file settings in both the DBASE and the Windows directories so dBASE will look the same no matter how you start it.

When dBASE runs under Windows, it uses as much memory as it can find. If you get a message that there is insufficient memory to load dBASE, try starting Windows in the Standard mode with the command WIN/S, then reload dBASE. If that doesn't work, you can try to limit the amount of memory dBASE uses. Exit Windows and dBASE, then modify the Autoexec.BAT file with the DOS SET command:

SET DOS16M = *max memory*

where max memory is expressed in MB and must be at least 3MB. Then reboot and reload Windows and dBASE.

Double-click the DBINFO icon to see information about the current system configuration, including:

- Operating system and Windows versions
- File and buffer settings
- Current path and network identifiers
- Total and available hard disk space

- Total and available standard, Extended (XMS 2.00), and Expanded (EMS 4.0) memory
- Config.SYS file
- Autoexec.BAT file
- Config.DB file

RUNNING UNDER OS/2

You can run dBASE IV 2.0 under OS/2 in a DOS session, but you must set the DPMI_MEMORY_LIMIT up from the default of 2MB to at least 3MB. dBASE will not load with less because there is not enough memory to load the DBASE1.RES resource file.

If you are going to have more than 20 files open at a time, you must also increase the DOS_FILES setting.

QUITTING dBASE IV

To quit dBASE, type QUIT at the dot prompt or select **Exit ➤Exit to DOS** from the Control Center. The syntax is:

QUIT (WITH *number* **)**

Using the WITH *number* option with QUIT returns a DOS error-level integer if dBASE terminated abnormally. The number can then be tested in a DOS batch file to find the cause of the error.

MULTITASKING AND MULTIPLE dBASE SESSIONS

The DOSSHELL, OS/2, and Windows operating environments let you run multiple sessions of dBASE and share local files among the sessions. You can run up to nine simultaneous sessions of dBASE and share files with other programs such as Paradox.

Set the command LOCALSHARE on in the Config.DB file to protect your files in a multitasking situation. With LOCALSHARE set on, dBASE makes sure that the DOS program SHARE is running. SHARE provides disk filesharing and locking features on a single-user, multitasking environment, just as in a network multiuser environment.

If you run dBASE under Windows without SHARE but with LOCALSHARE set on, you will get a message to load SHARE. To resolve the conflict, either load SHARE by putting the command in the Autoexec.BAT file or set LOCALSHARE off in the Config.DB file.

When executing multiple sessions of dBASE, each session is assigned a unique identifier: an integer from 1 to 9. This identifier acts just like the log-in user name in a network environment. Several commands and functions return the session identifier. For example, the third session of dBASE returns *SESSION 3* when you use ID(), LKSYS(2) or LKSYS(5), USER(), or LIST/DISPLAY USERS.

The session identifiers are recycled, so the number does not necessarily indicate the relative sequence of session startup.

OPTIMIZING dBASE IV PERFORMANCE

It takes time to search a large directory for a specific file. You can speed up processing by reducing the number of files in your working directory. If you have several dBASE applications, devote a separate directory to each one.

In addition, you can save time by sending all the temporary files to a separate directory. dBASE creates many temporary files that are erased when you exit dBASE normally. The DOS environment variable, DBTMP, defines where the dBASE temporary files will be stored. Add the following command to the Autoexec.BAT file:

SET DBTMP = *drive*:\ *directory*

If dBASE does not terminate normally, some temporary files may be left in the DBTMP directory. It is an easy matter to delete all the files that are left with the DEL *.* DOS command. Make sure you are actually in the DBTMP directory before issuing DEL *.*.

Efficient memory and buffer management may speed up dBASE applications. See your dBASE IV documentation for more information. Optimizing storage of memo fields and index blocks also improves the dBASE use of memory. See **SET MBLOCK** and **SET IBLOCK** in Part 3.

Several of the environmental parameters can be changed to improve dBASE performance:

- Set STATUS, SCOREBOARD, and CLOCK off to save screen refresh time.
- Set the ODOMETER to the highest value (200) to reduce screen activity.
- Set CONSOLE off before printing to the printer or a file.
- Set PRECISION to 10, the minimum, to reduce mathematical computation time.
- Set REFRESH to 0 to limit the number of screen updates.
- Set AUTOSAVE off so dBASE writes to disk only when the buffer is full (or you close the file), rather than with every change.

See Part 3 for details of these and the other SET commands.

CONFIGURING dBASE IV

There are three ways to customize your dBASE IV session: run the DBSETUP program, modify the Config.DB file directly, or execute SET commands at the dot prompt or in a program. You can change the default settings for the current session only, or for all subsequent dBASE sessions.

Many parameters can be set in any of the three methods, while others, such as memory allocations, are used only in the Config.DB file.

RUNNING DBSETUP

You can start the DBSETUP program in one of the following ways:

- Type **RUN DBSETUP** at the dot prompt, then select **Config.DB➤Modify CONFIG.DB**.
- Select **Tools➤Settings** from the Control Center menu.

- Double-click the DBSETUP icon in the dBASE group window and select **Config.DB➤Modify CONFIG.DB**.

Select the settings category from the horizontal bar menu to modify printer drivers, database settings, general environment parameters, display attributes, key functions, file path and directory designations, and memory allocations. As you highlight each selection in the corresponding pull-down menus, you will see an explanation of the selection and the range of acceptable values displayed in the message line. For settings such as DATE that have more than one valid entry, press the space bar to toggle through the options. Make your selection or enter a value, then press ↵. DBSETUP does not support a mouse.

When you have finished, select **Exit**. If you ran DBSETUP from the dot prompt, select **Exit to DOS** next. If you used the Control Center menu to invoke DBSETUP, select **Exit to Control Center**. From DOS or Windows, select **Save and Exit** from the Exit menu, then **Exit to DOS** from the DBSETUP main menu.

The changes are made to the Config.DB file and will take effect when you restart dBASE. If there are conflicting commands (such as FILES=99 in the Config.SYS file and FILES=40 in the Config.DB file), the setting in the Config.SYS prevails.

CHANGING THE CONFIG.DB COMMANDS

You can change the Config.DB file directly using MODIFY COMMAND or any other text editor.

The Config.DB file can include configuration commands to define the operating environment and manage memory for all dBASE sessions. While most settings can be made at the dot prompt as well as in the Config.DB file, some are available only in Config.DB. Table A.1 summarizes the configuration commands and options that are limited to the Config.DB file.

Table A.1: Configuration Commands Limited to Config.DB

Name	Default	Description
ASCIISORT	OFF	Enable ASCII sort order instead of Dictionary order.
BUCKET	2	Amount of memory allocated for PICTURE and RANGE commands, from 1 to 31K.
COMMAND	ASSIST	Command to be executed as soon as dBASE is loaded.
CTMAXSYMS	500	Maximum number of compile-time symbols, from 1 to 5000.
EXCLUSIVE	ON	Protects files in multi-tasking environment.
EXPSIZE	100	Memory buffer for storing expressions during compilation, from 100 to 2000.
FASTCRT	ON	Options are ON and OFF, where OFF eliminates video "snow."
FILES	99	Maximum number of open files, from 15 to 99.
GETS	128	Number of @...GET statements that can be active at any one time, from 35 to 2000.
INDEXBYTES	256(K)	Number of index file blocks in cache memory, from 2K to 2048K.

Table A.1: Configuration Commands Limited to Config.DB (Continued)

Name	Default	Description
LANGTABLES	OFF	Collation and extended alphabetic character definition tables.
LOCALSHARE	ON	Allows file sharing in multitasking environment.
MVBLKSIZE	50	Size of memory blocks for storing memory variables, from 25 to 100.
MVMAXBLKS	10	Number of memory blocks for storing variables, from 1 to 150.
NOCLOCK	OFF	Removes clock from menu bar.
PDRIVER		Name of the printer driver, as defined during installation.
PRINTER		Names of up to four printers, as defined during installation.
PROMPT		Prompt to show instead of the dot prompt, up to 19 characters.
RESETCRT	ON	ON resets CRT to default display mode when you access an external program from within dBASE. OFF does not reset display mode.
RTBLKSIZE	50	Size of memory blocks for storing memory variables in RunTime, from 25 to 100.

Table A.1: Configuration Commands Limited to Config.DB (Continued)

Name	Default	Description
RTMAXBLKS	10	Number of memory blocks for storing variables in RunTime, from 1 to 150.
SQLDATABASE	SAMPLES	Initial SQL database to use at startup.
SQLHOME	\DBASE\ SQLHOME	Subdirectory containing SQL files.
TABS	No stops	Specifies default tab stops
TEDIT		Installs text editor to use instead of the internal dBASE editor.
WP		Installs external word processor to use for editing memo fields.

Most of the SET commands listed in Part 3 can be pre-configured in Config.DB, to change their default value at startup. Some of them do not customize the environment, but instead apply to specific files or applications within a session and cannot be included in Config.DB. These commands are:

SET DOHISTORY	SET ORDER
SET FIELDS	SET PRINTER TO FILE
SET FILTER	SET PROCEDURE
SET FIXED	SET RELATION
SET FORMAT	SET SKIP
SET INDEX	SET TITLES
SET MESSAGE	SET WINDOW

In Config.DB, you do not use the keyword SET. Instead, you use the syntax *parameter = value.* For example, to have dBASE start up with financial numbers displayed in the format 123.456,78, you would include the following two commands in the Config.DB file:

```
POINT     = ,
SEPARATOR = .
```

To configure function keys in Config.DB, use the syntax *key label name = text*, where *key label name* is a valid key name, as listed under the ON KEY command reference in Part 2. For example, the next command configures the Shift-F9 key to enter the command BROWSE. See **SET FUNCTION** in Part 3 for other examples:

```
Shift-F9    = "BROWSE;"
```

CONFIGURING WITH SET COMMANDS

Use the SET commands described in Part 3 to configure a dBASE session from within an application or at the dot prompt. These commands do not change the settings in the Config.DB file and the parameters revert to the default settings when you exit the current session.

Appendix B

dBASE IV File Name Extensions

Table B.1: dBASE File Name Extensions

.$$$	Temporary file
.$AB	Temporary file, virtual memory
.ACC	Multiuser access control file
.APP	Application Generator design file
.BAK	Backup files
.BAR	Applications Generator bar menu
.BCH	Applications Generator batch file
.BIN	Binary file
.CAC	Cache file on install disks (renamed to .EXE)
.CAT	Catalog file
.CHT	Chart-master bridge file
.COD	Template language source code
.COM	Executable command file
.CPT	Encrypted memo field file
.CRP	Encrypted database file
.CVT	Converted multiuser database file with change-detection field
.DB2	Renamed dBASE II file for import/export
.DB	Configuration file
.DBF	Database file
.DBK	Database backup file
.DBO	Compiled .PRG or .PRS source code
.DBT	Memo field file
.DEF	Template language selector definition file
.DIF	VisiCalc Data Interchange Format file
.DOC	Documentation generated by Applications Generator
.DPP	Preprocessor intermediate source code file
.ERR	Error file created by forms generator
.EXE	Executable RunTime file

Table B.1: dBASE File Name Extensions (Continued)

.FIL	Applications Generator files list
.FMO	Compiled format (.FMT) file
.FMT	Format file source code
.FNL	Report binary name list (Template Language)
.FR3	Renamed dBASE III report format file
.FRG	Generated report format (.FRM) source code
.FRM	Report format file used by reports design screen
.FRO	Compiled report form .FRG file
.FW*x*	Framework *x* file for import/export
.GEN	Compiled template language file
.GRP	Windows group file for dBASE IV
.HLP	Help file
.ICO	Windows icon file for dBASE IV
.KEY	Keystroke macro library
.LB3	Renamed dBASE III label file
.LBG	Generated label-printing source code
.LBL	Labels design screen label file
.LBO	Compiled .LBG file
.LNL	Label binary name list (Template Language)
.LOG	Transaction log file
.MBK	Multiple index backup file
.MDX	Multiple index file
.MEM	Memory variable file
.NDX	Single index file
.NPI	Template interpreter report, label, form file
.OVL	dBASE IV overlay file
.PIF	Settings file for running dBASE IV in Windows

Table B.1: dBASE File Name Extensions (Continued)

.POP	Applications Generator pop-up menu design file
.PR2	Printer driver file
.PRD	Printer driver file, DBSETUP
.PRF	Print form file
.PRG	Command or procedure file
.PRS	SQL command or procedure file
.PRT	Non-ASCII printer output file
.QBE	Query source code
.QBO	Compiled .QBE file
.QRY	Query filter file
.RES	Compiler resource file
.RPD	RapidFile data file for export/import
.RTL	dBASE RunTime library file
.SC3	Renamed dBASE III screen (.SCR) file
.SCR	Screen file used by forms design screen
.SNL	Screen binary name list (Template Language)
.STR	Applications Generator structure list file
.T44, .W44	Work files used by INDEX and SORT
.TBK	Memo field backup file
.TXT	Text (ASCII) output file
.UPD	Update query source code
.UPO	Compiled .UPD file
.VAL	Applications Generator values list
.VMC	Configuration file, virtual memory
.VUE	dBASE III PLUS view file
.WIN	File of saved window definitions
.WK1, .WKS	Lotus 1-2-3 files for import/export

Appendix C

dBASE IV Specifications

Table C.1: dBASE IV Specifications

Open Files	
Maximum number of records	1 billion
Maximum number of bytes	2 billion
Maximum record size	4000 characters
Maximum fields per record	255
Field Sizes	
Character field length	1 to 254 bytes
Date field length	8 bytes
Logical field length	1 byte
Numeric field length	1 to 20 bytes
Float field length	1 to 20 bytes
Memo field length	8 to 64K bytes with dBASE editor; no limit otherwise
Characters in field name	1 to 10 characters
Index Files	
Maximum indexes/tags per file	47
Maximum key expression length	220 characters, 100 characters (evaluated)
Arrays	
Maximum dimensions	2
Maximum elements in one dimension	65,535

Table C.1: dBASE IV Specifications (Continued)

Open Files	
Maximum open files, all types	99
Maximum open database files	40
Maximum open index files per database file	11 (10 .NDX, 1 .MDX)
Numeric Accuracy	
Smallest number	$0.1 \times E^{-307}$
Largest number	$0.9 \times E^{+308}$
Numeric data type (see **SET PRECISION**)	10 to 20 digits
Float data type	15 digits
Memory Variables	
Number of active variables	25 to 15,000
Editors	
Maximum lines in MODIFY COMMAND	32,000
Maximum line length	1024
Maximum rows in custom forms	32,767
Maximum Nested Group (subtotal) bands in Reports design	44

Table C.1: dBASE IV Specifications (Continued)

Open Files	
Maximum number of locks	200
Retries of open lock (see **SET REPROCESS**)	–1 to 32,000, or infinite
Refresh interval (see **SET REFRESH**)	0 to 3600 seconds
Miscellaneous	
Maximum command line length	255 at dot prompt
Maximum procedures and UDFs per file	963
Maximum number of nested UDFs	32
Maximum procedure size	65,520 bytes
Maximum GETS per format file	2000
Maximum number of sort levels	16
Maximum keystroke macros in one library	35
Maximum loaded binary files	16
Maximum size of binary file	65,500 bytes
Maximum number of printers	4
Maximum fonts per printer	5
Maximum number of copies	32,767
Maximum label width	255
Maximum number of labels across	15
Maximum open work areas	40

Table C.1: dBASE IV Specifications (Continued)

Open Files	
Maximum number of open windows	20
Programmable function keys	29

Appendix D

Using the dBASE Compiler

The new dBASE Compiler for DOS allows you to develop an entire application and distribute it to users who do not have dBASE IV. The utility programs included in the compiler compile and link all your dBASE (both III PLUS and IV) programs into a single executable .EXE file. This file can then be distributed to the users on one or more disks complete with all the forms, reports, labels, and queries that the application requires.

The dBASE Compiler can build either a self-contained, standalone .EXE file, or a compact version. The standalone file links all the necessary dBASE source files, including command files and report and form designs, together with all the necessary RunTime library and resource files. No additional dBASE files are needed to run the application.

The compact version is for end-users who run more than one dBASE application and does not include the library and resource files. It saves disk space to have only one set of library and resource files to which multiple applications have access.

INSTALLING AND CONFIGURING THE COMPILER

The dBASE Compiler utilities are installed in much the same way as dBASE itself. The paragraphs below describe the system hardware and software requirements and the installation procedure for a single-user system. If you want to install the compiler on a network, refer to the network installation instructions that came with your compiler.

SYSTEM REQUIREMENTS

To install the dBASE Compiler for DOS you will need:

- A 286 or higher 100 percent IBM-compatible microcomputer
- IBM DOS or MS-DOS version 3.3 or higher
- At least 2MB RAM
- At least 5.5MB available on your hard disk, with an additional 2MB available during installation
- For network operation, Novell Netware 286 v2.2 or v3.11, Lantastic 4.1, Banyan Vines 5.0, DEC Pathworks for DOS 4.1, AT&T StarGroup 2.1a, or 3COM 3+Share 1.6.0

dBASE Compiler for DOS also runs under Windows 3.0 and 3.1 and the DOS compatibility box of OS/2 2.0.

INSTALLING THE dBASE COMPILER FOR DOS

Always make a backup copy of your system disks before attempting to install the programs. Then use the backups for installation, keeping the masters in a safe place.

To install with DOS, follow these instructions (if you are installing from a drive other than A, make the appropriate changes):

1. Insert Disk 1 into the A drive.
2. Type **A:** and press ↵ to switch to the A drive.
3. Type **INSTALL** and press ↵.
4. When the copyright screen appears, press ↵.
5. Press ↵ to accept the default source drive, or enter a different drive name and press ↵.
6. In the Directories window, you can change the default directory from C:\BDCOMP by highlighting the option line, pressing ↵, and entering the desired directory name.
7. In the same window, you can toggle the Code Page definition between 437 and 850 by highlighting the line in the box and pressing ↵. Make sure to select the same Code Page that the intended end-user's system uses.
8. When you finish with the options, press **F2** (DO-IT!).
9. Follow the instructions on the screen to copy and unzip all the system files.

You can also install the dBASE Compiler through Windows by accessing the Program Manager and typing **A:Install** in the command line. Follow the steps above to complete the installation.

COMPILER UTILITIES

The dBASE Compiler for DOS consists of five utility programs:

Compiler (BDC)	Preprocesses source code files and compiles source code into object files
Linker (BDL)	Links object, runtime library, and resource files into DOS-executable (.EXE, .RSL, and .RES) files

dSPLIT	Divides an executable file into segments that can be written to several floppy disks
dJOIN	Reassembles the files separated by dSPLIT into a single executable file
MAKE	A Borland utility that automates the application build process

The sections that follow describe most of these utilities, with their correct syntaxes and available options. The Borland MAKE utility is a versatile tool for developers to use to build and maintain executable files, updated with the latest modifications in the underlying source code, and to create complex control structures for generating dBASE end-user applications. It is a more sophisticated way of compiling and linking files using a metalanguage. Since it is not directly related to programming, MAKE will not be covered in this book. See your Borland documentation for more information.

To execute one of the utilities, type the command at the DOS prompt. You can also run the compiler from Windows, but the command line itself contains the options and, unless you always use the same file names and options, you will have to change the Windows Program Manager command line each time you want to run the compiler. It is easier to exit Windows before running the compiler.

INVOKING THE dBASE PREPROCESSOR

The preprocessor is actually a part of the compiler that is invoked by the preprocessor directives (lines that begin with #) embedded in the source code. The preprocessor scans the source code for directives, expands defined preprocessor macros into the source code, inserts specified text from other files, and retains source code commands that meet the conditions specified in the directives. The result is an intermediate program file of preprocessed source code that will be compiled by the compiler into object code.

• PREPROCESSOR DIRECTIVES You may insert preprocessor directives anywhere in your source file. Each directive line begins with # and can contain up to 1024 characters. There are three types of directives: those that define and undefine preprocessor macros, those that specify program text or dBASE macros from other files to include with the source code, and those that select parts of the source code for compilation by BDC based on predefined conditions. Table D.1 lists the preprocessor directives and shows their correct syntaxes.

Table D.1: Preprocessor Directives

Directive	Syntax
#define	#define *macro name* [*macro expression*]
#undef	#undef *macro name*
#include	#include *"filename"* / *<filename>*
#if	#if *expression*
#ifdef/#ifndef	#ifdef/#ifndef *macro name*
#else/#elif	#else/#elif *expression*
#endif	#endif

Defining Preprocessor Macros Use #define to define and name macros to be used by the preprocessor. When the preprocessor encounters the *macro name* in the source code, it replaces the name with the specified *macro definition*. You can use #define to specify sets of instructions or long strings that are used repeatedly. When the macro is no longer needed, release it with the #undefine directive.

For example, the directives below define the macro Group as a string that can be used in a report later in the application, then undefine it when it is no longer useful:

```
#define Group "Computer Intelligence, Inc."
...
...
@ 5,1 Say Group
...
...
#undef Group
```

Including Text The preprocessor creates *include* files that contain information for use by many of the programs in the application such as dBASE macros, constant definitions, and default values. Use the #include directive to insert the contents of the include file into the source code. If the file name is enclosed in quotes, the preprocessor searches the current directory first, then looks in the directories listed in the -I (#include file) compiler option. If the file name is enclosed in angle brackets (<>), the preprocessor searches only the -I path, but without the -I option, the #include directive is ignored.

You can also specify a complete path name, such as C:\DBASE\MYPATH, and the preprocessor will search only that path.

For example, the directives below both include the text from the Options.TXT file in the source code file:

```
#include "Options.TXT"
#include <Options.TXT>
```

The first directive looks for the file in the current directory, then in the directory named in the -I option line. The second directive searches only the -I directory.

If BDC can't find the file, an error message is displayed.

Conditional Directives The conditional directives let you specify which parts of your program you want to compile. The #if, #else/#elif, and #endif directives operate the same as the dBASE IF, ELSE, and ENDIF commands. The expression used by #if can include any of the dBASE operators except the substring operator (&) and exponentiation (** or ^).

For example, the directives below instruct the compiler to compile MyProg1 only if the macro COMPL evaluates to 0 and to compile MyProg2 only if it evaluates to 1. If COMPL is any other value, neither procedure will be compiled.

```
#if COMPL = 0
        DO MyProg1
#elif COMPL = 1
        DO MyProg2
#endif
```

You can also base your conditional compilation on whether or not a macro has been defined by using #ifdef to execute the code if the macro has been defined and #ifndef if it has not been defined.

For example, the directives below instruct the compiler to compile MyProg3 if the macro EDIT has been defined. If not, compile MyProg4.

```
#ifdef EDIT
        DO MyProg3
#else
        DO MyProg4
#endif
```

You can nest the conditional directives the same way as the dBASE IF...ENDIF pairs.

USING BDC

BDC can be used to compile only or to compile and link files. If you compile only, you can link the object files later with the BDL.

• SYNTAX

BDC **(***compiler options***)** **(***linker options***)** *file list* **(***@filename***)** **(***+filename***)**

• USAGE To compile and link, include both types of options with the BDC command. When compilation is successfully completed, BDC calls the linker. To link later, add the linker options to the BDL command line.

The compiler options specify the actions of the compile process and the linker options do the same for the linking process. Table D.2 contains descriptions of the compiler options, while Table D.3 addresses the linker options. The options may be specified in any order. Precede each option with a dash (-) or slash (/) and be careful to use the correct case, since upper and lower case instances of the same letter can mean quite different things. Include a space between the option switch and the associated value.

Table D.2: dBASE Compiler Options

Option	Description
- c	Compile but do not link.
-D *macro name*	Define a preprocessor macro.
-D *macro name=macro expression*	Define a preprocessor macro to the specified macro expression.
-I *path*	Search the specified path for #include files.
-n *path*	Write object files to specified path. If not included, current path is used.
-P *path*	Write preprocessed intermediate source (.DPP) file output to specified path, but do not compile.
-p *path*	Write preprocessed output to specified path and compile.
-t	Display code line that caused an error or warning.
-w	Disable warning messages. Error messages are still displayed.
-X	Set LangTables on and enable compilation of extended ASCII character set.
-x	Set LangTables off (US default). Error may occur if source code contains extended ASCII characters.

The -D compiler option allows you to define a single preprocessor macro. Use a configuration file to define an unlimited number of macros. Macros defined by a #define directive override macros defined by the -D option.

If neither the -P or -p option is used to write out the preprocessor intermediate files, they are deleted after compilation.

Table D.3: Linker Options

Option	Description
-B *program name*	Specify the first program to execute in the .EXE file. If not specified, the first .DBO in the file list is used.
- C *file name*	Link to specified file as the Config.DB. If not specified, file in current directory is used.
-E *file name*	Specify output .EXE file name. If not specified, name of first .DBO in the file list is used.
-L	Create a (large) standalone .EXE file.
-S	Create a (small) compact .EXE file (default).

The LANGTABLES setting determines how dBASE sorts data, converts between upper- and lower-case, and handles extended ASCII characters (>127). You can use the -X (on) or -x (off) options to ensure that the setting used during compilation is the same setting that will be used at runtime. You can also specify a Config.DB file containing the appropriate setting to be linked to the .EXE file.

The *file list* is a list of the source files you want to compile and/or the name of a text file in which you have stored the program file names. If you specify more than one source file, separate the names with a space. If you specify a text file, indicate that it is a text file by adding the character @ to the file name, as in @MyText. In the text file, each file name must be typed on a separate line with no delimiters. Blank lines and lines beginning with #, *, or ; are ignored.

A DOS command line may contain no more than 128 characters, so if you have a lot of control options or use the same ones each time, you can write these options to a configuration file. Use +*filename* to specify the whole group of options. Be sure to preface the file name with the plus (+) sign.

• EXAMPLE The following command compiles, but does not link, the CustOrd.PRG, CustInv.PRG, CustList.FMT, CustPaid.QBE, and CustList.FRG files and writes the object code files to the CustDir directory:

```
BDC -c -n C:\CustDir CustOrd.PRG CustInv.PRG ;
        CustList.FMT CustPaid.QBE CustList.FRG
```

The next command compiles and links the Master.PRG file and all the files contained in the MyProgs text file using the options specified in the MyOptions configuration file:

```
BDC Master.PRG @MyProgs +MyOptions
```

The object files generated by BDC have the same file extensions as the files compiled by the dBASE internal compiler.

The .EXE files created by the dBASE Compiler are to be used in a runtime environment and can not include any of the dBASE interactive commands. The following commands are not permitted in an executable file:

ASSIST	DEBUG	MODIFY COMMAND/FILE
COMPILE	DEXPORT	RESUME
CREATE (full screen)	DISPLAY/LIST HISTORY	SET (full screen)
CREATE/ MODIFY	HELP	SUSPEND

In addition, you may not include the following SET commands in your command file: DEBUG, DESIGN, DEVELOPMENT, DOHISTORY, ECHO FIXED, HELP, HISTORY, INSTRUCT, SQL, STEP, and TRAP.

If you have used any of these commands in your source file, BDC displays a warning and leaves them out of the generated code. If it finds SET SQL or RESUME , it will terminate compilation and display an error message. The use of a macro substitution for a dBASE verb will also cause an error message during compilation.

If the compiler detects an error during compilation, it does not generate object code for the program containing the error. It will go ahead and compile the rest of the program files, but will not generate an .EXE file.

USING THE dBASE LINKER

The dBASE linker utility (BDL) combines all the object files created by the compiler into a single executable (.EXE) file and, if you specify a standalone application, links it to the dBASE IV RunTime library and resource files to build a complete application.

• SYNTAX

BDL (*linker options***)** *file list*

• USAGE See Table D.3 for a description of the linker options. The options may be specified in any order. Precede each option with a dash (-) or slash(/) and be careful to use the correct upper- or lower-case.

The *file list* is a list of the object files to link and/or the name of a text file in which you have stored the file names. If you list individual files, separate the names with a space. If you specify a text file, indicate that it is a text file by adding the character @ to the file name. In the text file, each file name must be on a separate line with no delimiters. Blank lines and those beginning with #, *, or ; are ignored.

You can also include a Config.DB file and binary files. If you are building a standalone executable file, the RunTime library (.RTL) and dBASE resource (.RES) files are also linked. If you are creating a compact application, the library and resource files are treated separately. It does not link any data, memo, index, or text files.

You can link up to 2,500 object files, providing the executable file is less than two gigabytes.

• EXAMPLE The linker command below builds a standalone .EXE file out of the listed object files and links the Config2.DB file with them:

```
BDL -L -C Config2.DB CustOrd.DBO CustInv.DBO ;
        CustList.FMO CustPaid.QBO CustList.FRO
```

The next command links all the files in the text file MyProgs into a compact .EXE file named MyAppl. When MyAppl is invoked, StartUp is the first program to run, probably displaying a Welcome message and the opening menu.

BDL /S /B StartUp.DBO /E MyAppl.EXE @MyProgs

USING dSPLIT

If one of your application files is too large to fit on a floppy disk, you can use dSPLIT to break it up into smaller pieces and write them to several disks.

• SYNTAX

DSPLIT (-S *first segment size* **(,***subsequent segment size***))**
(-O *target path***)** *file name*

• USAGE *File name* is the name of the file to split. The file segments are given the original file name and a three-digit extension. For example, ThisApp.EXE would be split into ThisApp.001, ThisApp.002, and so on.

The -S option lets you specify the sizes (in KB) of the first segment and the remaining segments. Specifying the first segment as smaller than the rest allows you to add it to a disk that already has some files on it. The subsequent segments will all be of the same size. The size can range from 1KB to the size of the entire file. If you enter only one size, dSPLIT divides the file into equal segments of that size. Without the -S option, dSPLIT breaks the file up into 1200KB segments.

The -O option specifies the directory to which to write the file segments. If you leave out the -O option, dSPLIT uses the current directory.

If you are writing to a floppy disk drive, as each disk is filled, dSPLIT prompts you to remove it and insert another, empty disk.

• EXAMPLE The command

DSPLIT BigApp.EXE

divides BigApp into equal blocks of 1200KB.

The next command writes one segment of 500KB to a disk containing other application files, then writes equal segments of 1150KB each. All segments are written to the B drive.

DSPLIT -S 500,1150 -O B:BigApp.EXE

USING dJOIN

dJOIN reassambles the file segments written by dSPLIT.

• SYNTAX

DJOIN (-O *target path***) (-P (***message***))** *file name*

• USAGE *File name* is the root name of the divided file segments.

Use the -O option to specify the target path. If you omit the -O option, the current directory is used.

You can have dJOIN pause and display a custom message when it is time to read the next disk. If you use the -P option without a message, dJOIN will pause and display the default message "Please insert disk *number* into drive *drive name*. Press any key to continue."

• EXAMPLE The command

DJOIN -O C:\AppDir -P B:BigApp

reassembles all segments of BigApp and places the .EXE and other application files in the AppDir directory on the C drive. It will pause and display a prompt after each disk has been read.

Index

Note to the reader:
This index uses **boldfaced** numbers to indicate primary discussions of a topic.

E

G

H

I

N

O

S

Keys Used in the dBASE IV Program Editor

Action	Key
Abandon changes and exit	Esc or Escape
Access help screens	F1
Access pull-down menus	F10
Delete character at cursor	Del or Delete
Delete word to the left	Ctrl-Backspace
Delete to end of word	Ctrl-T
Delete entire line	Ctrl-Y
End line and move to next	↵
Erase character to left	Backspace
Insert a blank line	Ctrl-N, ↵
Insert/Overwrite mode (toggle)	Ins or Insert
Move left or right one character	← or Ctrl-A, → or Ctrl-D
Move up or down one line	↑, ↓, ↵ (insert off)
Move to beginning of line	Home
Move to end of line	End
Move to next word	Ctrl-→, Ctrl-F
Move to previous word	Ctrl-←,
Move to end of file	Ctrl-PgDn
Move to beginning of file	Ctrl-PgUp

9 781583 483961

Made in the USA
Las Vegas, NV
05 March 2023

68563175R00319